When the
Geese Come

When the Geese Come

The Journals of a Moravian Missionary
Ella Mae Ervin Romig
1898–1905, Southwest Alaska

edited with an introduction by
Phyllis Demuth Movius

University of Alaska Press
Fairbanks

Library of Congress Cataloging-in-Publication Data

Romig, Ella Mae Ervin, 1871–
    When the geese come : the journals of a Moravian missionary
  Ella Mae Ervin Romig 1898–1905, Southwest Alaska / edited
  with an introduction by Phyllis Demuth Movius.
        p.   cm.
    Includes bibliographical references and index.
    ISBN 0-912006-89-7 (alk. paper)
    1. Romig, Ella Mae Ervin, 1871– --Correspondence. 2. Yupik
  Eskimos--Missions--Alaska--Bethel. 3. Moravians--Alaska--
  Bethel--Biography. 4. Missionaries, Medical--Alaska--Bethel--
  Biography. 5. Moravians--Missions--Alaska--Bethel. 6. Alaska
  Moravian Church. 7. Yupik Eskimos--Social life and customs.
  8. Bethel (Alaska)--Social life and customs.   I. Movius, Phyllis
  Demuth. II. Title.
  E99.E7R647   1997
  266'.46' 092--dc21
  [B]   96-51588
                                                                  CIP

International Standard Book Number: 0-912006-89-7
Library of Congress Catalog Number: 96-51588

Printed in the United States by Thomson-Shore, Inc.

This publication was printed on acid-free paper that meets the
minimum requirements for the American National Standard for
Information Sciences—Permanence of Paper for Printed Library
Materials ANSI Z39.48-1984

Publication coordination, design and production by Deborah Van Stone.
Cover design by Deborah Van Stone.
Cover illustration by Louphena Hensal.
Cartography, pages 18–19, by Michael Wilson.
Photographic reproductions courtesy, Alaska and Polar Regions
        Department, University of Alaska Fairbanks.
Chapter goose ornament by Deirdre Helfferich.
Index by Paul Kish, Kish Indexing Services.

Contents

List of Illustrations

Preface

In 1992, I was first introduced to the Joseph Herman Romig Family Papers in the archives of the Elmer E. Rasmuson Library, University of Alaska Fairbanks, because of my interest in women who came to Alaska at the turn of the century. David Hales, Head of the Alaska and Polar Regions Department, told me that this collection contained several holograph journals written by Herman's wife, Ella, and I agreed that the material might be useful for my research.

As I read the journals and the associated manuscript material, I became intrigued with the wealth of information in this collection and with the character of Ella's writing. Simultaneously I felt a draw to this material beyond mere interest. The name "Romig" kept playing over and over in my mind, until finally I made a personal connection.

I am my family's self-elected historian and genealogist. As a result of that work, I knew, and eventually recalled, that several women in my paternal grandmother's family had married Romigs. When I discovered that Herman Romig's ancestors settled the Tuscarawas County area of southern Ohio, I knew I had discovered a link. My father's family is from the village of Gnadenhutten in that county. Once I had established a "shirt-tail relative" relationship with Herman and Ella Romig, I began my work with enthusiasm.

The results of my efforts are Ella's transcribed journals, with explanatory notes and introductory remarks about her life. I am indebted to David Hales for introducing me to the material. Margaret E. Murie, a Romig family friend, and some of Ella Romig's descendants graciously provided me with both information and encouragement. My thanks to William J. R. Daily and Molly Gilfillan, two of Ella's grandchildren, and Jean Romig, one of Ella's daughters-in-law, for their generous assistance. Staff at the Allen and Suzzallo Libraries at the University of Washington and the Elmer E. Rasmuson Library at the University of Alaska Fairbanks contributed in numerous ways with research assistance that was invaluable. I am especially grateful to Roy Bird, Lucile Childers, Mary Mangusso, Claus-M. Naske, and Richard Pierce for their editorial comments and suggestions. Because I consider this volume a companion piece

Ella Mae Ervin Romig in Bethel, Alaska, spring 1901.
(Courtesy, Alaska and Polar Regions Department, University of Alaska Fairbanks,
Joseph Romig Collection, acc. #90–043–929aN)

to work published by Ann Fienup-Riordan, I am grateful to her for the research assistance and encouragement she offered. When computer problems crept up, Patrick Farree's gracious assistance saved me hours of work. Project manager Debbie Van Stone's attention to detail and patience guided the entire project to completion. I also thank the Alaska and Polar Regions Department of the Elmer E. Rasmuson Library for its generous donation of the photographs from its collections used in this volume, and I am especially grateful to Richard Veazy who reproduced these images to his high standards of quality.

I dedicate this work to my husband, Jim, whose interest in Ella grew along with mine, and who agreed with me that Ella's framed photograph deserved a place of honor in our home.

Notes on the Editing and Presentation

Ella Romig wrote her journals in ruled student notebooks. They are presented here without omissions, with each chapter representing a separate notebook. Therefore, the chapters in this volume represent the amount of space provided for writing rather than thematic or chronological demarcations. The bulk of the journals were written by Ella as correspondence to her parents. The second half of journal number five, begun in December, 1904 and written at Carmel Mission, was directed to Ella's two oldest children, who did not accompany Herman and Ella to the Nushagak River region.

Because these journals were written as spontaneous correspondence to her family in Pennsylvania, Ella apparently did not edit her entries. I have corrected minor spelling errors and have added accidentally omitted words in brackets. Because the Yup'ik language was oral at the time, proper names were often spelled phonetically. For the reader's convenience, I have standardized these according to the scheme used by Ann Fienup-Riordan.[1] Words that Ella underlined for emphasis have been italicized in print. On occasion Ella wrote lengthy run-on sentences. I have broken these by adding punctuation where appropriate. As closely as possible, however, the journals are rendered with the same structure and format as those in which they were written.

---

1. Ann Fienup-Riordan, *The Real People and the Children of Thunder: The Yup'ik Eskimo Encounter with Moravian Missionaries John and Edith Kilbuck* (Norman: University of Oklahoma Press, 1991).

Chronology

Ella Mae Ervin born, December 28, 1871.

Joseph Herman Romig born, September 3, 1872.

Moravian Mission founded at Bethel (by John and Edith Kilbuck, William and Caroline Weinland, and Hans Torgerson), 1885.

Moravian school opened (Bethel), 1886.

Moravian Church call for physician to train in return for seven years service in Bethel, 1891.

Ella Mae Ervin graduates from Hahnemann University's Nursing School, 1894.

Joseph Herman Romig and Ella Mae Ervin wed, April 30, 1896.

Romigs arrive in Bethel, 1896.

Robert Herman Romig born, January 26, 1897.

Marietta Margaret Romig born, November 6, 1898.

Helen Elizabeth Romig born, January 2, 1901.

Romigs leave Alaska, 1903.

Herman, Ella, and Elizabeth Romig return to Alaska to try to develop a church hospital at the Carmel Mission near Nushagak, June 21, 1904.

The Romigs leave Carmel in the fall of 1905 (the mission is closed a year later).

The Romigs return to Nushagak, where Herman planned to open a government hospital and served as the Alaska Indian Service Superintendent of Schools at Nushagak, June 1906.

Romigs relocate to Seward, Alaska where Herman opened a private practice, 1910.

Howard Glenmore Romig born, January 28, 1911.

Herman accepts position as surgeon for the Alaska Railroad Hospital, 1914.

Romig family moves to Fairbanks, 1920.

Ella Mae Romig initiated into the Pioneer Women of Alaska, 1923.

Romig family moves to Anchorage, 1930.

Ella Mae Romig suffers a stroke, leaving her in failing health, 1936.

Ella Mae Romig dies, January 1, 1937.

Introduction

Disease of epidemic proportion killed many of the indigenous inhabitants of southwestern Alaska in the 1800s. The Moravian missionaries who had founded the Bethel mission in 1885 believed that medically trained personnel were needed to promote hygiene and physical cleanliness, which they hoped would relieve the personal suffering and devastation experienced by the Natives. The Moravian Church responded to the needs of the Kuskokwim region Eskimos when it sent Joseph Herman Romig, M.D., and his wife, Ella, to Bethel in 1896. Anthropologist and scholar Ann Fienup-Riordan has written, "The hope was that many souls seeking care for their afflicted bodies might come to seek the healing power of the Great Physician whom they served."[2] Through a calculated plan, the newly married Romigs were sent to provide health care and assist fellow missionaries in teaching the Christian plan for eternal salvation.

Herman, as he preferred to be called, descended from the founders of this central European pre-Reformation Protestant sect, his ancestors being among the early Moravian settlers in Pennsylvania in the mid-1700s. Dedication to church service kept the family on the American pioneer fringe. Herman, the sixth of eleven children and first son of Joseph and Margaret Ricksecker Romig, was born on September 3, 1872, in Salem, Illinois.[3] His missionary parents soon moved the family to the Moravian settlement in Independence, Kansas, where Herman was raised. In 1884, when Herman was twelve years old, his mother died. Due to insufficient financial resources and the difficulties of single parenthood, Herman's father faced the necessity of sending his children to the church-run boarding school. To avoid family breakup, the elder Romig replaced missionary work with teaching which, combined with his farming, provided adequate income and time to keep his family together. However, money was so scarce that when Herman graduated from high school he stifled his

---

2. Fienup-Riordan 1991, 212.

3. Joseph Herman Romig Family Papers, Series 1, Box 1, Folder 1, Archives, Alaska and Polar Regions Department, Elmer E. Rasmuson Library, University of Alaska Fairbanks.

The Bethel Mission in 1896 when Ella and Joseph Herman Romig arrived to
begin a seven year commitment as missionaries for the Moravian Church.
(Courtesy, Alaska and Polar Regions Department, University of Alaska Fairbanks,
Joseph Romig Collection, acc. #90-043-935N)

ambition to become a doctor and accepted a teaching position in
Independence in order to help the family. In 1891 the Moravian Church
sent out a call for a student interested in becoming a physician to commit
to seven years at the Bethel mission in return for a medical school
scholarship. Herman, "not daring to hope he might be selected to train
for the position, applied, and to his astonishment, was selected. He went
at once to Bethlehem, Pennsylvania to enter pre-medicine at the Moravian
College," later studying at Hahnemann Medical College in Philadelphia.[4]
During his senior year he met Ella Mae Ervin, an 1894 graduate of
Hahnemann's Nursing School, who shared his desire to help the less
fortunate.[5] The couple married on April 30, 1896, a few days prior to
Herman's graduation, and together they arrived in Alaska that July.[6]

Ella was the second of three children born to Albert Fisher and Marietta
Struck Ervin near Wilkes-Barre, Pennsylvania, on December 28, 1871.[7]

4. Ibid. Untitled manuscript, Series 2, Box 2, Folder 28, 3.

5. Judith M. Baker to editor, July 23, 1993, Hahnemann University, Philadelphia.

6. Joseph Herman Romig Family Papers, Series 1, Box 1, Folder 1.

7. Ella Romig membership application, Daughters of the American Revolution,
Washington, D.C.

Her family had also settled in Pennsylvania in the 1700s, and her great-grandfather, Henry Ervin, served as a private in Colonel Francis Johnston's Fifth Pennsylvania Regiment fighting in American Revolutionary War battles at Brandywine, Germantown, and Monmouth. His service granted Ella membership in the "Daughters of the American Revolution," which she accepted on June 5, 1935.[8]

Romig biographers have described Ella as a "fine-grained and reserved" easterner, whom they feared would not adjust well to the harsh and un-civilized Alaskan environment.[9] To the contrary, Ella thrived in the north and frequently remarked in her journal about the natural beauty around her, along with the healthy climate, the joys of living in a less populated area, and in particular, her gratitude for these "seven years of free easy life. That is to say, free from painful society and fashion. I often wonder how I could ever try to dress according to the 'latest style' again. I am certainly thankful for this blessed rest from all this."[10] It is apparent from her numerous comments about the never-ending housework that Ella took her homemaking responsibilities seriously, and prized cleanliness. She frequently expressed irritation with what she perceived to be the Natives' lack of interest in housekeeping, but once she described a unique method for ignoring her own domestic chores: "We are sleeping in our tent out on the bank. The children all like it so, and I am thoroughly disgusted with and tired of my dirty house, and find it such a relief to get out of it for a little while."[11]

Herman's oldest sister, Edith, and her husband, John Kilbuck, two of the original five founders of this mission, welcomed the Romigs to Bethel. The Kilbucks, along with William and Caroline Weinland and Hans Torgersen (who drowned not long after his arrival) had settled the Bethel mission in 1885. By the time the Romigs arrived twelve years later, these colonists had built adequate structures to house the missionaries and operate the school which they had proudly opened for six children in September 1886.[12] In addition to Bethel, they had established their presence at Carmel on the Nushagak River, and at the villages of Ougavig and Quinhagak. Native "Helpers" were converted to Christianity and trained

---

8. Ibid.

9. Eva Greenslit Anderson, *Dog-team Doctor* (Caldwell: The Caxton Printers, Ltd., 1940), 53.

10. Ella Romig, Journal entry October 12, 1899, Joseph Herman Romig Family Papers, Series 3, Box 3, Folder 42.

11. Ibid., May 11, 1902, Folder 44.

12. Fienup-Riordan, 85.

*Ella and Joseph Herman Romig joined other missionaries in the
Kuskokwim region who had established the Moravian Mission at Bethel in
1885. Shown in this photograph taken July 1896 are back row standing
from left to right: Reverend John Henry Kilbuck. Dr. Joseph Herman
Romig, Anna Lichty Helmich, Reverend Benjamin K. Helmich holding
unidentified child, Edith Romig Kilbuck (J. H. Romig's sister), Ella Mae
Ervin Romig and Reverend Ernest L. Weber. Front row standing at left
in front of J. H. Romig, young Joe Kilbuck. Women seated in front from left
to right: Mary Mack, Philippine King, and Caroline Detterer Weber.
Other children are unidentified.*
*(Courtesy, Alaska and Polar Regions Department, University of Alaska Fairbanks,
Joseph Romig Collection, acc. #90-043-855aN)*

to do the church's work in smaller outlying villages. One of the most fa-
mous of these "Helpers" was a Yup'ik shaman, Uyakok, who became a
Moravian pastor and took the name Helper Neck. As reported in Alaska
Geographic, "He was one of few native Americans to work out a system
for writing his language, developing his own letters to represent sounds.
Modern linguists say his writing system may be the only one in the world
for which there is a complete record of development."[13]

13. Penny Rennick, Editor, *Alaska Geographic, The Kuskokwim*, Volume 15, Number 4/
1988 (Anchorage: Alaska Northwest Publishing), 46.

Moravian Helpers, spring 1903, left to right:
Helper David, Helper Lomuck, Helper Neck, Helper Kawagleg.
(Courtesy, Alaska and Polar Regions Department, University of Alaska Fairbanks,
Joseph Romig Collection, acc. #90-043-858aN)

In retrospect, and by contemporary standards, the goals of the Moravians can be judged as intrusive:

> Like Protestant preachers and teachers working on Indian reservations throughout the United States in the 1880s, the Moravians wanted to change the way people were married, buried, clothed and fed. They planned to transform nomadic people who wore fur garments and lived in muddy, underground men's and women's houses into stable, hard working, Christian citizens who lived in single-family cabins and cut their hair.[14]

John Kilbuck's Delaware Indian ancestry and his physical likeness to the Eskimos made him an excellent candidate to accomplish these goals, and even though he represented an unfamiliar culture, the Natives respected and liked him.

---

14. Ibid., 47.

When they arrived, the Moravian missionaries were ignorant of the Yup'ik language. This understandably caused initial hardships for day-to-day life and thwarted their efforts at "proclaiming the gospel of Jesus Christ" to the Eskimos, and enhancing their quality of life—two of the stated purposes of the church.[15] John Kilbuck came to Alaska with a knowledge of American Indian herb medicine, a Christian theological education, and a proud heritage as the grandson of a Delaware chief. His understanding of Native Americans, his eagerness to learn the Yup'ik language, and his sensitivity to their needs allowed him to succeed in the Kuskokwim regions. His rapport with the Alaska Natives was evident in 1895 when John was on the verge of excommunication from the Moravian Church for adulterous activity with Mary Mack, a fellow missionary. The Natives, who did not necessarily share the Church's alarm regarding his behavior, organized an appeal based on the fact that he was the best loved and most effective of all the Moravians in the region. They were successful until a few years later when John confessed to subsequent adulterous behavior with Native women, resulting in the birth of at least one child.[16] For their transgressions, Mary Mack was given an early retirement, and Kilbuck was dismissed from missionary service and the church.[17]

Although we are given the impression that the Christian missionaries desired to change the Natives to Anglo-American ways, there was actually more of a merger of beliefs than an all-or-nothing credo, and it must be noted how quickly and easily Ella Romig adopted many Yup'ik customs and practices. She enjoyed the wild game and fish diet and quickly chose to wear the Natives' style of winter clothing. She defied a Church rule that young boys should have short hair when she allowed her son's hair to grow into "long curls."[18] The Eskimos believed long hair was necessary to keep disease at bay, and they balked at the missionaries' admonition for conformity to something different. In addition to cultural assimilation, Ella eagerly involved herself in outdoor activities. Winter became her favorite season, and picnics and tent camping, even at this time of year, had their appeal. In April 1900 she recorded in her journal that, "We spent a week in our camp and I must own I was more than sorry

---

15. Bernard E. Michel, *The Moravian Church, Its History, Faith and Ministry* (Bethlehem, PA: The Moravian Church in America, 1992), npn. *A Doctrinal Statement adopted by the Unity Synod of the Unitas Fratrum, or Moravian Church, The Ground of the Unity* (Herrnhut, German Democratic Republic: Moravian Church, 1981), 1.

16. Fienup-Riordan, 232-3.

17. Ibid., 225 and 229.

18. Ella Romig, Journal entry October 14, 1898, Folder 42.

Robert and Margaret Romig, March 1904.
(Courtesy, Alaska and Polar Regions Department, University of Alaska Fairbanks,
Joseph Romig Collection, acc. #90-043-922aN)

to have to return home…."[19] In January 1902 Ella described a "little picnic" in the woods, and in April of that year recorded her disappointment
that a snowstorm delayed a family trip "to the [rein]deer herd up in the
mountains…."[20] Part of her enjoyment of these outings was sharing the
pleasure of them with her husband and their three children born at Bethel.
The couple's son, Robert Herman, arrived on January 26, 1897, and their
first daughter, Marietta Margaret, joined the family on November 6, 1898.
Their third child, Helen Elizabeth, was born on January 2, 1901.

---

19. Ibid., April 28, 1900.

20. Ibid., January 28 and April 1, 1902, Folder 44.

Margaret (left) and Helen Elizabeth Romig, March 1904.
(Courtesy, Alaska and Polar Regions Department, University of Alaska Fairbanks,
Joseph Romig Collection, acc. #90-043-924aN)

Ella's attitude about life was buoyant, even though she occasionally complained about the drudgery, the loneliness, and the hard work. She had the ability to see the positive and to trust in God's will to maintain her emotional balance. One spring Herman was prepared to hunt geese as soon as the fowl returned to the area. Although Ella did not look forward to the chore of cleaning the birds, she excused the hardship with the optimistic remark that "when the geese come they bring Spring."[21]

An incident recorded during the winter of 1901 is testimony to Ella's resourcefulness, strength of character, and her trust in God. The Romigs'

21. Ibid., April 7, 1902.

third child, Helen Elizabeth, was born at Bethel in January. Within a few weeks, Herman left on a lengthy trip which left Ella alone to tend the house and children. Immediately after Herman's departure, a fellow missionary's infant son died, a fierce winter storm set in, and the Romigs' newborn became critically ill. Ella mourned the other infant's death, fought to keep the house warm by pinning up blankets to the wall that "bowed out like a sail in a full breeze," and nursed her own sick child.[22] She vented her frustrations as she wrote, "A man with a wife and family has no business to be a physician over such a wide territory."[23] Fear and grief caused her to remark that she had "never felt so blue and homesick in [her] life," but her ultimate strength came from her spirituality.[24] Ella confided in her journal, "But my dear little Helen Elizabeth I fear has but a short time for this world. Nor would I ask to keep her here if God thinks best to give her a brighter happier home."[25] By early March the weather and her baby had improved, and Ella's ever-optimistic outlook returned in full: "What a trial this is for me here alone with my little folks, but each day is one less of Herman's absence and one less of coughing for my babe.... We are having fine weather again. March came in like a lamb. I hope Herman may have nice weather when he starts for home. The long gloomy Winter with its traveling is nearly spent."[26] Herman returned home later that month to find his family healthy and cheerful.

Herman exhorted Ella to write more frequently to family and friends in the States. It is difficult to know his precise motivation, but it could be that he feared the Kilbucks, who both kept voluminous and detailed journals, would be credited with maintaining the most complete record of the growth and development of the Kuskokwim mission efforts. His apparent need not to be outdone by his sister and brother-in-law caused him periodically to make his own lengthy entries in Ella's journal, but she could hardly be considered delinquent in her efforts.

Ella wrote this series of journals expressly for her parents and children. She also kept a personal journal and wrote numerous letters to friends. Mail delivery from the States occurred only twice a year, during the summer months when sailing vessels could reach the mouth of the Kuskokwim River. Systematic entries allowed her to share a chronological account of

---

22. Ibid., February 26, 1901, Folder 43.
23. Ibid.
24. Ibid.
25. Ibid., February 27, 1901.
26. Ibid., March 1, 1901.

her life, whereas periodic letters would have been sporadic and incomplete. Apparently, the personal journal and letters have not survived, but the journals presented here have been safely preserved through the care of Ella's descendants. If Ella kept journals between her arrival at Bethel in 1896 and the fall of 1898, their whereabouts are unknown.

Ella tended to make her journal entries at times when her children were asleep, and when Herman was gone and she had more time to herself. She valued time to write, and once she commented that she sometimes stayed home from church for this purpose, a rare admission for a missionary. Another entry indicates she wrote in an effort to keep herself awake during a severe cold spell when she needed to stoke the wood stove frequently. During times of loneliness and emotional stress, journal writing provided relief from frustration and anxiety. A comparison of Ella's journals to those of other missionaries shows that she wrote more openly and spontaneously than did her peers. Her love for her family is unquestionable, and her integrity in honestly reporting the events at the mission is evident. Ella certainly knew the Moravian Church rule never to provide anything but the most flattering reports about her experiences.[27] She chose to ignore this guidance in favor of recording candid accounts of tension among the missionaries and periodic negative feelings about the Natives and their customs.

A relative who has only sketchy memories of Ella described her as the kind of person who kept to herself and remained on the sidelines, and frequent comments in her journal allude to this intense desire for privacy.[28] It was a desire not easily indulged in her life in the north. Once established at Bethel, the missionaries were expected to provide food and lodging to anyone who traveled through the area. In 1897, when gold miners began to arrive in the Kuskokwim region, the migrants frequently called upon the Moravians for hospitality. Bethel did not have transient accommodations, and therefore guests to the area shared the already cramped missionary quarters. Ella's frustrations at the intrusion and the extra work this caused were apparent when she wrote, "Our houses here are more like hotels in the states. Everyone on or around the place, and strangers coming from every direction all come in and make themselves at home. It is, no doubt, a good way to do missionary work, but I must confess, it galls me...."[29] Ella was not alone in harboring this attitude.

---

27. Fienup-Riordan, 179.

28. Molly Gilfillan, personal communication with editor, February 1993.

29. Ella Romig, Journal entry, October 12, 1899, Folder 42.

Feb. 26. 1901.

We are having such lovely weather, and fine travelling, Herman is doubtless making good time toward Nushagak, he will probably reach there in a week from here. I never missed him as much since we are here, it seems that he must come back. When he left he said that if he should meet the mail team from Nushagak and get word that Mr Rock is improving he would turn back. To think that each day he is going farther from home

A page from Ella's journal.
(continues on next page)

The frustrations to permanent residents caused by the increase in travelers were recorded by others as well. Joseph Grinnell, a half-hearted miner near Nome in the early 1900s, remarked in his journal, "We have to entertain so many visitors that it is getting tiresome naturally. I judge we have fed sixty men in the past week, or at least have served that many meals. We call our camp the 'Penelope Inn.' or 'Cape Nome Recuperating Station.'"[30] It is entirely possible that Ella had entertained these same guests before they headed north to Grinnell's camp.

Another irritation for Ella related to Herman's absences. When he was away, social custom dictated that travelers should not expect to be cared for in the Romig home. This resulted in unwanted isolation and loneliness. As soon as word spread that Herman had returned, people felt comfortable stopping in for anything from dinner to a week's stay. Ella remarked that she hoped the "time will come when we sisters here at the mission need not be slaves for the travelers. Natives as well as white men."[31] Not only did the guests create extra work for Ella, they were a drain on

---

30. Elizabeth Grinnell, Editor, *Gold Hunting In Alaska* (Elgin: David C. Cook Publishing Company, 1901), 74.

31. Ella Romig, Journal entry, June 8, 1899, Folder 42.

and that a month will pass ere he returns, makes me fairly sick. A man with a wife and family has no business to be a physician for over such a wide territory. Baby Bellie is coughing very hard poor little girl, she is so tiny to have such a cough. I try to act a woman and not a baby, for while medicine can do the boy no special good. Herman may be able to save a valuable missionary, but God knows it is hard to be alone during such a trying time in such a desolate lonely place. Margaret is far from well and at times is very troublesome. Robert had a very light attack and is almost well again. These two children nearly drive me crazy sometimes. They are so penned up indoors and grow milder no doubt. [aint unman] They fight and play in the loudest boy fashion from morning till night, but oh, my nerves suffer for it I can't assure you. Margaret is such a saucy little mite, if I scold her she tells me I am bad and she belongs to her papa: the next minute she will put her arms around my neck and tell me

already meager supplies, eroding precious time she preferred to spend with her family and invited guests. Ella also boldly expressed her opinions about the leadership offered the mission by the Moravian Church Board in Pennsylvania, and did not hesitate to chastise it for its periodic decisions to close the school and orphanage operated at Bethel, which Ella felt essential to the well-being of the Natives.

Ella's journals provide a comprehensive memoir of the importance of her family, and her relationship with her husband and her growing children. Herman's periodic entries also give us insight into his feelings about the family. Once when Ella was sick with suspected appendicitis,

*Ella's journals chronicled events at the Bethel Mission, and writing
provided an emotional outlet during difficult times alone.*
(Courtesy, Alaska and Polar Regions Department, University of Alaska Fairbanks,
Joseph Herman Romig Family Papers, Box 3, Folder 43)

Herman stopped all work to stay at home and care for her. Ella praised his
sensitivity when she wrote to her father, "I never want for anything when
I am ill, he takes the best of care of me. One morning last week he brought
my breakfast to me, and then threw his arms around me and cried great

manly tears because he could bring me nothing good. How sweet that breakfast of a roll, coffee, and rabbit stew was. Nothing ever tasted better to me."[32] Herman was always quick to compliment Ella's judgment in crises. When Helen Elizabeth had recovered from her almost fatal illness in 1901, he remarked that his "presence would have only been for company and help as Ella displays excellent judgment and good sense in her care of any she may look out for when sick. I am proud to have such an able and lovable wife…."[33] At the same time, he showed his consideration for Ella and the children with the announcement that he would halt all further travel that season because "my wife's babes demand some of my time,… so I am going to stay home with them this spring and stop traveling."[34] In addition to his demonstrated thoughtfulness, Herman was quick to praise Ella for her efforts to raise and care for his dog team, a responsibility she enjoyed.

Although she complained regularly about the lack of what she perceived to be a normal family life, Ella was quick to redirect her thoughts to her purpose at Bethel, which was to better the lives of the Eskimo people. In 1901, as her time in Alaska drew to an end, marked affection is evident in Ella's attitudes towards the Natives. That winter she and Herman had been at the village of Ougavig for two months to administer both spiritually and physically to the Natives. The Romig children had remained at Bethel in the care of fellow missionaries, and when ready to begin their return trip, Ella was particularly anxious to be reunited with her children. She also genuinely seemed to enjoy the journey, and remarked that "I always love to hear the bells jingle and see the dogs so frisky as they always are on a cold crisp morning. All along the road between villages there is nothing to be seen but God's own work save here and there a fish trap or fox trap."[35] The next day they could have pushed for home, but elected to spend the night at Akiak because "we had to hurry through all of our villages on our way up. We did not want to disappoint them this time, and they were so anxious for us to remain over night with them. So we are pleasing our people more than ourselves, for naturally we are very anxious to be with our little ones again."[36] Towards the end of the Romigs' tenure in Bethel, Ella had grown to know the Natives well enough to

---

32. Ibid., October 31, 1902, Folder 45.
33. Ibid., April 11, 1901.
34. Ibid.
35. Ibid., December 5, 1901, Folder 44.
36. Ibid., December 6, 1901.

anticipate missing them after she had departed: "When we first came, seven years ago, how long seven years looked then.... Now that the seven years are almost past... it will be hard to leave our Eskimos who grow more dear as the time comes to part with them...."[37]

The time did come, however, and in 1903 the Romigs left Alaska to establish themselves in the States. During this year's furlough, Herman divided his time between San Francisco, where he practiced medicine, and Pennsylvania, where Ella and the three children stayed with her father in Forty Fort, a small community near Wilkes-Barre. Both of the Romigs made numerous speeches to church groups about the success of the Bethel Mission, and Herman negotiated an arrangement with the church headquarters at Bethlehem, Pennsylvania, to return to Alaska and develop a hospital at Nushagak, where he would provide medical services to both Natives and the fish cannery workers in the area. In his agreement, Herman proposed that the church bear the cost of this experiment for one year. If successful, he would reimburse the church its expenses and continue the venture as a private enterprise. The church agreed to this trial offer, and Herman, Ella, and Elizabeth arrived back at the Carmel Mission near Nushagak on June 21, 1904. Their two older children, Margaret and Robert, remained with relatives in the states, where better educational opportunities were available to them. During this period, Ella's journals were directed to the children instead of her father, and she focused on telling Robert and Margaret about their Native friends and events that were familiar and of interest to the young children.

In the summer of 1905, Bishop J. Taylor Hamilton of Bethlehem, Pennsylvania, visited Carmel and determined that the church was not seeing results commensurate with its expenses. The Natives, lured away from the Moravian influence by cannery wages, had accepted worldly ways in the community, and the Russian Orthodox Church that first had a religious stronghold in this area continued to have its influence on the Natives' lives. After a year of medical practice, Herman decided, for many of the same reasons given by the church, that he no longer desired to practice in this isolated region. The Romigs prepared to settle in San Francisco where the family could once again be together and Herman could continue a surgical practice he had established with colleagues in 1903. The Romigs left Carmel in the fall of 1905, and the next summer the mission officially closed.[38]

---

37. Ibid., October 10, 1902, Folder 45.

38. Anna Buxbaum Schwalbe, *Dayspring on the Kuskokwim* (Bethlehem, PA: Moravian Church in America, North, 1985), 61-3.

Like other nineteenth-century missionaries, Ella arrived in Alaska with "noble intentions" to save heathen souls and heal diseased bodies.[39] She was handicapped by an initial lack of knowledge of the people and their environment; furthermore, the distance between the mission field and church headquarters caused frustration due to lack of understanding and delays in receiving direction or negotiating procedures. Yet Ella survived the human-caused difficulties and thrived on the natural ones. In a recent essay addressing conceptual research methods for northern regions, Kenneth Coates suggests that "the fundamental struggle in the North is between the people and the environment."[40] It was a combination of remoteness and the environment that characterized Ella's life in Alaska and lured her to remain.

As previously mentioned, Ella's adaptability to certain Native customs such as indigenous winter clothing, dog teams and boats for transportation, and a cyclical approach to food gathering, raising, and storage based on the seasons indicated her flexibility in new surroundings. Ella's willingness, with some relief, to abandon fashionable clothing styles dictated in the states allow us to understand her independence, which contributed to her success at life removed from mainland America. At the same time, however, it is evident that Ella was not willing to abandon all of the comforts to which she had grown accustomed. Although difficult at times, gardening provided a summer focus that resulted in the availability of familiar foods that could not withstand the long journey by ship from the states. As Coates suggests, the lack of products locally "generated a spirit of innovation" which certainly seems to be true for Ella because she apparently had never been much of a gardener before coming north.[41] The cost and time necessary for northbound shipments of goods resulted in Ella sewing most of her family's clothing which was a new, at times annoying, experience. She frequently recorded irritation in her journal that so much of her time was spent providing the basic necessities of life. It is therefore understandable that the arrival of the annual supply vessel caused relief and celebration. In addition to foodstuff, lumber, and other building supplies, the ship brought packages from home that contained

---

39. Julie Roy Jeffrey, *Converting The West: A Biography of Narcissa Whitman* (Norman: University of Oklahoma Press, 1991), xii.

40. Kenneth Coates, "The Discovery of the North: Towards a Conceptual Framework for the Study of Northern/Remote Regions," *The Northern Review* 12/13, (Summer 1994/ Winter 1994): 38.

41. Ibid., 33.

special fabrics for sewing, toys for the children, holiday gift items, and letters, albeit six months old, containing news of family and friends. The ship's arrival, which heralded a tie to the southern mainland, was without question the highlight of the summer season.

Like many Alaskans, Ella arrived in the north planning to stay only for a specific period of time. Her journals chronicle early observations and opinions, and the evolutionary process of change she experienced that resulted in seeing her surroundings and the people with whom she lived through different eyes. Her initial sense of opposition which originated from feelings of struggle against the Natives and the environment was ultimately replaced with an attitude of understanding and acceptance that allowed Ella to extend her stay in the north in relative harmony and peace.

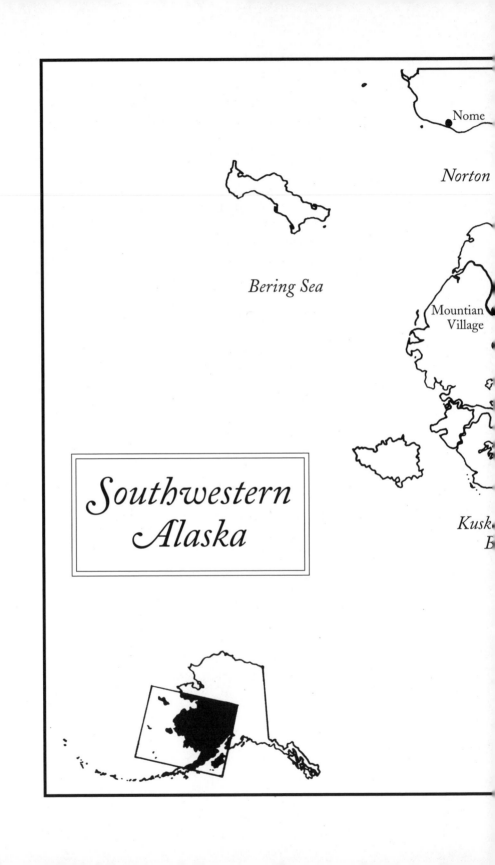

Nome

Norton

Bering Sea

Mountian
Village

Southwestern
Alaska

Kusk
B

Yukon River

Kuskokwim River

Saint
Michael

dreafsky

Paimiut

Russian
Mission

Holy Cross

ut

Aniak

kichak

Napamiut

Kolmakovskiy

Ougavig

Tuluksak

Akiak

Bethel ▲—— MOUNT ROMIG

Napaskiak

Nushagak River

Quinhagak

Nushagak
(Carmel)

Togiak

Bristol
Bay

cartography by Michael Wilson

chapter 1

September 18, 1898 to June 10, 1900

DEAR FATHER AND MOTHER:

I promised you in my mind a long journal this year and to begin it as soon as I returned from the coast.[42] But like many of my good resolutions I failed to begin as early as I had hoped to. But as to the long journal, I trust this part of the promise will prove true.

So many things have happened this Summer, sad unfortunate events in the Moravian Mission history. While you know of most of the particulars, I am going to write them all again, for there are many dates and circumstances I would like to remember which will in years to come be forgotten unless I have something to refer to, and I have not time to keep a private journal together with this one and one I have promised to the nurses in Philadelphia.

Herman often tells me that John's and Edith's [Kilbuck] fame is due largely to Edith's never tiring pen and thinks that unless I wake up and write more we will never have credit for what we do accomplish. Well, I wish I could write long and interesting journals for my friends' sakes, could I do so I would, but either Edith's journals have been much exaggerated or I fail to see the interesting part in the work.[43] Of course, our inability to speak or understand the language makes this people less interesting.

Then the past mistakes on the part of some of our missionaries makes the present or future look anything else but pleasant or interesting to us who are left here to battle against the discouragements.

Ever since last Christmas it seems we have had nothing but hard work, unpleasant trips and discouragements.

From Christmas until Winter travel [never] ceased, we had one party of travelers after another. This always means hard work for the sisters here at the Mission for we must always open our houses to everybody, native

---

42. Residents of Bethel usually met their annual supply ship at the mouth of the Kuskokwim River where the cargo was off-loaded into smaller vessels for the seventy-mile trip upriver to Bethel. In 1914 the river was charted, and by 1915 oceangoing vessels could navigate the river and anchor at Bethel. Freight costs were greatly reduced, and "this was the most significant historic change in Kuskokwim transportation until the advent of commercial aviation" (Oswalt, Wendell H. *Mission of Change In Alaska* [San Marino, CA: The Huntington Library, 1963], 44).

guides as well as white men. To feed as well as lodge them all with our scant supply of provisions and little house room keeps our minds busy as well as our hands to think of the "ways and means" and carrying out the ideas when once formed. Many times during the long Winter, with only our own family to cook for, we find the question what *shall* I get for breakfast, dinner or supper a very perplexing one to solve, for we have nothing but a small amount of canned vegetables and beans, not even potatoes. And sometimes it will be a week or even much longer when we are unable to get fresh meats or fish. Until this year we have gotten only a very small amount of canned or salted meats. You may imagine it very hard to prepare three meals a day for strangers with such a supply store to go to. Of course the natives receive only one piece of bread, a small piece of boiled sugar and all the tea they wish together with their fish. But it keeps one busy baking bread and boiling sugar, for both Summer and Winter natives are continually coming and going.[44] Any time during the day one must be prepared to give someone tea. For my part, all that a missionary sister's work amounts to is keeping the bread box and sugar can filled and serving free lunch at all hours. The native help do a great deal of the hardest work of course, but one must think of and order every minute duty of the household, even to the cutting of the bread else they help themselves too liberally.

Late in March Mr. Rock, a brother missionary from Carmel, arrived with two large teams of dogs and three native guides.[45] When he first arrived we were all very glad to see him. But later when he learned that he would not be able to return by dog team he made himself very disagreeable, as well as all the rest of us very uncomfortable, by his continual fault finding with the weather, our scant dog food or poor management of affairs in general at Bethel.

While at Carmel the run of fish will allow them to catch all they wish to keep servants, school scholars and any number of dogs, as well as

---

43. Edith's father, Joseph Romig, copied her Alaska journals for publication in *The Moravian* "so that through her words the entire church community might read about the work." The result was extraordinary support to the Alaska mission (Fienup-Riordan 1991, 30).

44. "Boiled sugar" was a form of candy made by cooking brown sugar and water until it formed a paste. The mixture was poured into a shallow pan where it hardened as it cooled. Pieces were cut or broken off and eaten like candy, or a piece was used to stir tea which sweetened the beverage (Smelcer, Clarence, personal communication with the editor, February 1995).

45. Reverend Samuel Rock served in the Kuskokwim region from 1896–1904 and from 1906–1916 (Schwalbe 1985, 300).

allowing the natives to put up enough fish to keep them until the next Spring thus taking all poor hungry natives off of their hands. But this is not the way here at Bethel. This Summer we had a large run of fish giving the natives as well as us the opportunity of getting plenty of food for the Winter. But the two previous years we nor natives could get enough to eat during the Summer much less for the Winter. All Winter after dog team-ing began, one team has to be kept making trips across the tundra for fish for natives and dogs. Years like these two, natives from all around, when their food runs out, generally come here for us to look out for [them]. We cannot see them starve so consequently have a multitude to feed. Our scant supply of fish, our good Bro. Rock attributes to poor management. We were all glad when the time came for him to leave for I know he was tired of us, and I am quite sure we were all very tired of him, especially we sisters who had to cook for him three times a day with almost nothing to cook, with an ever pleasant reminder that "Aunt Mary is an excellent cook" (Aunt Mary is Miss Huber, Mr. Rock's sister-in-law and a very lovely woman from all I heard). Poor Bro. Rock. Of course we had to make apology for his old maidish fussiness for he had just married, and three months was a long time to be away from his bride.[46]

After our trip to the coast, and Mr. Rock's departure, came the mail bringing so much sad news to us. Since Mr. Weber brought our mail on the morning of June twenty-fifth we have never felt the same happy party.[47] God alone knows how much John [Kilbuck] is missed here by missionar-ies as well as the natives who love him dearly, and truly he deserves their love for he is a kind just noble-hearted man, one whose advice and coun-sel is worth accepting.[48] While like many he has fallen, like few, I truly believe he deeply regrets his fall, and that his own conscience has punished him more than the sentence from the Board. Truly I have never known so lowly and child-like a Christian. Could you know him you would love and admire him. Truly God has used this man in His noble cause. To hear these many natives pray in their own tongue and sing songs, his translations, is proof of this. And who can fill his place? No one here, I

---

46. Reverend Rock married fellow missionary Emma Huber February 27, 1898 (Schwalbe 1985, 58).

47. Reverend Ernest Weber came to the Kuskokwim region in 1888, and with his missionary wife, Caroline Detterer, whom he married at Bethel in January 1890, served in Alaska until 1898. They established the mission at Ougavig, eighty miles up the Kuskokwim River from Bethel (Schwalbe 1985, 27, 46 and 300).

48. John Kilbuck was removed from missionary service in 1898 due to adulterous ac-tivity. In 1921 he was reinstated as a Moravian missionary at Akiak where he died in 1922 (Fienup-Riordan 1991, 232-3; Oswalt 1963, 85).

fear. But God is still with us and I trust will not let the work suffer too much from this blow.

After Mr. Weber had brought us the mail in which came this sad news on June twenty-fifth, he left us on the same evening confident that very soon he, his wife, and little Freddie together with the unfortunate fourteen men would in a few days reach Bethel. But God willed it otherwise. As the days passed by and we knew they had not gone up the river we feared they had lost their way in the two severe storms following Bro. Weber's departure. When the natives brought the news of the barge having been found with the tow line cut, we feared the worst for them. Five bodies, I believe, have been found only one of which, the first one, could be identified by the papers found in his pockets. His face was already past recognition. This one, Mr. Murphy, was the leader and Captain, and evidently a stockholder in the company. The company is the Columbia Navigation Co. of Seattle.

This unfortunate party and their poor ignorant pilot, our lost Missionary, were doubtless lost in a terrific wind storm and dense fog on June 28th. It was Mr. Weber's plan to go far out in the Bay to take their course up the river. These waters are dangerous in such a storm for a large vessel and of course their poor little steamer was utterly helpless. Had they kept near shore they doubtless had been saved. Early in August the steam boat was found bottom side up, her machinery all gone. Nothing I believe, with the exception of a shot gun, was found in her.[49]

Poor Mr. Weber, how much sorrow and disappointment has been spared him. He came back so full of confidence in his ability to fill Bro. John's place, and made his boast that he would show Kilbuck that the work could get along without him. But poor man, [he] did not know that the natives asked John to ask the Board at home to take him [Weber] away or that when he had gone, asked David to write and ask the Board never to send him back that they did not love him.[50] Now they dislike him more than ever for they blame him for John's dismissal. In this they wrong him. Then they did not wish to have him for their leader. One of the men said that the Lord knew just how much they could stand, and He knew they could not stand Weber so He took him away, and they are thankful to Him for it.

So poor Mr. Weber has been spared much disappointment in this work.

---

49. Ernest and Caroline Weber, and one of their children, were drowned in Kuskokwim Bay on their return trip to Alaska after a one-year furlough in the States (Oswalt 1963, 37).

50. David Skuviuk was a Native helper and interpreter for the missionaries (Schwalbe 1985, 39).

October 16, 1898

As of old, your poor journal has been neglected. I see the last, in fact the only date is nearly a month old. Well, negligence seems to be my normal state.

I think I have not told you of Herman's trip to the Yukon River. He made a trip to the Russian Mission by *bidarka* with a bill of furs for the steamer *Hamilton*, leaving here on August nineteenth with Mr. Lind, the trader who went to St. Michael, and three men from the Geological Survey party under the management of Prof. Spurr, who were on their way to St. Michael to take a steamer for the states.[51]

This Government Geological Survey party arrived here at Bethel on August eleventh after a long trip in wood or cedar canoes from Cook Inlet up the Skwentna River over a new pass never before known, to the headwaters of the Kuskokwim. From here the four remaining men in the party, Prof. Spurr, Mr. Post a topographer and son of the Illinois Senator, Mr. Rhone, and Mr. Hoffman went to Nushagak, from there they expected to go to Lake Clark back to Cook Inlet reaching there about this time, where they would take a steamer to the states.

Herman left for the Yukon on Friday returning two weeks from the following Sunday, after a very disagreeable trip, it having rained almost every day since he left home. During his stay at the Russian Mission he was entertained either by the Russian trader or the Priest. They were very kind to him. These Greeks are not always thus towards other church members but they appreciate the fact that Herman is the only M.D. near them and I guess think it well to keep in the good graces of the Moravians.[52] The Greek Priest is a very agreeable man and has a charming little wife. They both came up on the *Bertha* from San Francisco to Unalaska with us.

Mrs. Korchinskii, the Priest's wife, sent me some oranges and apples.[53] Oh, the apples were such a treat, the first fresh ones I had eaten in over two years. How hungry I get for fresh fruits up here.

---

51. A *bidarka* was an Eskimo kayak characterized by two or three manholes (Oswalt 1963, 20); Edward Lind was the Alaska Commercial Company agent on the Kuskokwim River. His common-law Eskimo wife frequently acted as an interpreter for the missionaries, and although Lind was a Lutheran, "he became a staunch supporter of the new mission" at Bethel (Oswalt 1963, 30).

52. The Russian Orthodox Church, also known as Greek Catholic, established themselves at Russian Mission in the early 1830s and considered their territory to include the Yukon-Kuskokwim Delta (Fienup-Riordan 1991, 133).

53. Father Iakov Korchinskii and his wife arrived at Russian Mission as the Russian Orthodox priest in 1896 (Fienup-Riordan 1991, 139).

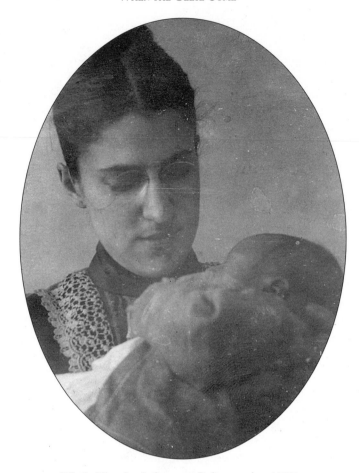

Ella holding her infant son, Robert, spring 1897.
(Courtesy, Alaska and Polar Regions Department, University of Alaska Fairbanks,
Joseph Romig Collection, acc. #90-043-916aN)

During Herman's absence I cleaned the house from one end to the other. Papered my little sitting room and put a brussels carpet on the floor, one Edith brought up fourteen years ago. When she left she gave it to Herman and me, and I thought it high time to make use of it.[54]

---

54. The official news of John Kilbuck's dismissal was received at Bethel too late in the season to allow time for John and Edith to pack their belongings and depart on the last ship. The church agreed that John could work in a "lay capacity" for one year at Quinhagak translating scripture and assisting in the construction of a new mission site (Fienup-Riordan 1991, 231).

Then the Board sent us fifty yards of pretty ingrain carpet so out of this I carpeted our bedroom. How nice it is to see the rooms carpeted. Bare floors look so forlorn especially here in this cold country.

Our house is so cozy now, it seems more like living. And I am glad for Bob's sake.[55] He enjoys the warm floors and the pretty red flowers in the brussels carpet.

Our little boy enjoys everything now; a very good time and good health. He is learning to talk very rapidly now at last. And is such a big boy. I am letting his hair grow. It is so pretty and curly, and I want him to have long curls this Winter.

Eddie, the native boy living with Edith, arrived from Quinhagak last Wednesday the eleventh. He came for medicine for Edith who has been ill for some time with throat trouble due to grippe.[56] Eddie left again on Friday. I am afraid he will have a hard trip as it is growing very cold, and paddling will be hard on the hands.

We have had such a balmy fall, such warm bright sunny days. Last year the river was frozen over on the second of October. The water is still clear but it is continually growing colder.

Herman sent for Edith to come up if she is not better, but this cannot be until dog teaming begins as the ice will soon form, making boating unsafe.

October 17, 1898

Last night was or seemed very cold. The thermometer registered twenty above zero when I looked at 7 A.M., but Herman thought it must have been down to zero before the sun arose.

The creek in front of the mission was frozen over and has remained so all day. In the main channel ice has been running all day. This is doubtless the beginning of a long cold dreary Winter.

All of the boys are thinking about skating and are getting their skates in trim.

Jesse, Daniel, and Dick and Fritz, two small boys, are all the school boys on the Mission this Winter. We miss the boys very much. I am afraid the Board will regret having closed school as the natives all appreciate the

---

55. Robert Herman Romig was Herman and Ella's first child born at Bethel on January 26, 1897 (Joseph Herman Romig Family Papers, Series 1, Box 1, Folder 1).

56. The word "grippe" was a colloquial term for influenza (Fortuine, Robert, *Chills and Fever: Health and Disease in the Early History of Alaska* [Fairbanks: University of Alaska Press, 1989], 207).

advantage of education now.[57] Many good scholars receive good salaries as interpreters on the steamers and at the different trading stations on the Yukon. The Catholics have a very fine school and naturally our members wish to send their children there since our school is closed, and this may mean the loss of some of our members. I hope the Board will have the school carried on next year.

Bob is getting to be quite an expert shot. Herman made a pop gun for him last week which he thinks very fine and amuses himself much of the time with it. He can't manage it alone yet but plays with it most of the time. Herman had him marching through the house today with it over his shoulder while he carried his shot gun. Two monkeys sure enough.

Robert is a genuine boy in every sense of the word. Such a noisy busy child I never saw. He sings and yells most of the day. I think he takes after aunt Sadie in singing for he sings away and hardly ever strikes a tune.[58]

We have a very small family now. Epuck, our hired man, and Patsy his wife, live in the old office or the little house where we keep our sick. We give them their flour, tea and sugar once a week, and they live to themselves. Nellie, my good faithful servant, and Daniel live with us in the house. These are all I have to bake bread for, and how strange it seems too for since we returned from the coast about July twenty-fourth it seems my principal occupation has been making bread. I have used at least six bags of flour in that time. I had two women sewing for me for some time and Bessie and Nellie in the house. Besides these all the time to feed, there were strangers continually coming and going.

Now travel can neither be by sled or water and thank good fortune for the rest, for I am tired of the multitude.

Bessie went home with her mother, Sallie, who had been sewing for me, a week ago yesterday, so Nellie and I are alone but I get along better with one servant than with two.

Bessie is a very nice little girl. We all love her, but I think I will not take her back again for her mother is such a terror to scold, and when she comes to visit she always makes trouble all around among the servants, and makes Bessie go home with her each time.

---

57. Due to a food shortage, the Bethel school was closed in the early winter of 1898. "However, a normal class, consisting of the most promising of the natives, was continued throughout the year" (Jackson, Sheldon, L. L. D. *Education in Alaska, 1897–98* [Washington, D.C.: Government Printing Office, 1899], 1765). A year later the Mission reported that "lack of means has necessitated the closing of the school" (Jackson 1898–99, 1392).

58. Sadie Ervin was Ella's younger sister born in January 1878 and married to William Hawke (Pennsylvania Census Records 1900; *Anchorage Daily Times*, January 2, 1937).

Bessie has been engaged to Eddie for some time. Last Saturday evening Sallie got in a tantrum, and declared she would not allow Bessie to marry him. I think the simple woman must have had a crazy spell for Eddie is the nicest native boy around and a good Christian. I hope Eddie will not marry Bessie for Sallie will only make them miserable by her scolding.

I am sorry Sallie is such a creature for she is such valuable help both in fur sewing and housework. She does such nice sewing. I would like to keep her were it not for her never tiring tongue.

I have most of my sewing done for the Winter. Bob has a new fur dress and a parka, and Herman and I have our boots and parkas done also.

Dear me, we have to make or worry about the making of boots, coats, caps, gloves and in fact every stitch we wear up here. We sew and work all the time and are never done either.

Sallie and I made Herman such a beautiful fur coat just before Sallie went home. It was my first attempt at cutting and fitting a man's coat, and I feel encouraged. I am going to try to make one for papa this Winter. I think he would find it very comfortable.

Saturday, October 22, 1898

The last three days have been much warmer. For awhile we thought cold weather at hand. The river and lakes froze over. We had one or two slight snow storms, but the temperature has gone up again, and we have had three more balmy Fall days.

The boys, however, have been skating right along and say the ice is perfectly safe. We missionaries have not been inspired as yet to go skating. Mr. and Mrs. Weinlick do not skate.[59] John has gone and Helmichs have gone to Ougavig for the Winter to take Mr. Weber's place, so we are a small party, so a skating party would be a slim one indeed.

We enjoy long walks along the river's edge now. The ground is dry and hard, no mosquitoes to bother us, and the reality that walks must soon end make them very enjoyable.

I dislike to think of the long dreary Winter. The days are so short, the weather so severe, and Herman will be away much of the time so the outlook is not a pleasant one.

Mrs. Weinlick and I made mince meat today, and I think it is very good. We followed as best we could a recipe of Mrs. Vorees. Many of [the]

---

59. Reverend Joseph Weinlick and his wife, Rosa, served as missionaries in the Kuskokwim region from 1898–1906 (Schwalbe 1985, 300).

things we cannot get so we substitute them by others as near alike as we can manage to find. We cannot get fresh meat so we used one can of roast beef and one of corn beef. In place of boiled cider we used some apple butter and fruit juice; the suet we simply had to leave out, for we had nothing like it in any way, only some dirty tallow which was not desirable.

It is very hard to cook now. Our potatoes are all gone. We have nothing but canned and salt meats. How we long for ptarmigans and Jack rabbits but it is soon yet; these or venison either.

Herman has asked for supper. I will have to grant the request but what *shall* I get?

Sunday, October 30, 1898

This is such a beautiful clear cold morning. The ground is covered with snow, the river is frozen over, and Winter is here again. This morning at 7 o'clock the thermometer registered about six below zero: this was the coldest morning thus far.

Winter traveling with dog team has begun. Four sleds arrived here from different directions during the past week. I am very sorry too that the ice is safe enough so soon. I had wished for a rest from the strangers. But our "hotel" and "free lunch counters" must again assume action. Any time during the day or night, when the doors are unlocked, we must be ready to serve tea and bread to the arrivals if they are natives, and the best we can find if they are white men. The principal missionary duty of the sisters seems to [be to] open her heart, her home, and bread box to everybody and anybody in the land. If she does not do the latter cheerfully she is not a good Christian.

I honestly believe that most of our Christians are Christians for what there is in it. They do not hesitate to ask for what they want and they always expect to get it too.

They will bring different things to trade for material or flour or something too much to ask for, and when they leave they invariably ask for a little soap, salt, matches, sugar, tea or some little thing or other.

It is very trying to get up at any time when they come and wait upon the miserable beggars. I can't truthfully say that I always do it with good grace.

And a more lazy set you could not find any where. But for this I can always offer apology, for they are very poor, have poor homes more like pig pens, have very little to eat or wear and therefore very little to do to keep house.

These poor destitute people surely deserve much pity, the best of them have but little and have no way of getting more.

May 28, 1899

Well, well, well, such an attempt at journal keeping. So many many things have happened since this poor forlorn journal was started. Well, I guess I never was intended for a scribe for I utterly detest writing.

I had thought [of] destroying these few pages and send only a letter, but then there may be something interesting in them so I will just add on to it.

Wednesday, June 7, 1899

I will make another attempt to write to you. Robert or Margaret generally manage to interrupt me at such times, but they are both asleep now for the night, I trust.[60]

I have not written one letter as yet, and the boats will leave for the coast in a few days. If I do not get to write to Ned and Duck you must assure them that this is meant for them too.[61] With my babies three, (for I tell Herman he is as good as a babe) my house, and my garden, I find most of my time taken up.

Robert is such an independent little boy. This Summer he is out of doors from morning till night or if not he is close beside his papa, whom he thinks is the sweetest being on earth. He talks nearly everything, but all in native. One of his favorite pastimes is playing at having prayer meetings. He gets hold of some rope or chain, [and] rings the bell. While he shakes the rope he sings, "tie lie, tulu, tulu, tulu." This is supposed to be the bell ringing. A few days ago I heard him ringing the bell and looked all around for him. Finally I found [him] behind the house with a dog chain that was at one end fast to one of his papa's dogs. The dog stood there half asleep while Robert rang the bell several times and had his

60. Marietta Margaret Romig was the second child born to Herman and Ella at Bethel on November 6, 1898 (Joseph Herman Romig Family Papers, Series 1, Box 1, Folder 1).

61. Ella's older brother, Edward, and his wife (Pennsylvania Census Records, 1880).

prayer meetings. You would scarcely take him for a white boy he is so tanned.

Margaret is a very dear baby girl. She has been such a good baby. She is quite a big baby girl now, and a very happy little girl. She has no teeth as yet. The picture I sent is very good of her. Robert would not allow his papa to take his picture so I cannot send you one. I wanted you to see him in pants. He wears pants altogether now and thinks it fine to be like papa. Edith gave him a pair of shoes last week. He is so proud of them. He had always worn fur boots before. When he had [to] give them up to have the buttons fastened on he went to the closet and cried as though his little heart would break.

June 8, 1899[62]

DEAR FATHER, MOTHER AND BRO. AND SISTER:

As my time is short, I will write a few lines for all in Ella's journal. A year ago today we started for the coast to receive our year's supplies and the mail which is as important as any part of the cargo and more sought for than anything on the boat. We were not disappointed in our expectation for many letters came, and we feasted on the stores the boat brought, first the letters and then the eatables for we had been at the coast about five weeks and were short of provisions when the boat came in.

One of our missionaries lost his life in coming to shore. He was in company with some miners, who were not any of them sea-faring men, and so when the storm arose all were lost. The storm was very severe, as the tents in which we were living had to be tied down, also the Bay was enough to wreck any boat of ordinary strength for the waves would dash above the bank as they were driven in by the storm. We succeeded in landing our goods all right and returned in safety. The trip was quite a sea shore outing to all of us and especially to Robert who learned to walk while away on this trip.

We are expecting to send you some pictures this year that will illustrate to you our Alaskan home and the people and surroundings in general that we have. Most of the pictures are what I have taken and are good illustrations of the people and of the place, though they often show defects in photography but that is the fault of the operator and not the camera.

---

62. Journal entry for this date was made by Herman.

Our home was again blessed by the birth of our infant daughter Margaret on November 3 [*sic*], 1898.[63] To us, as all parents who love their children, Bob and Margaret are about right. Bob runs after his Father all day and is rapidly learning native. Margaret, of course, as yet is not distinguished for much. Her mother thinks most likely for the colic at night if anything she excels in above other traits, however she is a very sweet little babe.

This year has been a very busy one owing to the loss of so many missionaries, some of whom were drowned and others recalled, for this reason the few that were left had much to do, and as I am one of the older missionaries by this time, I had to travel much this year. To tell the truth, I do not like to be from home so much, and in fact did not go as often as occasion really called on me to go, however home is all the dearer by having to leave it and go among so much dirt and filth, yet when we return, the very sight of home and Ella and the babies makes us happy before we finally arrive. Happy because we have finished one more trip, and happy to return to those we love. To me Alaska would be a very dreary place were it not for Ella and the children who make home a pleasure and life bearable in this far away land.

Missionary work is not as one would always think. To be a missionary is to give out, by word of mouth, by example, and often of the necessities of life. These people put their standard of living scarcely higher, if any, than the missionary they follow. True, they know no missionary is perfect and that there is a higher example than that of the missionary yet they scarcely expect to attain perfection above the example set them by their ministers. Of course they come short even in this, yet the missionary has an influence by example that words will hardly express. To work well with a native you must make him feel you think he is a man in every respect and that you treat him such, and all the while you are teaching him a higher standard and trying to get him to leave his former beliefs and superstitions and take your ideas of life. This he only does when he finds you to be a true friend and worthy of his following you as an example and also finds that you live up to what you ask him to believe.

One can entertain himself talking to and living with these people, yet their influence is not to keep you up with the times or to elevate your ideas of the world in general, yet they are a good people to study human-nature among as you can almost see their minds as they think. Your actions and words have so marked an effect on them.

---

63. Marietta Margaret Romig was born November 6, 1898 (Joseph Herman Romig Family Papers, Series 1, Box 1, Folder 1).

Herman Romig was the first medical doctor to practice in southwest Alaska. He is shown here in 1897 in his home office.
(Courtesy, Alaska and Polar Regions Department, University of Alaska Fairbanks, Joseph Romig Collection, acc. #90-043-949N)

Ella and myself are becoming more attached to the people and the work yet when our time is up we fully expect to come home, though I suppose to leave this cool refreshing climate and return to the warmer parts of this continent will be dreaded a little, yet this will only be a small item as offset by the seeing again of friends and home and the living among civilized people.

We are anxiously awaiting the mail from home and hope nothing but the best may be heard from you all.

My best regards to Aunts and Uncles and Cousins all of whom I am sorry to have so short an acquaintance with and hope to see more of, and my affectionate greeting to all.

I am your loving son and brother.

J. H. Romig

Thursday, June 8, 1899

Just one year ago today we started for the coast, and I must confess I heartily wish we were going again this year. Last year's trip did us all so much good. A change of surroundings and good sea air is just as enjoyable up here, and more so I think, than in the states. That trip was my first and last since I first arrived here in this lonely little Bethel. This is a very healthy climate I think, and I am sure I had rather be here than in the states just at this season of the year. But it would be nice to run in and visit with you all now and then. Staying in one little place grows very tiresome from one year's end to another. But just think, three years of our time has flown, and only four more years and we hope to see you all again. I don't know whether the time seems long to you or not, but here it flies so rapidly, and each year seems shorter.

We are learning the language, but slowly since I can talk some, and have become acquainted with the natives and their ways and customs. I enjoy their company, and like them very much. Most of them are very kind and friendly toward one another, as well as toward the missionaries. Only when I get the blues do I wish to flee from this free wild-like life. One is free to dress and live as he wishes and need not fear the criticism of society. You may know that Alaska agrees with us when Herman weighs 197 ½ lbs. and I 173, and we both seem to increase daily. If I continue in this way in the coming four years, I will be ashamed to appear in the civilized world.

The past Winter has been a fine one. Very cold at times but very few severe storms. We grew very tired of strangers arriving. It seemed we had someone here all the time. I hope and pray that a time will come when we sisters here at the mission need not be slaves for the travelers. Natives as well as white men. Herman was away much of the time but these were always times of quiet for the natives do not come so much in his absence.

I spoke of my garden. You will doubtless think, "Well, I would like to see the garden that Ella could get up." But you would be surprised to see my nice cabbage and rutabaga plants. Our lettuce, radishes and turnips are all up. The peas are beginning to peep through the ground. I have forty-eight hills of potatoes doing very nicely. These are my first potatoes. Mrs. Helmich raised the seed potatoes last Summer.[64] We cannot raise many varieties up here in this cold place, the seasons are so short. I have some celery plants. They are small but healthy looking.

---

64. Reverend Benjamin K. Helmich and his wife, Anna, served as missionaries in the Kuskokwim region from 1893–1908 (Schwalbe 1985, 300).

Ella did not consider herself a gardener prior to coming to Alaska, however,
her Bethel effort produced impressive results.
(Courtesy, Alaska and Polar Regions Department, University of Alaska Fairbanks,
Joseph Romig Collection, acc. #90-043-909N)

John and Edith are going to the states this Spring. Will probably return next Spring.[65] We will miss them very much, and [so] will the natives who love them so much. They surely have done good work here among this people.

Bessie, my nice little nurse girl, was married to Eddie late in the Winter. Eddie is a nice young man and a good Christian. He is a boy whom John and Edith have raised from a mere babe. I miss Bessie very much.

I have but one servant now, Mary, whom the natives call the big servant and they do not miss it much for she weighs, I should judge, about 250 lbs. But she is a very good, good natured, and willing girl which is the best of all.

---

65. John and Edith Kilbuck left Alaska in 1900. They returned in 1903 when the Bureau of Education offered John a teaching position at Barrow (Fienup-Riordan 1991, 246).

There are a few things I would like you to send to me next year. One thing I will probably want will be a nice rag carpet for a 15 by 18 room but of this I will write later in the Fall mail. If I send for the carpet, I will send you the pay from here. I do not wish the folks at Bethlehem to know of this as they sent me carpet last Summer. But even so, floors up here are too cold without carpet, and I have none for my sitting room. The Board will doubtless think me too extravagant, so I will pay for it myself.

Then I would like you to send me the black silk that is rolled up and in my trunk. Leave it rolled up and wrap it well before packing, and then my little brown cape too. This will be all. If papa or Ned have an old black suit I wish they would send it to me. We have to make all of our caps up here, and I have no heavy cloth. The dark blue will not do. If I thought papa would wear a cap such as we wear up here, I would send him one of otter.

We are having our great egg time now for the year. I am making noodles and drying eggs every day now for the Winter.

We had very few geese this Spring, about five hundred here on the mission, but these were plenty I am sure, for you may imagine that cleaning from fifteen to thirty geese in one day is no small job.

Now I am going to close for this time as I have noodles to cut and Marietta Margaret is fussy.

With love to all, I am as ever

Your loving daughter,

Ella

September 1, 1899

My dear father and mother:

How time flies, I surely thought I would get your journal begun before. A whole Summer with almost nothing to do, and yet I have done nothing. But I am most sure we all feel very little like writing to our friends these days. Our Summer has been so discouraging. After having waited since early in June for our supplies, we are still without anything. Our mail was fortunately sent by way of the Yukon or we had still been waiting for that. After having waited nine weeks at the coast for our goods the missionaries finally returned home, and Herman and Mr. Weinlick are now on the Yukon trying to get something for us to live upon this Winter, having left here on August seventeenth (17). As I have written you in several letters, a boat the *Bowhead*, having our goods came in Goodnews

Bay, but the captain could not find the Kuskokwim River and after having sent out three men to look for it, he left, probably on account of rough water fearing his vessel would be driven on the sand as it drew eleven feet of water, and at that place the water is shallow. The sailors, after looking for the Kuskokwim River, as well as for the return of their vessel, finally ran across a native who could speak a few words in English. He could count up to a hundred and say Mr. Kilbuck, Dr. Romig at the tea pot, so the men took his directions and after some time reached Quinhagak. Those who had been waiting at the coast for the goods returned Aug. 14th, Herman leaving three days later for the Yukon. John, who had started for Nushagak to try to get something to eat for the Winter, found the weather too severe and water too rough for so small a boat [so they] returned Aug. 19 of course with nothing.

While our provisions are almost gone, strange to say we get hungry just as often as when everything is full and plenty.

We obtained a few bags of flour two days ago from a trader passing here, and also some tea, all of which was somewhat damaged by water. Two men, whom we had sent to the Yukon for some very necessary things, returned the same day with a very few things. The trader being absent his son was afraid to give more. The flour they brought was wet and full of tobacco juice being near a bale in the boat. It does seem that we are doomed to starve this year.

The three sailors have all left for the Yukon River, will go to St. Michael, and from there home.

September 6, 1899

David, who left for the Yukon at the same time Herman and Mr. Weinlick left, returned today saying that after a very hard trip they all reached Pimiut just one week after they left here which would make it Aug 24; Herman having left the following day for St. Michael to buy our goods, as Mr. Hendricks, the trader at Pimiut, had no goods on hand. Herman thought he would be back to the Russian Mission again on Sept 3rd. If this be true they will probably return in two weeks. John thinks they will get back no sooner than Sept 20.[66]

---

66. In 1943 Herman self-published his account of this episode titled *In 1899 The Bowhead Failed To Arrive* (Joseph Herman Romig Family Papers, Series 2, Box 3, Folder 37).

David brought us states mail and among my letters was one from papa written in June. I felt quite cheered from Sadie's letters concerning mama's health. She wrote that she seemed decidedly better, but my letter of today [said] she was again so ill. Poor mother, will you ever get over your trouble? Herman and I think so much about you and wish too we could be with you. Herman could probably do no more for you than Dr. Cross, but he would gladly do all in his power. I am sure Dr. Cross will do all in his power for your best good, and he is so fully acquainted with your constitution. It is more a matter of time than of treatment in your case. Regarding a tumor, however, I would consult the best of medical skill. Why not go over and see Dr. Bullard? He is an excellent physician. I was surprised to hear of uncle Theodore's death. Had he been sick long? Poor fellow, and so much of his life wasted too. I hope he made his peace with his God before he died.

We have never heard a word from Ed this year, why does he nor Duck write to us? We have the news now that the vessel with our goods is in St. Michael. But we do not place much confidence in the report. Should it be true, Herman will doubtless try to get the captain to come around to the mouth of the Kuskokwim again where our goods can be landed as usual.

Our provisions are getting *so low*. I am really hungry sometimes, yes, many times. I miss Herman so much but if he were here what *could* I cook for him three times a day? My garden is quite fair, but not as good as in other years. The year has been so dry. For seven weeks after our garden was planted we had no rain. I have had the very nicest of lettuce, have very nice cabbage, beets, turnips, rutabagas and celery coming on, as well as potatoes. You see, I am quite a gardener.

Since it began to rain nearly four weeks ago it has rained almost constantly. We are getting so tired of this sloppy weather.

September 13, 1899

Herman came home on Sunday, the tenth, with a very good supply of provisions. Made a very quick trip to St. Michael. His trip from Paimiut, however, was anything but pleasant, the steamer being in a poor state for travel. In a wind storm she was driven on the wind, which was indeed fortunate for all on board, for had it not been for this they would have been driven out to sea and doubtless been lost, for the boat was perfectly unmanageable. Herman said that when he reached St. Michael he felt that he had great cause to be thankful. He arrived on one day [and] purchased his list of provisions. Officials from the different companies wanted to talk either about the wreck of last Summer at the mouth of the Kuskokwim or concerning a new mail route through this section, so Herman's time, you may imagine, was all taken until the following day when he returned to the Russian Mission. As soon as he arrived, and his goods were landed from the steamer, his boats that were in waiting were loaded, and in less than a half day were on their homeward way, reaching here in one week and one day afterwards. No one, save Herman, Mr. Weinlick and the good faithful natives who helped, can imagine how hard the work was to supply our mouths for the coming Winter. Over several marshy tundra portages, goods and boats had to be carried. I am always glad when Herman returns from these long dangerous trips. They are no jokes, I can assure you. I cannot help but worry even though they are getting to be old stories, and that each time he returns in safety. The *Bowhead*, our "would be" vessel was in St. Michael in August, but had left before Herman arrived at that place. The A. C. Co. [Alaska Commercial Company] men thought that the Captain would not venture in here again, as he was fearfully afraid of the Kuskokwim waters, but thought that should he go to Unalaska in time Mr. Grey, the A. C. Co.'s agent, would send our goods over. So they may yet come. I will not give up hope until the ice forms thus making it impossible to come. We so much need clothing. Of course we can manage to mend and darn and in this way pull through until our vessel next Spring, when we trust she will not fail to reach us.

September 26, 1899

We are still having rain, rain, rain. It seems that it will never clear again. On Saturday and Sunday last it snowed much of the day. Once on Saturday the ground was almost covered with snow. We have had only light frosts as yet. I have brought some of our garden stuff in already. I made a five gallon keg of sauerkraut today with the help of Mrs. Weinlick. It was real fun to make it. Will tell you later how it turns out. Now won't you be surprised to hear that I made, or tried to the best of my ability, to make sauerkraut. And still more so, that I raised the cabbage to make it with. Well it is true never-the-less. One must buckle down to most anything up here in order to have everything. I have nearly a bushel of potatoes, but will keep most of these for seed. Potatoes are a luxury up here. Oh, how potato hungry I get sometimes. My celery, though small, is very nice and such a pretty white too. But the chief things we raise here are dogs. I am now feeding twelve young ones for Herman, and while I am fond of them, they carry so much dirt into my entries, and howl and fight so much I am half tempted to switch them. I think that if you were to hear the dogs howl and fight for just one day you would [go] almost crazy. They even grate a little on me yet.

September 27, 1899[67]

DEAR MOTHER AND FATHER:

I hope to write a few lines this evening in Ella's journal, for this is the surest way for me to write, for at each mail sending season there is so much business correspondence that my friends have to take the will for the deed. Robert's large black eyes are watching me over the table and their expression is as much as to say that he thinks it bed time but I guess his mother will soon tuck him away for the night. He likes it very much when he can have a romp before going to bed but tonight I will forego the pleasure which is almost as great a pleasure for me as it is for him. To you the romps with your children and their many laughs are long since a thing of the past, however you can at least understand where we are on the ladder of life, and appreciate the cheer and comfort these little ones bring to us. Their little hearts and voices are not affected by being in Alaska, nor worried or restrained by care or responsibilities. Margaret is on the floor on a bear skin and doing her best at baby language. She will likely be animated and lively like little Helen was when we left to come up here.[68] I tell Ella that she and the children make home the happiest place in all Alaska for me so of this I have written first. Enough of our outside joys and cares to follow.

Of the daily routine of our life here, Ella tries to give you a good account, and so I will try to give a short synopsis of events since spring. We count from the coming of the birds or the leaving of the ice until the wild fowl migrate again and the Great White Bear's breath again congeals our river and paints everything white again for winter. At this time we are "putting on our mittens" as the natives say when they see the rainbow-like display of colors around the sun, which in the locality is indicative of on

---

67. Journal entry for this date made by Herman.
68. Helen was Ella's niece; Edward and Duck's daughter.

coming cold. So we are preparing for the cold, i.e. putting in our double windows, securing wood and cleaning up the place for soon nothing on the ground will be visible.

We enjoyed a very pleasant summer. The month of June was without rain, the mosquitoes were few, and the run of fish was large. Part of the Mission party were at the coast to meet the supply vessel (which as you already know failed us), and part of us were at home improving the place and looking after the fishing. Ella and the children often went with me when looking after the fish, and we had many pleasant boat rides.

We enjoyed a period of refreshment with our mail which came on July 21st. 1899. But soon [we] were forced to see we were left in a far away place with no supplies for a year. The tables were then turned, and we who had been having an easy time at home, if Alaska life is easy, had a little trip of 250 miles by river, lakes, creeks and portages to go to get to where supplies could be had. This was not all. We had to secure them from St. Michael about 350 miles still further away but this cost us little effort as the steamers landed our goods at the portage to this river which is about 200 or 250 miles from Bethel. The trip was far from what is usually termed a pleasure trip, yet we were all pleased when the trip was finished. Everyone that was on the trip was pleased to get home, and those at home were pleased to see us come for the mission was in need. Ella was not as plump, i.e. as stout, as when we left as they were on [a] rather restricted diet. She is now as stout as ever, since plenty of provisions are now on hand to do us until more can be secured in the winter.

I am thankful for the quiet rest at home I will now have in the next few weeks, for very soon the jingle jingle of the sleigh bells will mark the only season of rest that we get i.e. on the road while running or riding your brains are resting and being refreshed by good air and change of scenery, but when at home in winter my office seems to be the Court and Council room as well as Medical dispensary, and when on the road the village houses are poor and you are always surrounded by the sick or those to be talked to as friends or to council. Some may think this a good place for me to rest but in this work there is no rest summer or winter, except just at those seasons when the river freezes over and when it opens up again.

As the room is becoming chilly, I will close for tonight.

Your affectionate son,

Herman

Sunday, October 8, 1899[69]

We have been having some quite cold weather for the past week, but the wind is in the south now and it [is] raining quite lively for which we are very grateful as both of our boats are out yet and threatened to be frozen in for the winter. Ella says for me i.e. Herman to write some. To continue about the boats. One of the boats, *Swan* by name, came opposite the Mission today while we were in church and soon after attempted to cross to the mission. The channel the boat was in was free from ice which has been running for the past four days, but as they came around this island into the other channel the boat was caught in the flow of ice and taken down stream. By the work of those on shore and those on the boat we succeeded in getting her ashore and have her tied in a comparatively safe place. The second boat, the *Scow*, is about 15 miles from here against the river bank in a jam of ice. She also will likely come home safe tomorrow or the next day as we are having a warm south storm and rain which we hope will soon permit the river to clear itself of ice. As it has been new ice was formed each night and kept the river full of running ice but now with a south wind we feel quite hopeful of the boats both safely getting home.

We are all in fair health. The baby is teething and when entertained is also very entertaining but again does not wish to be neglected so she keeps her mother quite busy. The heavy stream of the work also gives me occasionally attacks of nervousness but they are so slight as to be scarcely worthy of mention. Ella retains her health and cheerful spirits, and when I am tired or worn with my work, she succeeds in dispelling all thoughts of myself and makes me change my tune to rejoicing over my happy home which she and the babies fill with sunshine.

Last week, by the aid of some natives, one of the missionaries and myself made a native house which some poor or helpless native families needed and then we ran the sawmill. It fell to me to be chief cook and bottle washer of the sawing as the other man knew less than myself about the sawmill, however, we succeeded in sawing what logs were on hand. Bro. Weinlick, the other missionary who assisted me, was badly scared since he had to run the engine and knew nothing about it. He stopped about every time a log was finished for me to see if everything was going well. Never the less, we got along well and I guess I was about as awkward handling the saw as he was the engine though I did not dare let on.

---

69. Ella began this journal entry, but Herman wrote the bulk of it.

One woman said she heard the *Kass'aq* or white men were running the engine even if they were afraid, and she was afraid in her house some distance away lest it would blow up. This puts me in mind of what I told the boys who were carrying water for me once while I was running the engine. I said if the water gets out of the water gauge this thing is liable to go off like many guns and kill us all, so when you hear me whistle twice hurry with water. I may add I did not whistle much that day for water. They think the sawmill dangerous, and it is good for them that they do. Today as the missionary who is trained to do the preaching was sick, it fell to me to keep the service. Ella as usual did her part with her music and we got along nicely. It is always a trial for me to try to preach, but what the Lord gives me to do I always try to perform and leave the balance to Him. I had the baptism of the infant son of one of our house servants, and Ella requested to name it; the child got Father Ervin's, i.e. Albert, named after Ella's father. He is a nice little boy, and so father must remember we will often hear his name as the child is almost as good as an orphan, and we are glad to keep its mother for her valuable services in the house. The mother, Jennie by name, is one of the first couple I have married, and as they have separated we have the woman as a house servant.

Well, I must close as one of the Helpers has come in to talk to me. Your affectionate son.

Herman

Thursday, October 12, 1899

Herman says, My! Ella you are a poor correspondent, why, how little you have written to your folks. Well, I said they know that of old so will not expect much from me. But privately, I think I am doing well this year, as least, well for me, for I am keeping a private journal and this one, together with now and then a letter.

I find that with two children, one a very lively little boy who is ever into some mischief or trouble, and a frisky teething baby girl, time for writing is not so plentiful. But man-like, Herman cannot see why I cannot cook three times a day, (not necessarily such a big task now, but however, a necessary one) oversee my house, care for my babies, and still write long flowing letters and journals. I tell him that as he can't or won't see such things that I will forgive him.

Our boats are both safely in. Still have south wind and rain. We have had so much rain, mud and muck for the past weeks or rather months, that I am getting anxious to see Winter come to freeze up this disagreeable mud business. Our kitchen floor and entry looks more like a pig pen than anything else, but there is little use to scrub now with so many coming in, and these large soft boot soles carry in so much dirt. Our houses here are more like hotels in the states. Everyone on or around the place, and strangers coming from every direction all come in and make themselves at home. It is, no doubt, a good way to do missionary work, but I must confess, it galls me to ever have a dirty house.

We have received sad news concerning one of our members, the wife of Helper Neck. She, together with another native woman, was out in a native canoe, they ran against a snag, [and] their canoe began to fill with water. Mrs. Neck, in trying to get to the other end of the canoe to tip it, fell over and was drowned while the other woman caught hold of the snag and held to it until help came to her. Bro. Neck is our best native teacher and a sincere good Christian man. Poor fellow, he has so much trouble, is sick much of the time, when his wife has always cared for him and his four little ones. Now that he is without a wife and his children a mother how hard it will be for him.

Wednesday, October 18, 1899

I am so tired tonight but feel that I must try to write some to you. Have been helping Mary with the washing today as Jennie's baby, Albert, is a very cross boy, and will not allow his mother to help me very much these days. One must work all of the time here if we would wish our houses be only half decent. And Robert and Margaret manage to add very much to the washing, so wash day is always a hard one.

The men were out hunting for rabbits yesterday and today, and really, for once or rather twice, met with success. In all, they brought in twenty-three yesterday, Herman and our men getting ten, and today thirteen, we having six. I can assure you we are more than thankful for this treat, for I may truthfully say that we have not been getting enough to eat for some time past. Living without meat and in fact, without many other common articles of the everyday living, is not much living. We simply exist this year. I guess we will have to eat like the old woman who fed her pig; eat well one week, and nothing the next, so that we will have a streak of lean and a streak of fat. Why even potatoes we eat as you would eat the finest of candy, yes, they are even more of a treat for only a very few times in a whole year can we have them. But as Herman says, all of these things we

Rabbit hunts provided meat and skins for food and clothing.
(Courtesy, Alaska and Polar Regions Department, University of Alaska Fairbanks,
Joseph Romig Collection, acc. #90-043-899aN)

will enjoy the more when we can have them again. But, while we must forego many pleasures up here, we still have much in our favor. A good healthful climate for one thing, an excellent climate for raising babes if not potatoes. With the exception of grippe which comes regularly once or twice a year, we never or very seldom have any of the many diseases of the states. And then for this seven years of free easy life, that is to say, free from painful society and fashion. I often wonder how I could ever try to dress according to the "latest style" again. I am certainly thankful for this blessed rest from all this.

Of course many things are very displeasing and disgusting. Just at the present time I am more than disgusted with the fact that Robert and Margaret both have the itch. This will seem horrible to you, I know, and surely it is no joke. Robert has it very slightly on one hand and Margaret on her left hip. I think they caught if from Mary who had it some time ago on her arm. They are all nearly well again. It is almost impossible to avoid such things at all times, where we are constantly thrown in contact with so many filthy, diseased persons. We shake hands with many every day who may or may not have anything from itch to any other filthy disease.

Thursday, October 19, 1899

Men are all hunting again today. I told Herman that more than rabbits are without heads these few last days. Oh, how much we enjoy the rabbits though. Are living fat on pot pies, noodle soup, and stewed or fried rabbit. On this kind of fare I can gain flesh again. During the Summer I weighed over 170 lbs but am very thin now. But no wonder, for such [a] slim diet as we have been having is not sufficient to nourish baby Margaret and mama too and both do well.

November 1, 1899

You must not think that Robert and Margaret have the itch all this while, they are both all right now.

Sunday, November 27, 1899

MY DEAR FATHER AND MOTHER:

Such a long time since I last wrote to you, and so much has happened. But of everything I have no time tonight to write about, only of the one that fills our hearts and minds with so much sadness at this time. Our poor brother John [Kilbuck] has had such an affliction. Last Tuesday morning he came over and said to Herman, "I wish you could tell me what is the trouble with my hand if you know, for I don't." During the night at about 3 A.M. he was awakened by a sharp pain between the first two fingers of his right hand as if by a needle. This kept growing worse, he feeling sick all over his body. His fingers and hand kept swelling until Thursday morning when Herman made an incision, but of no avail. The infection had already taken such a hold. On Friday A.M. Herman cut his hand in four places. On Saturday morning found his arm swollen, and made one incision in the arm and two more on his hand, putting in drainage tubes to drain the pus. But all this was not enough to head off the rapid work of this awful germ. This morning the hand looked so ugly, the arm swollen above the elbow, and working rapidly toward the shoulder. It was John's wish, as well as Edith's, to remove the arm, which Herman felt too was the only thing to do, which he did this morning. And so our poor brother has lost his right arm nearly to the shoulder. And we trust, may recover. But at this time his general condition is very bad, his blood being so badly poisoned.

Monday, November 28, 1899

John is still in a very critical condition, the wound is doing very well. I scarcely know who suffers the most John or Herman, for we all feel anxious for him, his blood poisoning may yet prove fatal. Then it was hard to take off the right arm of a fellow missionary as well as relative. I am so glad that Herman has so much surgical experience, for it would be still harder to do all this and not know much about it.

March 14, 1900

Dear father and mother:

While down at Bethel yesterday Herman brought this old, "intended to be journal for you," along with my own private journal which I had asked him to bring, so I am going to write some in it for you. You will wonder where we are if not at Bethel. Well, for some time Herman has been trying to induce me to do something out of my common way of living, make a trip or something else just as extra-ordinary, and finally he succeeded. This finds me, us rather, with our tent and stove a few miles above home in the timber where Herman has some men at work cutting fire wood. Herman declares the change and fresh air will do us all good, and I sincerely trust it may for with all the trouble I am having with Robert and Margaret I feel that some reward is due me. Margaret is just as naughty as naughty can be, she is such a spry active little girl, accustomed to having plenty of space to move around in. While here she is unable to walk over the uneven tent floor, and consequently is mad about it all the time. If it were not for Mary, her old nurse who is with me, I think I would be beside myself, but the little midget manages to keep us both pretty busy. But after all I am having a rest and I really need it, for we have had so many white men to entertain this Winter. The care of my babies and large house, with only one poor servant to help me, that I am ready for a rest. If this is to be the rest (?) I must make good my chance. The day before yesterday, the day we arrived here, while we were eating supper, we noticed our tent to be on fire from our tent stove. Two large holes were burned in the roof before we could put it out. Yesterday it snowed all day, and the heat from our stove melted the snow on the tip of the tent, the benefit of which we got inside as the roof dripped all day. Today is clear but a very high wind is whistling through our little nook in the trees almost carrying our tent with it. The stove pipe rattles sometimes coming off of the stove which fact frightens Robert until he trembles. The poor little fellow says, "The pipe is afraid, hurry and take me to Anna" (the native for mama). He wants his papa to hitch up the dogs and take him home right away.

April 28, 1900

Mr. Weinlick arrived at our tent from a trip to Ougavig just as I finished the above sentence, and since then I have either never had or taken time to write more.

We spent a week in our camp and I must own I was more than sorry to have to return home for although we live in an out-of-the-way place in the world, there are each day enough folks in our house to keep it in a perfect uproar from morning till night, and a little time in quietness is something to be appreciated by a missionary, here at least.

Much has happened since I last wrote you. When I wrote in the camp we were all rejoicing that the time for "white travel" was spent, but in the midst of our rejoicing, lo and behold, they began coming from the other direction. Within the past month thirteen men have gone through here from San Francisco, among them were five, who arrived a week ago yesterday, bringing a great deal of mail. We received your letters written in February with this mail. We were all so glad for mail but not so glad for more boarders [to] feed and fit out for their trip to Andreafsky.[70] We have had so little during this past Winter, and the white men have just about eaten us out of house and home. It is now nearly time for the ice to leave, and I fully expect to see more white men arriving on each cake of ice, they can scarcely get here in any other way, but we are ready to look for most anything these days.

Nearly three weeks ago we thought our time of plenty had come when the geese arrived but as soon as they were seen the weather turned cold and the geese made themselves scarce. Seven were killed in all these days. But today the tables turned. Edith's boy brought in three, and our man on the mission hunted twenty-one. We are very glad for these geese as we

---

70. Village on the Lower Yukon River north of Bethel (Lenz, Mary and James H. Barker, *Bethel The First 100 Years* [Bethel: A City of Bethel Centennial History Project, 1985], 33).

have four typhoid fever cases here and nothing to make soup for them, and as they can eat nothing else much it was often a puzzle to know what to feed them on. Then we have a private patient also, Mrs. Belcoff [Bel'kov], the Yukon trader's wife.[71] Herman removed a cataract from her left and only eye, but poor soul, she cannot see. Herman thinks the eye is diseased inside. While I was out of the room Herman played a trick on me. He says below that he leaves me enough room to finish, but you see he is mistaken.

April 28, 1900[72]

DEAR MOTHER AND FATHER:

I will leave Ella a few lines to finish up what she was saying and then add some for myself. It seems I can find little time any more for writing as there is so much to be attended to each day. The medical duties of this place have been of enough importance to keep me busy part of the time, and then the endless routine of missionary duties to fill up the balance. Since the middle of last August I [have] been from home about 86 days and in all traveled over 2000 miles making my time at home all the more enjoyable when there was not too great a press of work. Ella and children have been well and thus I have been spared worry when from home. We often wish we could come home for a short visit but must abide our time, and then a visit will be the one thing so often thought of and at last realized.

Ella has been raising me a fine young dog team, and so next year my trips from home will be connected with less hardships than some have been. I suppose you often wonder at the long distances we make in a day when on the road, but there are many days when the snow is soft and deep when we cannot make long runs, and when if your team is poor you can do no riding. I will often have occasion to thank Ella for my fine young dog team. If they live they will be worth from $300 to $500 next winter.

This summer I am Census agent for this river and also have a trip to St. Michael to make. I expect to be gone much of the time, however Mr. Kilbuck takes most of the Census for me, and I expect to take Ella and children to St. Michael when I go for a little outing and change, as I know the trip will do them good.

---

71. Ella may have been referring to Mrs. Bel'kov, the wife of Zakharii Bel'kov, a Creole Russian Orthodox priest who worked along the Yukon River (Fienup-Riordan 1991, 133).

72. This journal entry was made by Herman.

The mission work has progressed good this year, and with the exception of the difficulties of this, as all similar works, we can say the year has passed very smoothly and the Lord has greatly blessed our efforts for which we have great reason for thanksgiving. Though we have been short of some goods yet we have had plenty of the staples for our daily needs, and we have fully found the promise of our Lord faithful when he says, "And lo I am with you," even if it be to the ends of the world. We so much hoped that I might be relieved of the care of this work this year but it seems no change will be likely to occur for the present, probably next year. We feel that they ask too much for one man to be physician, minister and superintendent even at such a seemingly small place as Bethel.

Ella also has much to do besides the care of our home, and we will be glad when we can be just everyday Dr. Romig and wife, and not so much care and worry of the work. Yet while here, we are striving to make all of our talents count for the most, as we cannot always be on a mission field, and now we have the Golden Opportunity for doing good that may not come to us again or at least this time cannot be lived again, and we feel however wearing our duties may seem that they are a privilege granted us by One who has deemed us worthy of so noble a cause, and we dare not falter until we can be relieved.

I sent you some photos in an album by express which I fear were lost since you did not speak of them. I hope they may come yet. They were sent to you at Wilkes-Barre Express Office and should have reached you last September. If you do not yet receive them and will let me know, I will try and trace them up as I have my Express receipt yet.

This river is likely to open up for mining, and then we will not be so alone, and further a U.S. Mail will likely reach us from the states two or three times in the winter of each year.

Your letters were all very interesting to me. We always look forward [to letters] from home by each regular or chance mail to us, and though I am a poor writer I hope you will not think I am too busy to read, which though addressed to Ella, are just as interesting to me and greatly appreciated.

I must close as Ella is getting sleepy, and I can tell by her yawning she wonders when I will put out the light for the night.

Your affectionate son.

J. H. Romig

June 9, 1900

MY DEAR FATHER AND MOTHER:

We are already looking forward to the arrival of our supply vessel although the mission and trader's boats have not yet left for the coast. We sincerely hope nothing will happen to the boat this year, but sometimes feel that she may not reach us for this has been such a stormy Spring. We have had so many fearful wind storms, and if they serve our boat as they have served our garden she will surely go back on us. I had saved so many potatoes from last year for seed, and those that were not switched to pieces by the wind froze to the ground two nights ago. Everything indeed seems against us. We are all so hungry for something green, but I fear we will have to wait a long time for it. It has been so cold all Spring I sometimes wonder if we will have any Summer. Two weeks ago we had two fires going all the time for four days to keep warm, and today is almost as cold.

If anything happens to our supplies this Summer, I will insist upon going home or [at] least leaving Bethel for we could not freight enough to keep us from going hungry for there would be so many things to bring this time that we had on hand last year, such as clothing, soap, rice, beans and coal oil, paint and oil and lead, ropes for the boats and in fact everything to run the mission, for we are out of everything now.

I must confess that I would be glad for a rest for I am tired out and thoroughly disgusted too. The white travel through here have been a perfect nuisance this year, and they all said that this was nothing compared to [the] number who would go through next year. Whether we have little or much they will expect as much as if we were a well stocked company store. I often say that I did not come up here to run a boarding house but such seems to be the case for white men as well as for the spoiled natives.

Herman is, as usual, away. He was called to the Catholic Mission to amputate a foot for one of the school boys who accidentally shot one foot partly off with a shotgun. Herman left on the second and will probably return on the sixteenth unless he has been delayed by the heavy wind. Herman was also appointed census agent for the Kuskokwim River but he had Mr. Kilbuck sworn in for the greater part of the work thus leaving him only thirty days, but he will have other traveling enough to fill up the greater part of the year. Herman wants me to go to St. Michael with him, and while I will for his pleasure, for I know he gets as tired being away from home from the little folks and me as we get of being home all alone, still I do not look forward with much pleasure to such a trip with two restless children in the rainy as well as mosquito season. Herman thinks a change will do me good, but this remains to be seen.

Edith and her two children as well as Mrs. Helmich's two little girls will go down this Spring, John going out by way [of] St. Michael after his census is taken.

Edith's family have already gone to the coast, they left two weeks ago today. Our boats will leave on Tuesday the twelfth, if the wind is favorable; it is anything but favorable now. We feel that the boats cannot get down too soon as the vessel will likely be in early (if at all). You see I have my doubts about her coming at all.

I wish I could send you a nice fresh King Salmon for your dinner tomorrow. I am sure you would enjoy it. We are getting plenty now of fresh fish and eggs but these are all or about all we have to eat.

Well, since I wrote the last sentence one of my egg traders came in with eggs by the whole-sale. My other trader came in yesterday, so we have more than we know what to do with. I am going to count these and tell you how many I have. Of course we divide them between the three families. I guessed yesterday about three hundred and there are many more today. Herman is away missing all these eggs, but he will get what I crave most, potatoes and cabbage, as at the Catholic Mission they have a fine spot for a garden and raise enough of all the good [vegetables] to last the year around. If it were not for a confinement case due on June the fifteenth I would have gone with Herman, for a trip at this time of the year is much more pleasant than later in the Summer. But who knows, maybe I will go home yet this fall, for this I will do if our vessel does not come in. I would like to go to the states for more than one reason. I would love to see you all, especially mama who has to suffer so much, and who I know longs to see us all. Then too my eyes and teeth trouble me so much. My eyes have troubled me very much for a year, and for several months I have been unable to chew on any of my back teeth without being almost raised from my seat. But at the longest it will be only three years. It will depend upon circumstances as to whether we remain longer than next Spring. If circumstances are as they promise now to be, we will insist upon leaving the place.

You will want to hear something about Robert and Margaret. Well, they are human just like all other children. They fight and spat a great deal, and generally Margaret gets the best of Robert. Robert is as brown as a chestnut; he is out from morning till night. The natives call him "the little doctor" and truly he is, and looks like his papa. He delights in getting his papa's instruments and examining the natives' ears and eyes or with stethoscope and hammer examine their chests. Margaret is such a slender little mite but as spry as a cricket. She is better on her feet now than Robert, and she talks so much. The poor little folks miss their papa so much, they are always so happy when he comes in from a trip they scarcely know how to act. Margaret calls him her papa about every minute, pats his face, and hugs and kisses him until he goes to bed. And she never forgets him however long he may be away. I will be glad when they are in the states for they learn so much that is not of any good to them. Herman and I both feel that seven years are plenty for anyone to spend in such a work in such a place. The Board will try to keep us longer, as ten years is the regular number to serve before a furlough, and then unless one is completely worn out they ask them to stay until they are, but then they will be dealing with different persons when it comes to us, for we have them where the hair is short. We have a contract in black and white, or rather Herman has. I am not bound at all.

I told you I would count the eggs and tell you the number. Today there were 250 duck eggs, 242 goose eggs and 31 swan eggs, in all equal to about 885 hen eggs. I wrote Jessie Denniston yesterday, and told her I thought my trader brought 300 but according to this number there must have been at least 400, that is enough to equal that many hen eggs. You know my fondness for eggs, and doubtless Sadie will say I am glad Ella gets all the eggs she wants, but I must confess I have more than I want or know what to do with. I will go into the noodle business on Monday with full force. Last year I dried nine quarts but this was a great deal of trouble, while they were far inferior to La Monts New York dried, and so if it breaks the mission I will buy the La Monts dried eggs this year. I have plenty of work without drying eggs.[73]

Mrs. Bel'kov, Herman's private patient, left for home two weeks ago today, and poor soul, she could see no more than when she came. Her eye healed nicely but is doubtless diseased in some other way.

I am going to send three little work baskets made by native women, two by Jennie, the mother of Albert, papa's name-sake, and one by Fannie, the wife of David, Herman's interpreter. If you would send them something, just some little thing sometime they would appreciate it so much, a cup and saucer or an apron. They made the baskets for you, that is mama,

---

73. Exhaustive research did not reveal the technique Ella used to dry eggs. It appears, however, that the Natives did not use drying as an egg preservation method. Either Ella was previously familiar with a technique or she experimentally devised one.

Sadie, and Duck. Jennie made a larger and more beautiful one last Summer for Mama but it is too much to ask Mrs. Helmich to pack as she kindly grants me the privilege of putting these in her children's trunk. Her mother will express them from Ohio to Wilkes-Barre. I will send them to Ed as he will doubtless be in Wilkes-Barre more frequently than any of you.

I must bathe Robert and Margaret now so will close. I may find time to write more before the boats leave.

With much love from us all to you all, I am, your affectionate daughter.

Ella

Sunday A.M., June 10, 1900

The enclosed envelope I had addressed and stamped for a business letter but did not send it. So will send it to you. If you will write an answer in August or September first it will reach us by this address.

Yours,

Ella

chapter 2

October 19, 1900 to
June 19, 1901

MY DEAR FATHER:[74]

It is quite late, and I am very tired after a long day of house cleaning, sewing carpet, papering and caring for my little ones, but I am going to make a beginning at your journal however short it may prove to be. I would probably be downstairs working for some time yet as tomorrow is Saturday, and I have so much to do before Sunday. I was wishing for another day in the week this afternoon but Herman thinks any day will do as the work can wait. But as I was about to say that since I am cleaning the bedroom we are all sleeping upstairs, and I never feel quite safe with the children up here while we are below so you see you are having the benefit of my spare evening.

Robert and Margaret are both fast asleep. They are such busy little bodies all day long and when evening comes they are tired out and sleepy enough to wish to be tucked away in their little nests. The mother gets tired too, I can assure you, and is glad when their eyes are closed for the night. But they are the first ones awake in the morning and begin their work at once. But I am only too thankful that they are able to be so active for this has been a very hard Summer and Fall with us here. So many of our natives here died from an epidemic of grippe and measles. Here at Bethel, between fifty and sixty died. Our first village above here lost between forty and fifty, and all other villages lost about the same per cent of their people. The village above here, Akiachak, however is larger than any other on the upper river. We all had the grippe in a light form, that is, we missionaries and the children all had the measles, and all were very sick. We truly have much to be thankful for. All of our dear ones were spared while the natives were dying all around us. It seemed that no medicine could be found to benefit them. But this poor diseased people. It takes but little to carry them off. This late sickness took many of our very best natives, many of whom we feel could best be spared were left,

---

74. According to Ella's journal entry of October 21, 1900 her mother, Marietta Struck Ervin, had died after a lingering illness. Therefore journal salutations are now to her father.

while many of our very best were taken. But God's ways are not our ways. He above knows best.[75]

The natives who were left are having a hard time to recover, so slowly. It seems they will never grow strong. There are three sick now on the mission. Herman thinks they are getting typhoid fever, nor do I wonder for this mission is situated in a miserable place; marshy all around us and very poor water now as it all drains down from the tundra. We will be glad when the dirt is once frozen, and the creek as well, for we will then cross and bring water from the river.

This has indeed been a very hard and trying year or Summer, the early part having been cold and windy, while since late in July until only last week it rained about constantly. It did seem that we would never have clear weather again. Herman was away the greater part of the Summer taking census. The children and I accompanied him on his up-river trip, and intended going all the way to St. Michael, but we, as well as all of our crew, were down with the grippe while at Ougavig, and when we were strong enough, were glad to float down stream toward home. We found when we returned that this was our place for with all of the sick and dying we found plenty to do.

I am very sleepy and tired so will close, but I am going to have more time to write now I trust, as I have two pretty good servants now to help me. I have had to do all of my own work for the greater part of the Summer, as well as plenty for others, thus leaving me but little time to write. But I am going to try to fill this little book for you by the first Winter mail out, probably in December.

Ella

Sunday evening, October 21, 1900

DEAR FATHER:

Herman has gone over to spend the evening with Mr. Weinlick. I am upstairs keeping watch over my little ones who are fast asleep, so will spend my time in writing to you. How I long to be with you at home this Winter to help cheer your lonely home. I think of you almost constantly.

---

75. Despite his efforts during the epidemics of 1900, Herman was unable to cure many of the sick Natives. This inability to demonstrate that his method of medical care was better than shamanism caused him to lose stature among the Natives, and he never fully regained his reputation (Fienup-Riordan 1991, 235).

How very sad and lonely you must be since our loved one was taken from us. I can scarcely realize that she is gone. It seems that she must be there as always. It is so hard to think of returning home and not to find her anxiously waiting to see me as she always was when I visited home while living in Philadelphia, and now that she is gone forever from the house seems almost impossible. Yet who can tell how soon any one of us may be called home. What a blessed hope we have of Heaven and of meeting all of our loved ones again. That meeting will be sweeter than any on earth could be. Poor mother; how much she had to suffer during the last few years of her life. I could never wish her back into this world of suffering again. None of us know how much we may have before us yet. How I wish I could have been at home with mother through her long and painful suffering. When I think of all the hard work one must do here for these ungrateful natives I cannot help thinking at times t'were better I had been at home with my poor mother to work for and comfort her in her last sad days. Yet these poor people have souls to save, and if God has placed me here for their use it must be for the best.

I will be glad to go home next year for a rest for I am tired out. The hard work here from day to day, and the worry together with being at home so much of the time alone with the care of little ones, house, and servants are very wearing. Five years are quite enough for me, period.

Robert is restless, he does not seem well. I hope he will not be ill. He has never been quite well since he had the measles. I must close for the night and go to him.

Affectionately,

Ella

Sunday evening, November 25, 1900

DEAR FATHER:

It is over a month since I last wrote you. How time flies, and how little I accomplish at writing. I had so much wanted to write you a long journal for the first Winter mail, (we are promised regular mail through this part of Alaska during the Winter) but as usual I will probably have but little written as the first mail should go soon. But my time is not spent in idleness, I can assure you, for it does seem that my sewing will never be finished this Fall. When one must make or oversee the making of caps, mittens, coats, boots and in fact, every article of clothing one wears, and care for children and house, there is but little time left for anything else.

Since I last wrote Robert has been quite sick. We thought first he was getting typhoid fever, but Herman thought afterwards that he had, I believe he called it "army dysentery," as he had every symptom of it, and then again he thought it to be one of the afflictions that frequently follow the measles. Whatever it was he was a pretty sick little boy and lost a great deal in weight, but he seems quite well again and is getting so fat his clothes will hardly hold him. He and Margaret are two very busy little youngsters and now that they are in the house most of the time they keep their mother's time pretty well filled. Margaret is the dearest little chick, and just as spry as a cricket. She talks almost everything now and her tongue is scarcely ever quiet, nor is her body quiet from the time her eyes are opened in the morning until she closes them in the evening. I am sorry to say that she is not very religious. She goes to church for a good time if she can manage to have it. One Sunday morning during prayer she slipped away from me and played a tune on the organ. The same morning while her father was saying grace at breakfast or repeating the "Lord's Prayer" she thought it too long, I guess, for she told him three times, "That's enough!" We think her a very sweet cute little girl. All the strangers going through love her for she is very friendly. But Robert is a very independent little fellow for outside of his father and mother, he thinks he can live just as well without friends. He has very little to do with anyone. But he is our darling boy and a very loving little fellow toward his father and mother. He is a thorough boy. His pockets are stuffed just as full of every sort of thing he can find during the day: strings; nails; patches; his handkerchief; paper and matches if he can manage to find them. I always worry lest he do some harm with these; either set fire to himself or the house.

Last Saturday night a trader was here, and among other things to sell he had mouth organs. Robert wanted one so much but his father objected to him having one for the native children play on them too whenever they get a chance, and they are such a filthy diseased set I don't like my children to put their lips to anything after a native. But Robert was so disappointed that Herman gave his consent finally, but they were all sold by this time, and the poor little fellow cried as though his heart would break and sobbed for a long time in his sleep. There are so few things to make the little hearts happy here, in the line of toys, that I never like to see them disappointed when now and then they do see something they want. Herman has promised to bring him one from the Yukon station if they can get it so Robert seems happy again and talks of his promised "sing," as he calls it, all day.

Christmas is nearly here again. How time flies. But we never look forward with much pleasure here to the holidays for they are always the hardest days of the year for the missionaries when the natives, or many of them, come to spend them with us. I suppose we ought to feel happy at seeing so many others so very happy, but I am growing tired of so much hard work and long for a few holidays myself.

This will be a sad Christmas for you at home too, with our dear mother and Helen gone from our midst.[76] It does not seem possible to me that they are gone. It seems like a sad dream from which I must yet awake, but I will never truly awake to it all until I return home, if God permits my return, and find the dear faces missing. Poor Ed and Duck. My heart aches for them in the loss of their dear little blue eyed girl. But it is all for the best. God never makes a mistake. That that seems our very hardest trial may sometime prove our sweetest blessing. Yet it is hard to see it thus. If we would only trust more fully to our ever-loving Savior how truly he would comfort us through our deepest sorrows.

November 27, 1900

Herman left this morning on his first Winter trip. This is the beginning of a long lonely Winter for me as well as one of many hardships for him. But I often tell Herman that these trips are not nearly as hard on him as they are on me, for while he seems to enjoy them, and in a few days after each return he is restless to be off again, while I do not enjoy being left alone, with the care of my little ones and keeping them warm, in the least. Herman has gone to Andreafsky to set up stakes between here and there for a new trail which is to be for the "promised mail" route. How nice it will be if we can write and receive letters more frequently. Three white men accompanied Herman on this trip. Mr. Hubbard, one of Mr. Lind's partners, Mr. Hall and Mr. Barrey or Mike as we all call him, two miners who were frozen in here this Fall. Another miner of this same party, Mr. Noreen, left this morning for down the river on a prospecting tour. Herman furnished him grub, dogs and guide, and if he finds gold, or we hear reason to believe he will, half of all claims will be ours. So you see Herman is somewhat of a miner this year, and I must confess that I will be glad if we too find gold for truly we need it. Mr. Noreen is going in the vicinity of Mount Romig, a mountain named for Herman by Prof. Spurr

---

76. Helen, the daughter of Ella's brother, had died as well.

and Mr. Post of the U.S. Geological Survey party that passed through here in '98.[77] But now you must not think we are rich when you receive this for like many other poor unfortunates, we may not find a cent.

This has been a very late Fall. Not until now has traveling been safe, while in other years men have been here from all parts of Alaska north before the middle of November. After the first freeze-up, which was late, and we had all felt so thankful that the rainy season was over, we had several warm spells accompanied by south rain. The ground is bare of snow now. In the morning everything is white with frost, but soon this disappears, and the same brown tundra is left to look upon. But no doubt we will have plenty of snow and the great white sheet of earth to look at before Spring comes again. While the Winters seem so long and lonely, yet how time flies. I can scarcely realize that we are beginning on our fifth Winter in Alaska. But even though the seasons fly around so rapidly, they wear on one severely. The grey hairs are already appearing among the black ones, and wrinkles [are] coming on my brow. You must not expect to see me as fresh and young as when I left home.

Herman took some pictures of the children a short time ago, and I trust we can finish some to send with this journal. They were taken by flash light, and Robert was afraid and seriously objected to having his taken but Herman did take it any way with his face all screwed up to cry. He got a very cute one of Margaret in Mike's lap. Mike is a very funny Irishman and a great favorite with Margaret. We asked him over one night to pop corn for us and when all was in readiness to begin Mike put corn, ear and all, in the frying pan, and when I told him how to shell and pop it he said, "Well mum, I niver did the likes o this afore, for sure, and I niver knowd how t'was did." Mike is an old sailor and often amuses us with his yarns, for like all old sailors he was talkative in his own line. He is not much of a lover of Dewey for he says "they writes too much about him, but I'd like to own the house their just often given him in Washington."[78]

It really seems warmer tonight. I wonder if we are going to have another soft spell again. So many of the natives are sick, and we all think it due to the damp warm weather at this season.

---

77. Mount Romig is a 4,000-foot peak in the Kilbuck Mountains seventy miles southeast of Bethel (Orth, Donald J., *Dictionary of Alaska Place Names* [Washington, D.C.: Government Printing Office, 1967], 814).

78. On May 1, 1898 George Dewey defeated the Spanish fleet at the Battle of Manila Bay during the Spanish-American War. His victory resulted in the acquisition of the Philippines by the United States. Dewey was welcomed home a hero and promoted to the rank of rear-admiral. In March 1899 the U.S. Congress created for him the rank of admiral of the navy, the highest rank ever held by a United States naval officer. In 1899–

November 29, 1900

This is Thanksgiving day, and such a quiet day it has been. There were very few in chapel this morning, in truth there are only a few to come this Winter. We miss so many faces that were always good and faithful church goers. We miss all of those who were taken from us during the last severe epidemic of grippe and measles, more now than we have yet, as the natives during the Summer and Fall are more-or-less scattered either fishing or hunting, but at this time they are always settled for the Winter, and then the natives from up and down the river are always coming and going. But those who come and go are but few this year.[79]

Robert, Margaret, and I took dinner with Mr. and Mrs. Weinlick today and had a very nice dinner as well [as] a very pleasant time. Of course turkey was not the bill of fare. But I live in the anticipation of eating turkey next Thanksgiving day.

I was just thinking of all the Thanksgiving days since we came here. The first year we all spent the day with Mr. and Mrs. Helmich. We were then three families, and as usual Mr. Lind the trader was of the party. The second we were all at Edith's: Miss Mack was living here then, and Mr. Lind and Sipary and wives were down from the post.[80] The third we were but two families here at Bethel, and Mr. Weinlick was absent so I had the dinner: Mrs. Weinlick, Mrs. Lind, John [Kilbuck] and a Mr. Hendericks who were then here, took dinner with us. The fourth, a white man from the Yukon, Mr. Dunn, was here. He, Edith, Herman and I were over at Weinlick's. And today the party was still smaller. I wonder where we will all be next year?

Just a year ago at this time John had his arm taken off. A year ago on the twenty-sixth Herman amputated his arm, that being the fourth operation, and the third under ether. I often think how hard Herman tried to save John's arm, and how he prayed for a more skillful Hand to guide his hand aright, but God willed it otherwise in this. He above knows why John's right arm was demanded, and God forbid that we should judge

---

1900 there was talk about him as a possible Democrat candidate for the presidency. Instead Dewey spent the last seventeen years of his life in Washington, D. C. as president of the general board of the Navy. (Encyclopedia Britannica, 1910 and 1994 Editions. "George Dewey.")

79. Records of the Bethel population indicate that "half of the adults and all of the babies died" during the 1900–1901 influenza epidemic (Oswalt 1963, 94).

80. Reinhold Sipary was the Alaska Commercial Company agent at Kolmakovskiy Redoubt on the Upper Yukon River (Oswalt 1963, 109).

Reinhold Sipary was a Finnish trader who established a post for the Alaska
Commercial Company at Kolmakofskiy on the upper Kuskokwim River.
This photograph shows Sipary's Yu'pik wife and their son, George.
(Courtesy, Alaska and Polar Regions Department, University of Alaska Fairbanks,
Joseph Romig Collection, acc. #90-043-906aN)

as to the cause. John and Edith are in the states this year, and such a sad
homecoming after all these years of hardest toil and severe trials. Truly
"life is real, and life is earnest," here in Alaska and on a mission field. God
grant that every man and woman here may profit by our poor fallen brother.
God alone knows why he suffered him to fall.

Mr. Weinlick will start out on his or rather the first missionary trip of
the season next Monday.

A reindeer herd arrived at Bethel in the spring of 1901. Sheldon Jackson,
the General Agent of Education for Alaska, hoped that reindeer herding
would provide the Alaska Natives with economic opportunity.
(*Courtesy, Alaska and Polar Regions Department, University of Alaska Fairbanks,*
Joseph Romig Collection, acc. #90-043-915aN)

I look for Herman home next Wednesday or Thursday, but he will start
out again very soon to the mountains to look for moss and a suitable place
to locate the herd of reindeer we are compelled to take this Winter.[81] We
trust that grippe or some other plague has so diminished the herd at the
head station as to make it impossible to give us a herd as these deer are
only a great expense and trouble. They cannot compare with the dogs for
travel. We will feel like killing them off for food and clothing; reindeer
meat is excellent.

November 30, 1900

Your letter written August 31st has just reached me. Mr. Dunn who
was here over last Thanksgiving, arrived here from St. Michael this
morning, and among other letters, he brought yours and Sadie's. I have so
many letters stacked up to answer, so while yours is new I will answer that
I may number it among the "answered ones."

81. In 1890 Sheldon Jackson, the Presbyterian missionary and General Agent of Education for Alaska, had decided that bringing herds of reindeer to Alaska from Lapland
would give the Natives an opportunity to develop an industry that would help to feed
them as well as provide income (Jackson 1894–1895, 1437).

You speak of your great loss in the death of mother and that of our darling little Helen. Yes, I can realize how deeply you feel them both. I can well remember while at home how very lonely and empty the house seemed if mother for some reason was absent for a few days, and how tasteless the meals if she were not at the table, and too, I well remember how lost you were without her. Now that she has gone forever from this earthly home seems too sad to be true. Yet it is a comfort to know that we alone suffer, for after years of suffering she is at last resting where sorrow and pain never come.

How I long to be at home with you this year if my little ones or I could be of any comfort to you. Margaret is such a dear loving little girl now as well as so bright and spry. I am sure she would add much to your happiness were she there. She and Robert are both asleep now after a very busy day. Robert is out of doors much of the time now, as the days are very pleasant. He is looking so well again, his face is round and rosy, and he seems more like his old self. He talks so much about the "sing" his papa has promised him. When he is asked where his papa is, he says he has gone to buy a "sing" and some candy for him. I do hope the poor little fellow will not be disappointed this time.

I am glad you are to have someone to help in the house this Winter, and trust she will be satisfactory. If all goes well I will keep house for you next Winter. I hope Herman will be able to go with us. I would not like to leave him alone but I do need and must have a rest and change.

Herman is to some extent engaged in mining this year. He has had some very good reports of gold from the natives and will look them up. If gold is everywhere else in Alaska, why not on the Kuskokwim? It would be nice to have something to make us a little more comfortable in the states after all these years of hard toil for simply love.

December 5, 1900

It is nine o'clock, and from the length of time the lamps have been lit it seems as though it might be midnight. The days are so short now there are only a few hours of day in which to work by daylight. We get up every morning in time to have breakfast over in time to begin sewing as soon as we can see. Robert and Margaret begin their song at about five a. m. each morning. This is always a signal to me to get up and make a fire for when they are awake there is little more peace.

I rather looked for Herman today but he did not come, but without a doubt is somewhere near home and will be in tomorrow. Mr. Dunn is still here waiting for Herman to take word back to St. Michael in regard to the mail route between St. Michael and Katmai. Mr. Schoechert has the mail contract but as he does not know it, Herman will probably be expected to help it along at this end until word can be sent to Carmel.[82] I hardly know whether he will act on this business or not as he told the Home Board in the Spring that he would not have anything to do with any outside matters. There are to be two mails in and two out between December first and April first. The contract I believe is for six thousand dollars ($6000). This mail will be a great nuisance to the mission as we will have to board and fit out the carriers who will have to wait over for the return to take the incoming or outgoing mail to their more special points. It seems there is no end to work and worry on a mission field.

A poor unfortunate man by the name of Mr. Barney arrived here on Saturday from down the river. He and his partner had been wrecked in the Summer having lost all but their very lives. They were picked up by two other men when nearly starved who have been keeping them ever since, but as their supplies are now nearly gone, they have brought the one to us for care. Poor fellow. My heart aches for him he seems so down cast, and well he may for truly this is not a very desirable country to be thus unfortunate and especially at this time. We have given him warm clothes and are feeding him. He is a Wilkes-Barre man, although it is eighteen years since he left there. We have more white men on the place than we care for, and they all must eat. Although they can earn what they get, still we do not need white men to do our work, and natives do not eat white man's food. Last Winter we had to manage in every possible way to make our provisions hold out, and from all appearances we must soon begin this again.

Sunday, December 9, 1900

Herman is still away. He can scarcely travel during these last three days as they have been very stormy, windy ones, and on the tundra such days are always much worse than on the river. As Herman's road is all on tundra this blizzard is doubtless keeping him. While it is hard to have him gone so much during the long cold Winter with all responsibility of house, sick, and children on my hands, yet I scarcely know whether to wish him

---

82. Reverend John Schoechert entered the mission field in the Kuskokwim region in 1889. On March 20, 1893 he married fellow missionary, Lydia Lebus, and they served together at Carmel until their departure from Alaska in 1911 (Schwalbe 1985, 56 and 300).

home now or not, for when he is here there are nearly always white men here from some part of Alaska to be fed and waited on, and when he is away I do not worry my head about them. Mr. Dunn is still here on the mission partly waiting for Herman but now on account of the wind during the three last days. Although Mr. Dunn is a very nice man still I must confess that I had rather have Herman away than have *any* boarder for I have plenty of work of my own to do without cooking for any white men. We have a white man up at the trading post this year who counts on entertaining all travelers though here, but he charges and we scarcely ever do, so we will doubtless be preferred, and then he is not well liked either but all this matters not to me. If the travelers do not like him and his price they will have to move on, for we are not here for the benefit of the traveling public. Mr. Hubbard, the trader, is with Herman now so Mr. Dunn stays here with Mr. Noreen and Mr. Barney in a mission house.

Robert still talks about his "sing." On Friday the water sleigh was coming in from the lake and Robert said, "Here comes papa, see! He has my 'sing' too." Poor little fellow. I do hope he will not be disappointed. Mr. Dunn is coming again from St. Michael later in the Winter and has promised to bring Robert a mouth organ from there, so he will have one any way though he will have to wait a long time. Robert talks so much. [He] asks so many questions that sometimes when I am busy I get out of patience with him. It seems his tongue is never still. He always wants to know just why everything is as it is, or likely to be. Then one thing, I can't always understand him for he talks native, and can go ahead of me by far in the native language. He is getting so fat I must make him all new clothes as he is like a pudding stuffed in a bag. Margaret is just the other extreme, such a slender little midget, but just that much more quick than Robert.

I am so sleepy I will have to stop for tonight. I have been working very late every night since Herman went away, and Robert gets awake every morning as regular as the clock hands move on the five stroke, Margaret soon following, so I have had but little sleep. When Herman is absent the hours are always golden for me. When I have prepared three meals a day for a hungry man or sometimes for men, and cared for the children there is little time left to sew.

December 27, 1900

Christmas is over, and how glad and thankful we all are too for this part of the year is always an awful strain on the missionaries. There are always so many natives here and all to be entertained by the missionaries. This year it was much more easy on us as we had two native families to take charge of dealing out to the guests, but still we had all of the baking to do which amounted to about sixty loaves of bread and about one thousand cakes, besides all of the sugar we had to boil and cut. There were, as near as I can guess it, two hundred guests on the mission from Saturday until Wednesday morning. Oh, what a blessed quiet it was yesterday morning when they all had left.

There were three strange white men on the mission over Christmas all [of] whom Herman met last winter. Captain Newcomb, his son, and a Mr. Bosworth, the carpenter from the Captain's boat. Captain Newcomb has the *Sarah*, one of the finest and largest Yukon steamers owned by the A. C. Co. He will probably run a steamer on the Kuskokwim next Summer. How nice it will be to see a little of civilization on this lonely old Kuskokwim, and the best part of it is the fact that Mrs. Newcomb and daughter always accompany the Captain on his boat. He thinks some of bringing them over by the last dog teams in Spring and leaving them here until he goes down to Goodnews Bay for his steamer. The Captain and party left this morning for upriver partly to look over the river for navigation and partly to look for gold.

Herman came in from the Yukon on Thursday the thirteenth after a long hard trip. He was on a three day trip up the river since then.

Tomorrow I will be twenty-nine years old. How old I am getting.

Robert and Margaret had a very happy Christmas. The poor children; it takes very little to make them happy. Robert had a new sled, the hoe, rake and shovel you sent him, new mittens, a pair of home knit stockings and a "sing," as he calls it. Margaret got a picture book, the little cradle that was in your box, and a new doll that I made for her. A little native girl made a pair of boots and a parka for her, all of which Margaret is very proud.

Margaret is a cute little youngster. This morning in bed I had occasion to spank her. After crying a very short time, she took her baby, which was between us, and said, "Come over here or mama will spank you." Later in the day she wanted some sugar which was on the table. I told her no, so she climbed up on a chair and said, "Well, I'll just help myself, or rather steal some." She and Robert have their little spats, and Margaret generally gets the best of him. Robert spends much of his time out of doors with his new sled and enjoys it so much. He comes in with such red cheeks it makes me feel refreshed to look at him. I have so much work to do I scarcely ever get out.

Mr. Barney, the man of whom I wrote you before, accompanied Christian, a native boy, to Nushagak. Christian carries the mail contract to Mr. Schoechert. We were glad to see Mr. Barney go as we had no use for him here.

January 2, 1901[83]

DEAR FATHER:

I will add a few words to Ella's journal this evening as she is not able to write as yet, but we hope soon will be. She is doing well, and so is our latest addition to the family, which came this morning and as yet has no name in English, though in the native language she has many names being one of the first children born since the sickness, and from the custom of the people must have the names of all those who died just previous to her birth. The child is a girl and a plump healthy baby, and we are expecting to call her Helen after Mr. Ed's little girl Helen. Bob and Margaret, when they came downstairs this morning, were highly pleased and Margaret thought her mamma had a new doll baby for her and would not give it up, so she made a big fuss for the baby and finally had to be paddled in order to get her dressed. I went out a short time today and the both of them got on the bed and wanted the baby. Their Mother had a time until I came in. Ella says she thinks she is breaking your family record for children, and though she once said she wished for ten boys she now is more than pleased that Margaret has a little sister. Our little folks are much company to us, and were you to visit us you would likely find them full of enough life to keep you also from getting lonesome. If we succeed in coming home in the spring you will find us a more lively family than when we left. We hope for a year's rest soon as our work is very trying, and we are feeling the strain of the work more each year.

I am taking every advantage that presents itself on this river as the river is opening up for mining, and hope to realize something for my efforts.

We are to have two mails a year out and two mails in from the states during the winter months and so can get word to you and hear from you oftener than in the past.

Margaret is just in again on another of her trips for the baby. She says "Mamma Kaka" (my mamma) and "Baby Kaka" (my baby) and is searching for the nose and eyes of the babe. She has just brought in a dipper of

---

83. Journal entry for this date was made by Herman.

Ella with Helen Elizabeth, 1901.
(Courtesy, Alaska and Polar Regions Department, University of Alaska Fairbanks,
Joseph Romig Collection, acc. #90-043-914aN)

water to her mamma and spilled about half on the floor. These are some of their remarks: (Com-mi) in there is the babe; (Tong-man-tuk) look here at it; (Whi pika ka) my babe; (Una blanket Baby Kaka) that is the babe's blanket.

Yesterday we were out for a sleigh ride, and I photographed the team and Ella and children. The picture is not good as the dogs would not stand so that I could get a tin picture. My dog team is as good as any in this part of Alaska, and is composed of young dogs Ella has raised for me. You should see some of our sleigh rides. The dogs always trot if they are not fighting or running. Some times we can go for a mile or two just as fast as the team can run, and at all times faster than a horse could go, i. e. on the average for a day's run. Bob and Margaret enjoy the sleigh rides and sing, play the mouth organ or sleep and feel as safe as in the house. The older folks feel about the same as when driving a horse that runs away by spells.

Ella is as much in love with the dogs and sleighing as I am, and we will part sorrowfully with our dogs when we leave Alaska. You would hardly think it, but the team I send you a picture of would bring, if for sale, $500. without any trouble. Just now I am anxious about my dog team for a mad dog (not exactly mad as in the states, but very similar to it) was here and fought my dogs all of one night. We fear we may lose part of the dogs, and when you realize that the dogs are worth about $50. a piece, you can imagine I am anxious about them. However much we like the dogs and the beauties of the road, they like every rose that has its thorns, mean many long miles from home in a bleak and barren country. Your imagination alone can do more than my pen to picture the team as you see it, and two lonely looking fur bundled men miles from home or sight of human being on a waste and frozen plain, the driven snow as endless and desolate as the sea and nothing to divert your mind but the beauties of nature, and in this alone there is company. Surely as the Bible says, "The earth is the Lord's and the fullness thereof." So here the sparkling frost, the glowing Aurora, or the falling star. The traits and homes of the wild bird or beast as it watches you from a distance or springs from before you and runs down to the drifted snow all speak of a God that rules the universe and who feeds the sparrow and clothes the grass of the field, and how much more that the same God cares for us and will some day make clear to us many things that now we can only see and wonder at the infinite wisdom and grandeur of His power. We surely miss much of the good things of life by being up here but in return there is much in our work with the people and much that God has placed in nature about us that we can enjoy. Were we not so placed as we are, we might pass many of the beautiful things about us by without more than a chance thought.

Since fall there have [been] many white men come onto this river prospecting for gold, and there is promise of a steamer for this river [in] another year. We hope so, for if a steamer comes on this river we will be saved much work and great risk in landing our goods as of old. We have lost many of our people from the sickness of last summer, but expect more whites on the river, and thus our work will remain about the same though we think that the people will be improved in our time, and that is mining will offer them an opportunity to earn some of the necessities of life which they now secure with much difficulty. I must draw my letter to a close for today. Your loving son,

J. H. Romig

Sunday, January 20, 1901

The first out-going mail arrived from St. Michael last Wednesday by Mr. Dunn of whom I have written before. Mr. Schoechert from Carmel arrived on Thursday so the mail will doubtless start soon for Katmai. I did want to fill this book for you by the first mail but as usual have failed. I surely counted on writing a great many letters during the days that I was too weak to work, but it takes me to have a baby to bring the white man, for no sooner had I crawled out of bed when two arrived, although we did not entertain these two yet they sat around in our house a great deal, and then they also brought another ship wrecked man whom we had to fit out with food and clothes. When baby was two weeks old Mr. Dunn and Mr. Corbisher from St. Michael came. These two are still guests in our house. Mr. Corbisher is a very nice young man, in fact I think the nicest one who ever happened along here. You may have heard of his father who is a surgeon in the U.S. Army. He also has a brother, a surgeon in the Army, and two more who are officers, all having served in the late war with Spain. Mr. Corbisher, who intends going down the river to buy dogs, is storm-bound here. We are having a severe snow and wind storm. During the past week we had a very severe cold spell, really the only one of the Winter. The thermometer having reached as low as thirty-five [below zero].

Our baby Helen is a very dear little girl, and a perfect picture of Robert although fatter than he was at her age. Robert is very proud of the fact that she looks like him and tells everybody she looks like "tu ya tu ya," which is himself. Robert and Margaret both have whooping cough, so you see things are quite lively here in every respect.

January 24, 1901

Here it is four days since I began my little epistle on the opposite page, and this is the first opportunity I have had to finish it.

Mr. Dunn and Mr. Corbisher both left on Monday morning; one for down river and Mr. Dunn for St. Michael, and poor fellows they are having an ugly trip for it has been blowing fearfully ever since. Yesterday morning it was calm long enough for Mr. Schoechert to make a start, for which I am most heartily thankful, for now that the white men are all off again I can again breathe and have space in my own house. Oh, how tired I am of this kind of a life, and how I long for a quiet home life. I am growing to almost dislike the face of a white man. If all who come are not guests in the house they are my frequent callers. They and the natives just about take full possession of the house when Herman is at home. The only times during the Winter when I have any rest or quiet from this kind of life is when Herman is on the trail, and to have him away makes it hard for me too especially during these long cold nights. To keep three little ones warm as well as myself is no small task. Tonight I will probably write until late in order to keep the fire up for the wind seems to find its way in on all sides. It is almost impossible to keep warm.

Herman and Mr. Noreen left yesterday afternoon to stake out some mining property. On Mr. Noreen's last trip he was more than encouraged over his find. He found quartz and thinks it will prove very rich. God knows I hope it may mean a little something for us. I would like Herman to have a nice little start in practice in the states for I feel that I have had about as much of this as I can stand. Herman says that he likes this free easy life. It is not a very hard one for the men, but far from free and easy for the women who scarcely know what it means to rest, and never know what it means to have a little change from home cares.

But, I must not complain. I have much to thank a kind Heavenly Father for. While we and our little ones are warm and well cared for in food and clothing there are many poor destitute natives in Alaska. The sickness of last Summer left many poor fatherless and motherless little ones, and in every village can be found many half-fed half-clothed little ones. If our church were to open a school now we could soon fill [it] with the poor helpless homeless children. But no, they deem it wisest to run around the country preaching to old case-hardened sinners. Herman has written to Dr. Sheldon Jackson asking him to give us a manual training school here, but in as much as we are not Presbyterians we will probably not get it. Although Dr. "Shellgame Jackson," as old Alaskan miners call him, represents "Uncle Sam" in Alaska, he is very partial toward his own church. It may be that if we praise his pet scheme, the "reindeer," enough he will give us our school.[84] We are getting a herd of reindeer this Winter, but are not very joyous over the prospect as they will doubtless be a great nuisance and little gain. I don't know whether we will be allowed to kill one now and then or not, but hope so as the meat is very good. By the way, I had a nice little treat when Mr. Dunn arrived. Mrs. Dunn sent me a Porterhouse steak weighing between ten and fifteen lbs. and Mr. Hastings, the A. C. Co.'s agent at St. Michael, sent us a turkey. I am saving them until Herman returns, and we are free from visitors, save those we choose to invite.

January 25, 1901

The storm is growing worse instead of better. I have been putting wood in the stove all evening, and yet I am shivering from cold. I hope Herman is somewhere in good shelter, poor fellow. I guess he wishes he were at home, and so do I.

Sunday, January 27, 1901

It does seem that nature has joined all her forces to see just how perfectly wretched a storm she can get up. I never knew such [a] blizzard in our time here. The wind blows a perfect gale continually while the thermometer ranges from thirty-five to forty below zero. It keeps the boys pretty busy getting wood, poor fellows. I feel sorry for them, but then if they have not enough good common sense to work a little extra in fine weather, to be in readiness for such storms, they will have to work in all kinds of weather. But it does seem that this storm must soon blow itself out for it has blown almost steadily for nearly two weeks. I feel sorry for the poor travelers on Alaskan trails in this storm for they have anything but pleasant accommodations in the dirty smoky native huts. Poor Herman. I guess he wished the weather would turn good. He was so restless to be on the road. He planned to start so often before he really got off. First he was kept by David whose nose started to bleed, and the boy would probably [have] bled to death had Herman been away for I was too sick

---

84. In the missionaries' report for 1901–1902 to Sheldon Jackson, they remarked that a school was maintained at Bethel (Jackson 1903, 1251), so evidently their plea succeeded.

and weak to go out, and Mr. Weinlick was on a trip. There next came the white men to bother not only Herman but his wife also who, of all things, kicks (if you will pardon the word) more against the entertaining of these miserable nuisances than any other duty she [has], if such is her or any missionary's duty, which I very much doubt. I got really out of patience with Herman before he got started. He was so disgusted over the state of affairs and scolded a great deal about always being kept by some sick native or white travelers. I wonder what would become of the poor men up here if they were obliged to stay at home with their children from one year's end till another. However, I do wish they could be compelled to try it just for one round year. Just to see how it goes. I guess if Herman were to read this he would [say] well, if Ella were to travel awhile in Winter she [would] find it not all fun, but I always tell him he has this much change from home and many days, according to his own account, are pleasant on the road, and the most pleasant part of the trip is the thought of getting home again. On the other hand I am ever thinking how nice a little change from [all this] would be.

Ugh! I am glad to [be] in a warm house tonight. It makes me feel cold to hear the wind howling without. Last night I had to hook up a damper for the bedroom stove pipe. It sounded at times that the draught would take the wood up the pipe and out of the chimney. By the use of the damper I burn less wood, and have more heat.

We are having a great deal of sickness around here this year. David, the doctor's interpreter, has been sick all Winter. First he had typhoid fever after he had something the trouble with his "insides," as the natives say, and this is really the nearest I can get to naming it. I only know that he was an awful trial to Herman sending for him all hours of the day and night. Poor boy. He was quite sick, but not as sick as he thought. Now he manages to keep all hands busy with his nose. When it starts nothing but packing gauze will stop it. Herman told Mr. Weinlick and Mr. Hall, a white man living here on the mission, that between them they would have to plug his nose if it got to bleeding badly while the doctor is absent. Mr. Hall said, well, he could plug it with his fist but of gauze he is [not] acquainted with its use in the medical or surgical form.

Sunday, February 3, 1901

Well, well such weather since I last wrote you. We have had all kinds of changes. On last Tuesday it grew ever quiet. One day we had a severe south snow storm, the temperature going up several degrees above zero, and in the evening going down to fifteen below again. Since yesterday morning it has been blowing and raining and thawing until now. The snow that was banked above windows in many places is all gone. If it keeps on at this rate the tundra will soon be bare again. Such a difference from last Sunday for we are nearly suffocating in the house today.

Herman returned from his running trip last Wednesday evening having experienced his hardest trip in Alaska, and I am sure he is right for it was the worst I ever knew here at home.

You will doubtless wonder about our gold mine. Well you must not say or think much about it. We do not, then we will not be disappointed if it does not turn out well. However, we think and trust it may prove rich. Henry (Mr. Noreen), who thinks a great deal and says little and who is an experienced miner feels very encouraged over the prospects. We all know there is gold there as Herman and Mr. Noreen pounded up some of the rock and found very good colors. This kind of a mine must be very rich in order to sell it, as it will take probably a hundred thousand dollars just to set up all necessary machinery. Placer mining they call "poor man's mining." But a quartz mine takes almost a good rich mine to work it, so unless we can sell it, it will mean nothing to us. Alaska is a very rich country. How nice it would [be] if we could have a little taste too.

Margaret has the whooping cough very badly. Poor child. She coughs so hard most of the time, and retains but little of her food. I think and hope her cough is at its worst now. In this case we can look for a change for the better. Our dear little Margaret has had a hard time for some weeks. Soon after the baby came she had an abscess on her neck and had to have it lanced twice, and it is only now getting better. These abscesses seem to be an epidemic as several of the natives have had them, and now Mrs. Weinlick's baby is getting one in the same location as Margaret's was.

Robert has the cough only lightly thus far. I told Margaret and Robert that we would go to the states in the Spring, and they have talked all morning about the states. Poor little folks. They don't know how much they [will] miss living up here.

We had our beef steak yesterday noon and some for breakfast this morning, and will have our turkey tomorrow dinner as we are unable to keep it during this thaw. It seems like states sure enough. Porterhouse steak and turkey. I told Mr. Noreen yesterday, when they showed me the gold they had found in the rock, that that would [buy] plenty of Porterhouse steaks and turkeys. I just make fun of him and Herman with their gold, but Henry always assures me that there is gold there.

I wish you could see my dear baby Helen. She is such a sweet fat baby girl. I tell Herman the nicest one we ever had. She looks so much like her papa and Robert.

February 17, 1901

Much has happened since I last wrote. The most important thing is the fact that the gold mine is all up. Poor Mr. Noreen, he is so disappointed, and we tease him so much. After making a test of the mercury they found it to contain gold while a test of the rock with some of Herman's dental mercury revealed only rock. Henry says he won't give it up yet, for the rock has every indication for gold. So we tell him it is all there but the gold. I told him that if I had a few wolf collars to sell, I would own a mine yet before he and the doctor. Mr. Corbisher, of whom I wrote before, offered me eighteen dollars for the collar on my Winter parka, and really meant it. I hastily made up [my] mind that should I refuse so good a thing, I would be a greater fool than he, as money is not such a plentiful article here. So I accepted it. The real value would probably be four dollars. A sure case of "more money than brains." Although wolf is very scarce and very high in St. Michael.

I have a pretty basket here that Mr. Lyons, the census agent who was on the Kuskokwim last Summer, wanted very much and offered me fifteen dollars for, and a Mr. Bales would have given more, but I refused to sell it. Since then I have concluded that such golden opportunities to make money easy would seldom occur in one's life, and I am quite sure that in the future I will grasp all such. But then there are more important things for a missionary to write about than gold and money making.

Our poor people seemed doomed to die. So many were taken by the grippe and measles last Summer and now many of [the] poor children are going from whooping cough. If only we had a place, a hospital, where we could give them attention and good food, this at least could probably be avoided. Robert has had it in a light form, while Margaret has had a pretty severe attack. Now that they are both better our dear baby Helen is getting it, and I am very much worried about her as it goes hard with so young a child, but I trust [she] may have only a light attack. She is such a bright strong baby, so fat and pretty. My dear little ones are very much to me for they are all that I have much of the time to cheer the long lonely hours in this far away land.

Herman has had a call to Nushagak which he will no doubt have to attend. Mr. Rock is very sick and has been much of the time since last

September. Herman is now at Ougavig since last Wednesday. I sent the letter on from Carmel. He will probably be in in two or three days. It will be hard for me to have Herman gone so long, the children not being very well. As it is I have not known a good night's rest for weeks. Herman will be gone at least a month. The mail carrier came from Carmel on Thursday morning but brought no mail from the states. Mr. Schoechert's team had been to Katmai but no steamer had yet arrived. A stormy season was reported and very rough coast for some time, it may be that the steamer was lost. The carrier will leave for Nushagak with the second and last outgoing mail as soon [as] Mr. Dunn arrives from St. Michael with it. We hope that at least one home mail will reach us. Herman will probably accompany the mail carrier, Mr. Blandoe, to Nushagak.

We are having such lovely weather now for nearly a week. After the rain we had another fearful wind storm for some time, but it is perfect weather now. Almost like states weather.

Henry left a week ago yesterday for the herd of reindeer. This will be a long trip as the station is above St. Michael, and coming back with the deer will be slow. It remains to be seen how this reindeer proposition will turn out. We all feel that they will be a great expense and trouble.

David is still the same troublesome patient. He had another hemorrhage from the nose yesterday. Poor fellow. He suffers a great deal and causes the missionaries a great deal of trouble as well for he always thinks he is much worse than he is, and thinks that the missionaries have nothing to do but to wait on him.

February 21, 1900 [sic][85]

The second and last mail for the states arrived from St. Michael tonight. I am sorry that I have been so negligent about writing. I wanted to fill this journal for you for I know you would enjoy it, but it seems I can never find enough time to write to my friends.

Herman started for Nushagak this morning in answer to Mr. Rock's call, but I am sorry he did so, though we all thought it best as Mr. Rock has been sick a long time. Mr. Weinlick's little boy, eight months old on the twenty-third of this month, who has been very sick with whooping cough for several weeks, died tonight at nine o'clock. He was such a nice bright sweet little fellow. Always laughing. How they will miss him. He was such a strong looking fat boy. What will this cough do with my poor

---

85. The year was 1901.

little baby? She is so fat and sweet now, but that she is beginning to cough pretty hard too. Oh, how I miss Herman, yet if it is right and best that he should go to Carmel I must not complain. God can and will wonderfully care for His own. Now that Mr. Weinlick's baby has been taken, I can scarcely look for my little Helen to get through if she has a hard attack. But God gave her to us, and He has a right to take her if He sees fit. We love the dear little one so much, it would be hard to give her up. Yet how much pain and suffering they who are early taken home to their loving Heavenly Father are spared. If only Herman were home. It will be so hard to have him gone so many long lonely weeks. My heart aches for Mr. and Mrs. Weinlick. They are heart broken over this their first sorrow.

February 26, 1901

We are having such lovely weather, and fine traveling. Herman is doubtless making good time toward Nushagak. He will probably reach there in a week from here. I never missed him so much since we are here. It seems that he must come back. When he left he said that if he should meet the mail team from Nushagak and get word that Mr. Rock is improving he would turn back. To think that each day he is going farther from home and that a month will pass ere he returns makes me fairly sick. A man with a wife and family has no business to be a physician over such a wide territory. Baby Helen is coughing very hard poor little girl. She is so tiny to have such a cough. I try to act a woman and not a baby for while medicine can do the baby no special good, Herman may be able to save a valuable missionary, but God knows it is hard to be alone during such a trying time in such a desolate lonely place. Margaret is far from well and at times is very troublesome. Robert had a very light attack and is almost well again. These two children nearly drive me crazy sometimes. They are so penned up indoors and grow restless. No doubt I don't wonder they fight and play in the loudest boy fashion from morning till night, but oh, my nerves suffer for it I can assure you. Margaret is such a saucy little mite. If I scold her she tells me I am bad and she belongs to her papa. The next minute she will put her arms around my neck and tell me I am hers. I always speak English to them, and they are taking it up too. When I tell Robert to do something, and he does not start right away, I often say "go on" to him, and of late he has taken it up too. No matter what he asks anyone to do for him, he always says "go on." Margaret is trying to say "you" in native, which is "ilpit." I can't begin to tell you on paper how to pronounce it. It was one of the hardest words for me to get. The best that Margaret can do is "ifit." She talks so fast it always sounds very cute. But she will soon be able to twist her tongue enough to say it no doubt.

Evening: It is blowing a fearful gale again. Another big wind storm no doubt. At our north window I have two blankets pinned up and a chair up against to keep them from blowing out in the room. Really they are bowed out like a sail in a full breeze. Ugh! How dismal it sounds, the wind howling and every now and then the house cracks like a cannon ball exploding. I am sure I never felt so blue and homesick in my life as I do now. I am completely worn out too from loss of sleep. The baby coughs so much during the night, and each time she coughs I have to take her up and help her or I am afraid she would choke. Then the fire must be going all night, thus my night's rest is always broken to such a degree that I feel as though I had had none at all.

Mrs. Weinlick's baby was buried on Sunday up in the little cemetery on the hill. He is the second white person buried in our cemetery.[86] Mr. Hubbard, the trader, made him a very nice little coffin and covered it inside and out with white flannel padded with cotton. The dear little fellow looked so sweet and peaceful. Mr. Helmich held the funeral services, and he and I sang "Jesus Born of My Soul," "When He Commeth" and "We Shall Sleep But Not Forever." Then he was taken to the cemetery in a sleigh and laid to rest, or rather his body was, while the dear little soul is resting where I trust we all may sometime. But I must not dwell on this subject. It is too sad and gloomy, and I am too much that way as it is.

February 27, 1901

We had our baby baptized this afternoon. I asked Mr. Weinlick to come over and baptize her, and Mrs. Weinlick held her. I gave her Helen's name but instead of Louise I named her Elizabeth for a very dear friend of ours in Philadelphia. But my dear little Helen Elizabeth I fear has but a short time for this world. Nor would I ask to keep her here if God thinks best to give her a brighter happier home. This is a very gloomy world to me just now with Herman gone and my darling babe so sick. Even the weather is so dismal and gloomy. Very little can be heard over the howling of the wind which finds its way in the house from nearly every corner.

---

86. Hans Torgersen, one of the founders of the Mission, was the first non-Native to be buried in the Bethel cemetery (Schwalbe 1985, 14).

March 1, 1901

My little Helen has been brighter between her coughing spells all day and seems quite like herself. But how hard the dear little thing has to cough. I am sometimes afraid she will choke. What a trial this is for me here alone with my little folks, but each day is one less of Herman's absence and one less of coughing for my babe. The darling baby, she cost me so much, I scarcely knew a comfortable day for months before her birth and have never gotten real strong since. All of this discomfort but makes my baby more dear and precious to me. If God gives her back in health and strength how thankful I shall be.

We are having fine weather again. March came in like a lamb. I hope Herman may have nice weather when he starts for home. The long gloomy winter with its traveling is nearly spent. I can scarcely realize it. It will soon be Easter then we look for the geese, then the ice leaving and next the boat. How soon the time will fly now until vessel time. We will soon have to think about seed sowing again, that is, in the house, but mine will not be very extensive this year. Gardening is too hard work for the little we realize from all the work, and then when one thoroughly dislikes it as I do it is still harder. I have about all I can manage to raise these little Romigs without going too much into the garden raising.

Robert and Margaret are fast asleep and tired enough to sleep, I am sure, for I am tired enough listening to their noise from morning at six until about eight in the evening. Of course, whatever Robert does is all right in Margaret's eyes so she follows suit, consequently they are as good as two noisy boys. Margaret puts her cape on and her hands in the sides of her drawers which she calls her pockets, and struts around as proud as a peacock. I guess I will put pants on her and call her Jimmy.

April 11, 1901[87]

DEAR FATHER:

Ella says I may add to your journal that Ella is writing you, and so I begin on a new page. To take up the link of her story is hard for me, and so I will write independent. The winter will soon be a thing of the past and right glad are we for of all the years spent here none have exceeded them

---

87. This journal entry made by Herman.

Herman's children were very important to him,
and he enjoyed family-centered activities.
(Courtesy, Alaska and Polar Regions Department, University of Alaska Fairbanks,
Joseph Romig Collection, acc. #90-043-909N)

in hardships. Sickness has not spared our family as nearly everyone has been more or less affected by the various epidemics of the year, but thanks to an all-wise and all-compassionate Heavenly Father we are all spared and are looking with pleasure for the spring. I have been from home so much this year that this season of home to me [is] a precious one of rest and happiness with my family. There is a trip or two yet that I could make but my wife's babes demand some of my time, and so I am going to stay with them this spring and stop traveling. Thus far I have made about 1700 miles by dog-sled and been gone about half the winter from home. This is a hard land when one must be from home so much, and some of the time know that the dear ones at home are not as well as they might have been. On our trip I came near rupturing myself having an accident with my sleigh in the mountains, and I may add, to be sick far from home in the mountains is not pleasant, and [is] dangerous in addition. I tell Ella that I am now going camping, and wish to take her and the children along for a change. She protests as she has [the] garden to make, yet I say to her she can spare a week to camp in the woods when we are getting our fire wood. For I know camping will be good for both her and the babes.

Helen is much better now and I think will fully recover in a short time. She was very sick during one of my trips, and poor Ella had to care for her all alone. Yet I dare say my presence would have only been for company and help as Ella displays excellent judgment and good sense in her care of any she may look out for when sick. I am proud to have such an able and lovable wife and babes.

I must close for today. Your son,

Herman

Sunday, June 2, 1901

MY DEAR FATHER:

Herman, Robert and Margaret have gone to church, and while baby Helen sleeps I will try to write to you. I stayed at home for this purpose but baby took another view of the matter by starting to fuss. When I can do nothing else to quiet her I play the organ. This she always likes, and it has had a splendid effect upon her this time. After listening awhile she fell asleep.

It is almost three months since I last wrote you. All that I passed through during the two weeks after my last writing God and myself alone know. Baby Helen was so very sick. Many times I thought she would choke to death. Poor little babe. She coughed so hard. The night before Herman came home from Nushagak I thought she had gone. She had a very hard coughing spell, and [it] seemed such a long time until she breathed again. After this hard spell, for four or more days, she lingered between life and death when she slowly improved. God truly has been good in sparing our little one for she is such a sweet babe. I trust I may never have to be alone in this dreary land with so sick a child. I shudder now when I think of those long, lonely sad days. But all the hours of trial truly bring us nearer our savior who, after all, is the only true comforter.

Tuesday, June 18, 1901

Truly I am having a hard time to write a little. Baby is so troublesome. She wants someone to entertain [her] all the time and the little nuisance she gets awake every morning at about four o'clock, and sleeps but little during the day.

June 19, 1901

This leaves us all well. The boat starts now. Your loving Son and Daughter,

Herman & Ella

chapter 3

July 14, 1901 to
June 1, 1902

Bethel, Alaska, July 14, 1901

Mr. A. F. Ervin
Forty Fort Luzerne Co. Pa.

My dear father:

We are still waiting and even looking for some word to come from the vessel. We all thought that this year the goods would surely come earlier than in previous years but it is the same old story. Although I must confess that I am very thankful for this long rest and quiet. It is our only one during the year. When our boats come in there is so much work always dividing goods, and then the natives come from every direction to trade and to visit.

Ougavig, Alaska, November 1, 1901

My dear father:

Whatever may have interrupted the above, I cannot tell. I suppose a baby cried or some native wanted something, but I am sure there is no excuse for not writing sooner than this, for we had plenty of time last summer for most anything before the mail and goods came. As near as I can remember the mail arrived at Bethel about the fifteenth of August, and about a week later the boats got in, that is the first boats. Both boats made a second trip to the ware-house.[88] Last summer was certainly a very trying one, we were never so low in provisions, there were many days that I simply did not know what to cook, and then Herman and his faithful bird dog would start out on the tundra for a long tramp for grouse, and they never failed to bring us something, anywhere from one up to six. Mrs. Helmich says that the doctor and his dog kept us from starving, and I believe it was almost so, at least they gave us many a good meal we would not have had otherwise.

---

88. The location at the mouth of the Kuskokwim River where goods were transferred from large ships to smaller boats for the trip upriver (Oswalt 1963, 19).

Fourth of July picnic upriver from Bethel, 1901.
(Courtesy, Alaska and Polar Regions Department, University of Alaska Fairbanks,
Joseph Romig Collection, acc. #90-043-918aN)

Well as I said before I was very glad for a good rest, although the rest grew rather long and provisions got very low, and we finally gave the boat up for lost, yet with it all we had many nice times. Mrs. Helmich stayed at Bethel while Mr. H. waited at the coast for the vessel. We had a number of picnics during the summer. On the "Fourth of July" we all clubbed together and made up as good a dinner as we could, got in a large family boat and went up the creek to a favorite spot and had a very enjoyable time. The day before, three white men had arrived from up river; three unsuccessful miners and we asked them to accompany us. And how they did enjoy their dinner, it meant so much to them who had roughed it so long. It is not always convenient to cook for the many white men who happen along here, but I am sure we never miss anything in the little kindness we may show for nearly everyone of them has, somewhere a mother, a wife and children or a sister who I know would appreciate any kindness shown a dear one in this desolate country. These three men who were with us on our "Fourth" picnic told Mr. Helmich when they got to the coast how much they enjoyed that little picnic, and they said they would never forget it.

Thus passed our summer, the early part was pleasant but the summer almost passed before we ever heard from home or knew that we would have provisions for the coming Winter. One day when we all felt that we had waited long enough we all got together and made out a requisition with the idea of sending [it] to St. Michael for provisions, but the following day word came that the boat was in. Mr. Lind had heard from some men who came from Dutch Harbor that the A. C. Co. would send a steamer to the Kuskokwim so he and one of his partners, Mr. Hubbard, and Mr. Helmich put their heads together and planned just how this steamer would come all the way to Bethel as well as to the head waters of the Kuskokwim, and when in their minds she had gotten to all of these Kuskokwim ports, they accordingly started home; boats, crews and all. (Mr. Lind had bought a little steamer). One Sunday about noon a native came in and said he had heard a whistle and sure enough here was the little steamer with two boats in tow. Well we all thought they had given up the boat for a bad job but not so, they had just returned to wait here for the steamer of the fairy story. On Tuesday while they were sitting in the doctor's office telling just how it would all be, of course, a messenger arrived from Quinhagak saying [the] vessel was in and to hurry up about coming back again for their goods. You may imagine there was a scattering of men. They all started for the trading post on a run. Mr. Lind, who scarcely ever walks faster than a man of perfect ease, and Mr. Hubbard, too fat to walk very fast, both started on a trot. How we did laugh. Mr. Helmich, who had not gotten home yet, had not so far to go back but when he reached the vessel he found that only Mr. Lind's goods were on board. Of course he helped him to unload. Our boat came in a week later with Mr. and Mrs. Stecker on board for Bethel and Mr. and Mrs. Zucher of Nushagak.[89] Mr. and Mrs. Stecker are very nice people. Very lovely Christian people.

You will wonder why I am at Ougavig. Herman and I are both here for three weeks now and will probably remain for two weeks more when we will return by dog team. It will soon be four weeks since we left our little ones. It seems such a long time. Mr. and Mrs. Stecker are keeping them,

89. Reverend G. Adolph Stecker and his wife, Franziska Pitschmann, served in the Kuskokwim region from 1901–1910 after sixteen years of experience working with the Labrador Eskimos. Following his wife's death in 1913, Reverend Stecker returned to the Kuskokwim with his two daughters, Anna and Marie, where he served until 1927. Reverend Ernst Paul Zucher and his wife, Elizabeth Arnstadt, who had previously served in Africa, were missionaries in the Kuskokwim region from 1901–1908 (Schwalbe 1985, 86, 124 and 300).

and I am sure they have good care. The children all like them, and baby Helen loves Mrs. Stecker very much. She always cries to go to her. We are enjoying this visit very much, especially Herman. He is just in clover here or more like it in rabbits. Mr. Helmich and Herman are hunting most of the time. Yesterday and today in the whole drives 248 were killed and fifteen from steel traps. Herman shot thirty-eight yesterday and twenty-one today. The way they hunt rabbits here, a number of men, anywhere from ten up, get lined up at the end of an island and drive toward to [the] other. They generally shoot a number through the brush, but when the fun comes in is when they get to the other end. Here the rabbits run every direction. Mrs. Helmich and I are so tired of this everlasting butchering. Tomorrow we have a hundred and forty to attend to. We think we have good grounds for a divorce. I am sure that hunting them is far more fun than cleaning them.

Ougavig, Alaska, November 6, 1901

MY DEAR FATHER:

Christian and Charlie arrived yesterday from Bethel with Herman's team. How good it was to hear from our little ones, and to know that they were and have been well. Mr. Stecker wrote that Robert ran away when he realized that we had gone. He decided to run after us. Nellie, Christian's wife and [a] very faithful servant, had quite a time getting [him] home again. He was going to his papa and mama whether or no. But now they say that he runs along after Mr. Stecker like he does after his papa. Margaret is learning to speak German so the story goes. (Bro and Sr Stecker speak German, in fact are German people). Baby Helen is as thick as she is long and is beginning to walk. The children all seem to love their new papa and mama. We are growing very homesick for our babies. It will be five weeks day after tomorrow since we left them. That is a long time and the only time that I have ever been away from them. I am however, enjoying this visit very much, it is such a treat to be among God's own trees, and to hear the wind making music through their branches. Ougavig is situated almost a quarter of a mile from the river bank in a woods, while Bethel sits out on a barren tundra where the wicked Alaska winter winds have full play from every side. In Winter Ougavig is protected from the wind by the trees. But in Summer the mosquitoes make life unbearable. The missionaries generally spend their Summers at Bethel. How lonely it must be living here alone. I am sure Mr. and Mrs. Helmich are more brave than I, for I am sure I would be very unwilling to come here unless another family were to come too. Often Mr. H. goes on trips leaving his wife alone with her children. Of course there is no danger of anyone bothering a mission. The natives are very kind and friendly and especially when a missionary sister is left alone with her children in Winter time.

I always dread to see Winter come; Herman is gone so much of the time on missionary trips. But we are here for the welfare of the poor Eskimo, to teach them about a dear loving savior and as their villages are so scattered they can but be reached by traveling from village to village.

We had a very late, as well as a very pleasant Fall, it seemed the river would never freeze over. Not until Oct. twenty-ninth did the river freeze over to stay. For several days before this there was a run of ice from up north thus making very rough roads. I don't anticipate a very pleasant trip home.

Wednesday, November 11, 1901

It really seems like Winter tonight. We have been having such mild weather, I don't know whether it is because we are here in the trees or whether it has turned a mild spell. Mrs. Weinlick wrote from Bethel that she hoped it would not be so cold when we would return, and that Mr. Brown (a miner living on the mission ground in a new little house of his own) could not keep warm, so it seems that they have had cold weather down there.

Mr. Brown has been on the mission since last Spring. Sometimes he works for the missionaries or goes on trips for us; one time during the Summer he went up the river for a raft of wood for his little house. He is from Montana and I believe a quite well-to-do man, and is a genuine frontiersman. [He] has lived in the west since he was a boy. It is quite interesting to hear him tell how he ran away from his home in one of the southern states when only eight years old with several other boys who all but Mr. Brown grew homesick and returned home. But Mr. Brown stuck to his resolve, and was over twenty-one when he next saw his mother. He is trading this Winter and will probably send for his wife and child next Spring. Mr. Brown has spoken to Herman about practicing medicine at his home town in Montana, a gold and coal mining town, and has promised to build and furnish a hospital for him. We will soon have to begin to think and plan for the future if we do not wish to continue in missionary work. We often feel discouraged at having so little medical work and no hospital. Not that we wish everyone to get sick for us to practice on, but we know that there must be places where more of our kind of work must be needed.

The doctor and Mr. Helmich are talking over the last year's sickness and its ravages among our poor people. It carried off so many of our poor natives. Herman has just said that when he took the census for a part of the Kuskokwim he numerated about fourteen hundred and now there is scarcely half of that number. It seems hardly worth while sending any more missionaries up at so much expense, and yet our church [is] sending more out next year. The old people are all dying off, and one can scarcely find a living child born during the last three years. These natives think so much of their little ones, but they are born to them to lose so soon.

We have just learned of the sad news of the murder of our noble president.[90] The world truly is poorer for having lost so good a man. He ruled over a very trying time. My heart aches for his poor invalid wife. She must be broken-hearted. We only know that the president was shot at the Buffalo exposition on September the sixth and that the murderer had been caught, but who this cruel wicked creature was we know not.[91] We are all anxious for the particulars. God pity such heartless creatures. I often wonder why such things are permitted. God above knows why He permitted our country such another hard blow. We have lost three such good noble presidents.

Sunday, November 17, 1901

Mr. Stecker arrived yesterday from Bethel on his first missionary trip. We were glad to hear from our children again. They are quite well now but have had somewhat of a cold. Something like the cough that goes with the grippe. The natives are all coughing in every village. They are troubled with this same slight affliction. Ever since the Summer of ninety-nine we feel more or less worried when all of the natives start coughing, and the poor natives worry very much until a change for the better is

---

90. William McKinley, President of the United States, died on September 13, 1901, due to injuries inflicted by an assassin's bullet (Weisberger, Bernard A., *Reaching for Empire* [New York: Time Incorporated 1964], 155).

91. Leon Czolgosz, a twenty-eight year old Polish immigrant, was apprehended and charged at the scene. He was electrocuted within eight weeks of his crime (Weisberger, 1964, 154–55).

noticed. Our poor natives. They all suffered very much at that time and so many died. These natives are not a strong class of people but since the "big cough," as they call it, so many have died from the effects of that severe epidemic. David, who came with Mr. S. [Stecker] yesterday, tells us that Jennie, an old and faithful servant of mine, is dead. Poor girl. She had been poorly ever since that severe grippe attack, and like all of these poor people she had not a strong enough constitution to work against its effects. I will miss her very much for she was always very good and faithful. I could always count on her to help me in every way especially fine sewing when she was able. Jennie was the mother of Albert, your little name-sake, who died a year ago last Summer of measles. The father, a worthless scamp, lives here in Ougavig. I am sorry that he is free now to neglect another wife if he ever gets one. Jennie left him over a year ago. He was not good to her. Abused and neglected her. She came down to Bethel with him and would have nothing more to do with him afterwards.

Wednesday, November 20, 1901

Christian arrived again today. He left only a week ago yesterday with a load of our things and some rabbits for the school and was told to stay at Bethel to rest the team, but I think they are getting anxious for us to come home for they sent him back in three days after he got home. We were all in chapel tonight when Christian came. I thought when I heard bells that it might be him, and as we were not looking for him so soon, I could scarcely wait until chapel was over thinking someone at Bethel might be ill, but thank God, they are all getting better. Some of the natives are sick here, and Ernest Helmich, Robert's little chum, has been quite sick today; naturally I worry about my little folks.

Mr. Stecker and David left this morning for Tuluksak, one of our Christian villages, where he will give communion tonight. Tomorrow he will start for the deer herd in the mountains about eighty miles by trail from Bethel, and expects to return to Bethel on or near Thanksgiving day.

We hear from home that Robert goes to school sometimes; he likes Mr. Weinlick, the teacher, very much, and no doubt Mrs. Stecker is glad when he is gone for a little while. I think my little ones must keep her quite busy, but then she is accustomed to the care of children, for she has three of her own in a mission school in Germany. She and Br. Stecker miss their children very much nor do I wonder for I am homesick for mine and they are only eighty miles away.

Saturday evening, November 23, 1901

Have just finished our supper work; have all enjoyed a Russian bath; the children are asleep, and to tell the truth I am too sleepy to think. I have been sitting here for about fifteen minutes trying to collect my thoughts, but find it a pretty hard task. One always feels very sleepy after a Russian bath. I wonder how you would like a bath like this. The room is made as hot as possible, the stove is covered and surrounded by rocks; in one corner of the room is a bench about five or six feet high. After sponging the body you climb upon this bench, throw water on the hot stones and then sweat, (and you sweat too I can assure you) after a time you get down, take another wash and then get up on the bench for another sweat. It gets pretty hot sometimes but by bathing one's face and neck in cold water you can manage to breathe. When you think the dirt is all out, you take a dash of cold water and go to the dressing room to dry yourself off and dress. How clean one feels after a bath of this kind, but last Saturday I found it almost too much for me, it was so hot I almost fainted.

The first white man arrived here today from the Yukon, is said to have come to buy dogs. Last Winter long before this date miners and prospectors were arriving from every direction. We have often said of late that it seemed strange that there have been no white travelers yet. This man has only one dog, but his business here is to buy up dogs. The arrival of a white man three years ago was quite an event, but now it seems like an every day occurrence.

This is such a beautiful still clear moon light night, bitterly cold and the dogs are howling, it truly seems Winter-like. The dogs always seem unusually frisky and happy when it is coldest. I too enjoy these clear, cold moonlight nights when the trees and everything is covered with snow and frost that sparkles like diamonds. Herman says that traveling with the dogs when every dog is working and the bells jingling on a night like this is delightful, and I am sure I would like it too. How I wish we were on our way tonight for the dear babies.

Sunday, November 24, 1901

We were all invited down to drink tea with the native trader Ma-gax-i-lick (this name means rabbit skin parka) and enjoyed ourselves very much. The natives like the missionaries to mingle with them in this way; tea drinking among them is almost as much for a courtesy as it is among the fashionable ladies in the states with their little afternoon teas. But in the size of cups and amount of tea they drink there is a marked difference, for the natives here like large cups frequently filled. But the joke today was on me they claim, for I could only eat my bread, butter and sugar, while the others seemed to enjoy their tea very much. The way this all came about; a few days ago Herman and I had an argument on smoking or rather I read him a lecture on smoking, as to it being a selfish, extravagant, and unnecessary habit which had not one good point in its favor, and at the same time he was setting a bad example for our son, and Herman claimed that tea and coffee could be counted in for the same and asked me if I would give up my coffee and tea, which I enjoy very much, if he would give up his pipe. I at once said "yes," and have kept to my word. Herman tried hard today to get me to drink tea and declared that I would be very deficient in courtesy not to drink a little, but I only explained to my hostess why I could not drink tea, and feasted on bread and water. For this one time I did not eat and drink what was "set before me for conscience sake," for my conscience told me that that would be wrong. I have given up this tea and coffee drinking and the price of my share of both of these articles I will save up for on toward the education of my boy and girls. Herman still keeps the right to drink tea and coffee and so I will claim the right to the cost of an equal share.

After our visit and chat with the natives, Herman and I took a long walk, and enjoyed it very much, it was about forty below zero but not a bit of wind blowing so that we did not mind as we were dressed in furs and the lovely sun shine and exercise did us good. When we returned the natives were firing the *Kashima* (men's council house) for a bath, the big volume of smoke that rose toward the sky with the sun for a background together with the snow laden trees made a pretty picture. These baths are somewhat like the Russian bath of which I spoke last night. When the *Kashima* is hot enough the men climb on the benches for a good sweat but I don't believe they ever use water. Herman says he has seen some of the young men run out and jump in a snow bank after a good sweat and then into their clothes. This is rather a sudden cooling off I think. The *Kashimas* here serve for church (in villages where there is no chapel) court-house, town hall, hotel, working house for the men, and in fact for all public meetings; in these nearly all men travelers sleep. The *Kashima* here at Ougavig is one of the largest and nicest on the river as well as one of the oldest, one of the benches about forty feet long and two feet wide was hewed out with a stone adz before the time of white man's tools were known of here. About twenty-five years ago there were two *Kashimas* here and the natives say they were both full of men then. Now there are less than a hundred men women and children in the village.

Dear Father:[92]

I will steal a line to you in Ella's journal. It seems she has been telling you of the village at this place. Each village has its particular history but this one in particular is an interesting one. They came from up the river being a branch of some other village leaving for a better home and landed at this place for a camp one night. Being [settled] in the camp they tried fishing and found the waters to abound in fish. Thus they stayed and the village prospered. As the years went by the growth of the people necessitated the building of two *Kashimas,* and later the founders of the next two villages below here left this village to fish in the summer. They stayed for the winter and the two villages of Kwigogluk and Tuluksak sprang into existence.

One incident of interest happened that put a historic reputation to this place. A child was known to be a bad boy and unruly. [He] was often chided for his waywardness, and his especially wayward carelessness tanning of his clothing. If he was to stay at home he was sure to follow the hunters or if to work he would neglect his duty. Thus his mother often scolded. Finally in a fit of anger he started for the woods and his steps were traced to a tree and then ended. No trace or sign of him was further to be found. Then the tree was cut and blood came from the core and it moaned like a child. The limbs and bark were taken and made into dolls and masks which being used and consulted by the Shaman, or medicine man, gave forth the warning of the seasons of game or fish or sickness or health, and many other items of interest. Thus, dolls were regularly consulted by the villages and the people of adjoining villages, and the answer was to be an auspicious one. A special tree was selected to hang these idols in and no one ever molested them. When the village gave up heathen customs and embraced Christianity they gave these up and they are now in my possession.

This is one story and is for sure that the tree and its dolls are a creation of the Shaman's. The boy was lost, and the dolls were consulted, and the tree upon which the dolls were hung still stands. The people also inquire at times of the safety of these dolls.

---

92. The remainder of this date's entry was made by Herman.

Monday, November 25, 1901

Today, at twenty-five minutes to two, a little son was born to Mr. and Mrs. Helmich. The day has been very cold, and a perfectly beautiful one as well; so clear and sunny. Tonight the thermometer goes down to twenty-eight below zero. The night is a perfect one. The moon is full, every object in view is robed in white, and not a breath of wind blowing. Baby Helmich will never have a prettier birthday.

Tuesday, November 26, 1901

The temperature this morning at sunrise was thirty-seven below zero, and tonight at dusk it was thirty-four [below zero]. But we do not mind the cold while it is so still.

Herman held a preparatory service this evening for communion. Tomorrow he will talk personally with the members, and on Thursday evening will administer the Lord's Supper. Mr. H. does not care to be ordained as his term of service is almost up. He feels that if he were ordained the church would have a stronger hold on him and try to make him serve a longer term. They would probably try to make him stay another five or ten years. They always try to have their missionaries nearly worn out before they give them a furlough.

Nearly all of the natives in the village came up to see the baby this morning, and each one brought him a dish full of ice-cream, fish or berries. It is a custom to take a present when they go to see a newborn baby for the first time.

Friday, November 29, 1901

Mr. Helmich had a wood cutting frolic today to get wood for the chapel. He and several of the natives sawed and split wood for a half day, and when they had finished we gave them a good supper of tea, sugar and bread. After this they had boiled pink beans, and last, dry fish and ice-cream. They all seemed very happy, and there is no doubt about their enjoying their meal. If there is one thing a native loves more than anything else it is filling his stomach, but who does not like to eat.

Herman held the communion service last night. Thirty-five natives communed. The service was such a nice one, everything passed off so smoothly. Sometimes the natives get mixed up; they either sing too much or not enough, or shake hands at the wrong time, but last night everything went well. I always like Herman's communion services anyway. He has a sincere earnest way that some of the other missionaries have not much, to their own misfortune, for the natives do not like a service of this kind hurried. The natives always like to talk over their little troubles before communion and leave it to the missionary to tell them whether or not they are fit to commune. Sometimes, in fact very frequently, they have the silliest trifling little troubles to bring up, and a missionary will sometimes lose their confidence if he treats their little trials lightly. This is one way in which John [Kilbuck] won their love and confidence by entering into all that was of interest to the natives, and this is one way in which Herman fills, to some degree, our brother's place. I am very proud to say that there is not a doubt as to which missionary is most loved now. Some of the missionaries think that it is Herman's profession that makes him so popular with the natives. Whatever it may be, there is no missionary more loved than my Herman, and I can truthfully say there is not one who loves the natives more than he. This may be another reason why they love him.

Wednesday evening, December 4, 1901

This is our last day at Ougavig, and although we have enjoyed our visit here very much I am glad it is at an end as we can now speed toward our darling babies, and to our own people again who claim to be very homesick for us.

Herman baptized baby Helmich last night, and I held him for baptism. Little Paul Herbert Helmich is my only God-child living now, little Paul Weinlick having died last Winter. All of my native babies have gone, like nearly all native babies do. I often wonder who will make up our future congregations here. The old ones fast dying out and as it now seems, no new ones to take their place. Herman gave the baby, for his baptismal text, the thirty-third verse of the hundred and nineteenth Psalm: "Teach me, O Lord, the way of they statutes, and I shall keep it unto the end."

We had thought to start home today but Herman could not finish the sleigh in time to make any distance by daylight. The days are so short, one scarcely sees the sun rise until it sets again. But how time flies. We will soon have passed the shortest day and then we will be looking toward Springtime again. The seasons seem to come and go so rapidly up here. This has been a full day for me with getting ready for the trip and helping Mrs. H. all that I could, as she is not very strong yet. I am truly glad for this good rest before starting out on our long trip. We had planned a love feast for last night but gave it up. A Moravian love feast means a good sized cinnamon bun and a cup of coffee for each person, and of course this all means work, something we have had plenty of for the past two days.

Made sausage from rabbit meat this morning to take home. This rabbit sausage is certainly excellent. We always mix a little salt pork with it. We are taking plenty of rabbits home with us as they are not so plentiful down at Bethel.

Tuluksak, Thursday, December 5, 1901

We left Ougavig this morning at about nine o'clock reaching here at two, the distance being twenty-five or more miles. Although the road in some places was very rough (owing to a run of ice in the Fall just before freezing up) nevertheless I enjoyed the trip very much. I always love to hear the bells jingle and see the dogs so frisky as they always are on a cold crisp morning. All along the road between villages there is nothing to be seen but God's own work save here and there a fish trap or fox trap. I enjoy riding and running over the pure white snow, through the trees, on the bare tundra or on the river and creeks whichever it may be, if it is not too cold, and today has certainly been a perfect one.

We climbed a very steep bank at one place to go through a little stretch of woods from the river to a small creek. After reaching the top a native took charge of our team while Herman stayed back to help get Mr. Helmich's sleigh up (a native is taking his, Mr. H's, team down to help us home). When the team reached the top they started through trees like crazy, the native holding to the sleigh, down the bank into the creek and down the creek as fast as they could go. The native held on as long as he could but finally had to let loose, or did, at least. After running about a mile, in making a sharp turn in the road the sleigh overturned stopping the team. When I reached the sleigh I was pretty tired but had time to rest before Herman and the other team reached us.

Dogs do not travel like horses, they go much faster and are not so easy to handle. When they take a notion to run they will run like the wind, and there are no reins to hold them in with. The harness is attached to a long lead line which is fastened to the under front of the sleigh. When you are ready to start all good-byes have been given, the last thing done is hitching up the dogs, and when the last dog is in the signal is given and gladly by the dogs for they are all howling to start. I always travel like Herman sitting on the side of the sleigh ready to jump at any minute. Edith always rode in state, propped up in the sleigh, but oh no, not this chicken, I value my head too much for this, for the sleigh is just as likely to be upside down as it is right side up. Herman has a very fine team but it takes two wide awake men to handle them for they go like crazy. I think I am getting younger for I can jump off and on the sleigh almost as well as my better half, and it truly behooves one who travels behind a dog team to be supple.

We are staying in the mission house here with Waska and his mother. Waska is a very nice boy, and one of our old school scholars. His mother is one of the kindest women on the river. Such a good motherly old soul. This was once quite a large village, but since the "big cough" there are scarcely enough to tell the story. Living here with Waskas are three of his cousins, a boy and two little girls left motherless and fatherless by the epidemic of '99. Also another little girl, Nannie, the adopted daughter of Anna and Sumpka, of whom I may have written before. They were old faithful servants of Edith's for many years. They too died during the cruel epidemic; Anna on one morning and Sumpka the next morning. Well, back to Nannie, she has a father, one of the best hunters on the river and who always lives well, but generally when husband and wife separate, as Nannie's did, the children go with the mother, the father scarcely ever having anything to do with them afterwards.

Some little girls are sitting on the floor playing with their rag dolls. They have beds made of patches and scraps of fur and chairs of little pieces of wood. How little it takes to make these poor people happy. I just gave each of these little girls a needle and three blue beads and how happy they seem. If you should ever send me another box send some nice patches and a few cheap mouth organs, they would gladden the hearts of some poor fatherless and motherless children. How good it is that we are running school this year. It feeds, clothes, and gives a warm home to some of the many poor children on the river.

I guess Herman is tired. He is lying here beside me fast asleep. He had drunk tea twice since we arrived, but as I already wrote you, I do not drink [it] anymore. Waska's mother is boiling some [fish] roe for me, and as I write I am munching a piece of dry fish, of which I am very fond. Someone sent Herman ice cream made of seal oil, tallow, and snow and berries. He ate nearly all of it, but I think only for "conscience sake." It is sometimes hard to "eat what is set before you" up here.

Herman did not hold service tonight as he has no interpreter along, and is not good enough in the language yet to speak it alone.

Akiak, Friday, December 6, 1901

We arrived at this place about noon today, the most of the trip being very pleasant. We left Tuluksak just at dawn, and such a perfectly lovely morning it was too, overhead at least, but the first part of the trail was very rough, the ice wall piled high all around, while on either side of the trail was open water. I jumped from the sled for it turned over first on one side then on the other. I managed to keep hold of it, sometimes up and sometimes down. I wonder that my bones were all whole climbing over all this rough ice but they were, and as you see I am alive to tell the story. When one travels with Herman there is no chance to pick one's way over rough ice. If your hair stands on end, no matter, it is a case of holding fast to the sled and hoping for the best. After we had passed over this rough part of the trail, we had a fine run all the way into the village. Just as we neared the village we met a white man, a prospector who was here buying furs. He had the ordinary miner's team, not like ours, but one that has to be pushed along. Poor fellow, he was having a hard time to move at all while we were just spinning along.

This is our largest Christian village, and the one to which we belong. They always count us and Kilbucks of their village, and this is John's favorite people. The people here are very friendly. No more hospitable people can anywhere be found. The family with whom we are staying, as well as some of our other friends, have brought us so much to eat of dry fish, ice-cream, dried venison and berries. Not wishing to be deficient in courtesy, we have eaten a little of each, consequently we are somewhat uncomfortable. I managed to eat my share of all with the exception of the ice-cream. This I cannot bring myself to like well enough to eat ever so little. We are the guests of Kawagleg, our native helper here at this village. His is the dirtiest house in the village and his wife the most untidy of all the women, but she is the kindest and best old soul of them all I think. She has been flying around ever since we arrived trying to entertain us, and not-with-standing all the dirty surroundings, we are truly enjoying ourselves. At such times we must throw aside our very refined tastes, and try to be interested in all that interests our people. If one were to look upon the outside of these natives there would be nothing to keep us up here, but under all of these dirty clothes, [there are] many a kind, true and loving heart. When we first came to Alaska it was indeed hard for me to tolerate such filthy dirty creatures. But the more I know them and their language, and of their home life, their joys and sorrows, the more I love them. We could have reached home tonight had we pushed on, but as we had to hurry through all of our villages on our way up, we did not want to disappoint them this time, and they were so anxious for us to remain overnight with them. So we are pleasing our people more than ourselves for naturally we are very anxious to be with our little ones again.

We were over to the *Kashima* a while this evening to see the folks dance or practice for their plays.[93] Such a noise I never heard with the beating of the drums and each man singing to the full extent of his singing ability. The way the directors swing themselves and jerked their bodies and yelled I am sure they will be pretty well tired out. While this so called singing is going on some of the women in their dancing caps are dancing. According to my way of thinking their dancing is not very graceful, although very orderly. They bend their knees and nod their heads; make motions with their arms somewhat like gymnasium exercises, all in perfect time with the music. I would like to be present at the time of the play but of course cannot leave home so soon again. While the natives play nearly everything away that they own, still these plays are harmless too, and afford the natives much amusement and pastime, something we all need at times. One village plays against another, each one of course trying to out-do the other. In their songs they ask of each person what they want. A native will go any distance through storm or sunshine and pay any price to obtain the article asked of him. It would be somewhat of a disgrace not to give what is asked and a little more. As they sing and dance in the *Kashima*, as each article is asked for, the person walks in and lays it on the pile. When it is all over all of these things are dealt out to the villagers, the old people and the poor are remembered first consequently those who play the most away get the least although they get the most praise. Thus the man who has the most is not or does not remain the richest one. These plays generally place them on pretty much of an equal. You could scarcely find one native who is worth much more than another, and if there are any such persons they are always very kind to those in need.

Bethel, Saturday, December 7, 1901

We arrived at home about three o'clock, and how good it is to be here again with our darling babies. Robert was so glad to see us. He hugged and kissed me several times, laughed, nearly cried, and asked several times

93. The winter festival was an occasion for feasting, dancing and gift giving. The missionaries participated in these events until they realized the pagan implications (Fienup-Riordan 1991, 189).

why we stayed so long, and wanted to know if we were going away again. Margaret too is very glad to see us again, and how they do talk. They try to tell everything in one breath. They talk more English than when we left home and some German. But about baby, she would have nothing to do with us and looked so cross and just clung to Mrs. Stecker for quite awhile. Finally she looked at me and smiled, and then held out her dear fat little arms to come, and stayed with me until bed time. I think she knew me after all. It is very evident that Mr. and Mrs. Stecker took good care of them while we were gone. They look so well and are all much fatter than when we left them. We had to stop at Akiachak on our way down to bury Toni's and Mollie's baby. This took some time as the cemetery must be over a mile from the village. My heart aches for the father and mother. This is their second child and both are gone. After the funeral services were held at the house we started for the cemetery and about a quarter of a mile, up in a tree, was the remains of the little one together with a little box containing all of its belongings. When the coffin was lowered in the grave, the mother took these little things from the box and laid them around the little coffin. How her heart must have ached, poor soul!

We had very rough roads between Akiachak and here, worse than any, I am sure.

Monday, December 30, 1901

I am trying to do my own work now as Nellie and Christian were getting tired and wanted a vacation. I find that my house and three little folks takes almost all of my time thus leaving me no time to write. Herman scolds because I am not willing to take another native girl and train her, but I prefer to do my [own] work than to take in a raw native girl whom after I have dressed and cleaned up and taught to wash dishes and scrub, some man will be sure to want, for so many more women died two years ago than men. Consequently there are many wife seekers.

We had a very pleasant quiet Christmas this year, the first since we are here. On other years so many natives came from all the villages, making it very hard for us to entertain them all over this time. So Mr. Stecker told them they were not to come this year, but that they should have their celebration at home.

We had no presents for our little folks, save a suit of clothes I had been keeping for Robert, and a rag doll which I made for Margaret. But they had a very pretty tree with plenty of candles on it, and truly Robert did enjoy lighting the tree up several times during the day. I let him enjoy it just all that he wanted for this was all the pleasure we had to give them. It is always hard over this time for me. I would love so much to make my children happy, but there is so little one can get. I am thinking of sending out to the states on the next mail for Christmas gifts for next year. A prospector who happened to be here at Bethel, who is an excellent artist, painted a beautiful picture for me to give Herman, otherwise I would have had nothing for him. We all took dinner with Mr. and Mrs. Stecker, and had a very enjoyable day. We had no turkey but a fine roast of venison took its place.

January 1, 1902

MY DEAR FATHER:

Were I at home now or even at a distance where a letter might reach you in a week or two I would wish you "A Happy New Year," but as this will not reach you for some months, such a greeting would seem very old and stale to you. But I pray that God's richest blessing may rest upon you and *all* of my dear ones at home through the coming year. Oh, how I wish that it might be made more pleasant for us all by a visit to the dear old home again, but this I fear will not be added to the pleasures of the coming year.

We were all together last night, the missionaries and our three white neighbors, (Mr. Brown who lives in a little house of his own on mission ground; Mr. Ryfcogle the trader; and Mr. Peterson a surgical patient of Herman's) to spend the last hours of the old year and see the new one dawn. About nine o'clock we had a nice lunch, and then we played games until twelve o'clock. We did not usher the new year by a display of fireworks and firing of cannons, but rather Mr. Stecker read the CIII Psalm and offered prayer to the God of all mercy and comfort, and truly He has wonderfully blessed us all during the past year, and how little we do to repay Him for all His kindness toward us. After we had all wished one another a Happy New Year our little party broke up. Today the men and school boys are hunting.

Tomorrow will be another great bout; our darling baby will be one year old. I am going to make her a doll and dress it for her birthday present for she always likes to play with Margaret's. Our Babe is such a sweet fat romping little girl. How she does love to get undressed in the evening and then get on the bed with Robert and Margaret and have a romp. She talks some, or rather says a great many single words, and stands up beside chairs. I think she will soon walk.

It has been bitterly cold for the past week but now is quite warm, and we are having a lively little snow storm. In one night the thermometer went up from forty degrees below zero to twenty above. But I prefer the colder weather. In this weather I always feel so lazy and sleepy. Herman has a new typewriter now, so in the future we will both write mostly with that which, no doubt, my friends will be thankful for. Really I can scarcely read my own writing of late. Herman says I may learn to use the machine too and will find it easier to write than by hand. I think too that it will not be so hard on my eyes.

Monday, January 6, 1902

The old Laplander who has charge of our deer herd, together with his wife and daughter, and the wife of Wassili a native herder, arrived at the mission today.[94] The herd and herders are stationed a good many miles back in the mountains so this trip down here is for them like going to town sure enough. We expected them at Christmas time, but the mountain streams were all open at that time making it impossible for them to travel. Wassili and the young Lap were down a few weeks before Christmas for some supplies. The party who arrived today are here for the same reasons as well as for a little visit. They all took supper with us tonight. The girl speaks some English so we can manage to make one another understood. They all seemed to enjoy their supper, especially the old father. He drank so much coffee and said it was such good coffee: ("they are great coffee drinkers"). I am sorry that Mr. Helmich is not here. He dislikes the Lapp girl so much, he always calls her the green cheese because she almost ran over him with her deer last Spring and then giggled at him. Mr. Helmich, naturally a very serious long faced fellow, saw no fun in this act. I believe he told her as much at the time. The Laplander's wife is almost as broad as she is long, and very good natured looking and is much younger than her husband. In fact, she is his second wife and step-mother to his four children. They dress very oddly, nearly always in

---

94. The Laplander to whom Ella referred was probably Per Nils Bals and his family (Lenz and Barker 1985, 29).

*Per Nils Bals and his wife with their daughter standing behind them
celebrated the Christmas season in the Romig home. Sami reindeer herders
from Scandinavia were brought to southwest Alaska to teach
herding techniques to the Alaska Natives.*
(Courtesy, Alaska and Polar Regions Department, University of Alaska Fairbanks,
Joseph Romig Collection, acc. #90-043-913aN)

black or dark blue trimmed in yellow or red, the women wearing a queer looking cap of red and yellow material (they wear these all the time) and very short skirts. They wear such funny boots made with sort of a hook turned back from the front of the toe. This is to hold the skis on I believe. Herman will take their picture, and I will send you one if they are good.

We are having such cold weather again it is almost impossible to keep warm in the house.

Sunday, January 12, 1902

Herman is on a missionary trip over the tundra. He left last Wednesday morning when the thermometer registered forty below zero, and until today it has been from that to fifty-five below. I expected him home yesterday, but he did not come nor has he arrived yet. I am just a little worried about him not coming, but of course he is all right or someone would come to tell us. In this kind of weather it is so easy to freeze a foot or a hand or in fact freeze to death if one is not properly clad, but Herman is well dressed and is doubtless somewhere near home.

We have just had our Sunday evening reading. Every Sunday evening one of the men reads a sermon, generally Moody's. I like the custom very much. It was Mr. Weinlick's turn tonight, and he read from a book on Sowing and Reaping. How carefully we Christians ought to walk before God. In our every thought and action we are sowing seed that at some future time we must reap whether it be for good or evil. How many many seeds we sow that we will have to reap in sorrow. Oh, how I hope to see my little ones grow up to walk in God's way. Whatever else they may choose in life to do, above all other wishes I have for them is that they will be true followers of Christ and be useful instruments in His hands.

I have not attended services since Herman left, having no servants it is hard to go out of doors. Baby is very fussy. She wants to be on the floor all the time, and it is so cold I am afraid to leave her down at all. When Herman returns we will fix up the upstairs room over the kitchen where she will be warm. She would soon walk if she had a chance to learn. She is the dearest baby, so cute and smart. She talks so much already for her age and is so full of fun. She loves to play with Robert and Margaret, and how she loves Margaret's doll. She holds it and sings to it.

The dogs are so restless tonight I am afraid the deer are near. The Bals are thinking of leaving tomorrow. The deer are at pasture over two miles from the mission. The Bals man goes out every morning to them. These deer may turn out well. I trust so, for the board have put so much money in them. As for me, I think they are best in the pot. They are fine eating.

Thursday, January 16, 1902

A little son was born to Mr. and Mrs. Weinlick today at 5 A.M. How glad I am for Mr. and Mrs. W. as they were called upon to mourn the loss of a little boy last Winter. This baby is such a frail looking little fellow he was nearer dead than alive when born. I hope the little one may live.

Mr. Helmich, who is down from Ougavig on a visit, took ether to have a tooth pulled. He has a very poor heart, and when nearly under the influence of ether he stopped breathing. How glad I was when he breathed again, for I was worried having seen a man stop breathing during an operation at Hahnemann who never breathed again. It seems very childish for a man to take ether to have a tooth pulled, but Mr. H. was determined to have it and took it at his own risk.

This has been a full day for Herman and for me too. But sometimes I wonder if Herman really is a physician. He has so little to do up here in his profession, that is, it would seem little to a physician in the states.

Herman returned from his missionary trip last Monday about noon having frozen his nose and chin slightly during the trip. One village he visited, who are Greeks, expressed a desire to belong to us and have asked for communion.[95] I don't know what the Greek Church of Russia is like, but here a Greek is a pretty poor excuse of a Christian. Scarcely better than heathen.

Sunday, January 19, 1902

The mail arrived from St. Michael tonight, and Bro. Stecker will start for Nushagak tomorrow carrying it that far. He expects to be gone about a month or more. This will be a long and very hard trip as Herman had a dose of it last Winter and will testify that it was not a pleasant trip.

January 22, 1902

The white men are beginning to come now. Who can tell when they will stop. One arrived at about two o'clock just as we had finished our dinner yesterday. Of course we had to set up a meal for him. Today, just as we were through with dinner, Mr. Koltchoff (our sticking plaster) arrived. He too had to have a meal. This man to me is thoroughly disgusting; he can not take a hint nor a kick either. He comes so often and always expects us to board him three times a day. He was a Moravian at Nushagak while he lived there, but I think he is a pretty expensive member. People evidently think we run a hotel, only they never think of paying for their meals and all the other trouble they make. I declare, if this man does not know enough to cook for and wait on himself, I will tell him to get out. I have enough work to do without keeping boarders.

The man who arrived yesterday told some heart-rending accounts of freezing during the last cold spell. One man was frozen to death in the mountains. Another froze both feet and both hands. According to his

---

95. Russian Orthodox Church members were frequently referred to as "Greeks" (Fienup-Riordan 1991, 133).

accounts he is in a pitiful condition [and] will probably come here for treatment. And still another man froze one big toe. The poor men, and all for the sake of gold which they find not.

Mrs. Stecker, Mr. Ryfcogle, Herman, Robert, Margaret and I were all out riding today. Herman took pictures of his team and all of us. We like the ride very much, it is such nice weather, about ten above zero.

Tuesday, January 28, 1902

The nice weather continues [and] today it has been perfectly beautiful. We were all up in the woods for a little picnic. We had all of the children along, and how they did enjoy it, especially baby who had such a good time. We had our tent and stove, and while Mr. Ryfcogle and Herman took pictures, Mrs. Stecker and I prepared lunch which consisted of cold meat and bread, canned pears, coffee and coffee cake. Nothing elaborate, you see, but it was enjoyed heartily by all. Several of the natives were along. We made quite a party. Herman, Mr. R., Mrs. S. and myself occupied the first outfit; next came Robert and baby in Robert's little sleigh with three dogs to pull them; then came Annie Weinlick and Margaret in Annie's sleigh with three more dogs. There were two natives with each of the children's outfits to guide the sleds. Just as we arrived at the old camping ground (the same place where Herman had a logging camp two years ago when we were along), David and Fannie, who have been visiting at Akiachak, arrived. They stopped to take dinner with us, and homeward their outfit added one more "car" to our "train." We returned about 5 P.M. all feeling much benefited by the outing. Herman is developing his negatives now, and Mr. Ryfcogle is helping him.

Mr. Koltchoff left for down river today. After we had failed for several meals to invite him in, he finally began cooking for himself and was then no trouble. Poor fellow, he has not a home in the world (his only child is in the states in school). I do feel sorry for him and like to do him little favors, but we all think that he expects too much.

Robert was five years old on Sunday. I gave him a new rain coat, a pair of outing flannel night drawers and a handkerchief. Made him a coconut birthday cake on which were five lighted candles at breakfast. How the pretty brown eyes sparkled when he came out, he was so glad for them all especially his ticking rain parka which he has worn ever since. Herman, Margaret and I went for a little drive on Sunday, and when we returned Robert had been up among the trees and brought home with him five little "Christmas trees" as he calls them, and wanted me to decorate them and put candles on them too. Of course, as Xmas is passed, we did not decorate Robert's trees, but Herman placed three upon his instrument case; one over the bed-room door; and one among some curios on the wall which gladdened Robert's heart. He seemed to feel quite satisfied. Robert goes to school. I sent him to keep him indoors; he wants to be out all the time and that would be too much during very cold spells. Mr. Weinlick tells us that Robert has a good time in school, helps himself to the boys' pens, tells them to speak loud when he thinks they speak too low; in short, I guess he is somewhat of an assistant teacher.

Saturday, February 1, 1902

Herman left for Carter City, (a little mining camp about one and a half days run from Quinhagak) the day before yesterday to see the man who froze his feet and hands of whom I have already written about. The man, a Mr. Johnson from Nushagak, who we thought would bring the poor unfortunate man here, took him from Goodnews Bay to Carter City, but the man declared that the doctor had gone to Nushagak with the mail carrier and would attend to his wounds on his return. From all accounts, the poor fellow will have to have both feet and hands amputated if he is still alive when Herman reaches him, which Herman doubted from what Mr. Johnson told concerning his condition twelve days previous. Herman expected to reach Carter today and everything has been in his favor since he left. Mr. Brown and Mr. Ryfcogle went along to assist in the operation. They expected to over-take Mr. Koltchoff, who is very good at such cases, and ask him to go also.

Mr. Johnson met Mr. Stecker at Quinhagak who was having a very disgusting as well as discouraging trip. [He] had everything wet when he arrived at that place from the tides. He will probably reach Nushagak today. I am so lonesome when Herman is away which is pretty often during the Winter. Baby is rather troublesome, especially at night, and having the full care of the children day and night is tiresome. George's wife is with me now until George returns from Carmel, and I am very grateful for her help. She is very good with children and the baby likes her very much. I was planning to go to Paimiut with Herman last Thursday but his professional call, or rather what seemed to be his duty, changed my plans, but we will go when Herman returns. I told Robert he might go with us, but he said he did not want to go to Pimiut he wanted to go to the states. Rob often asks when we are going to the states. The little fellow has no idea where they are. He evidently thinks it something like going from Forty Fort to Kingston.[96]

Friday, February 7, 1902

Herman returned last Wednesday having learned at Quinhagak that his would-be patient had died. Poor fellow, how much better he is dead than living with both feet and hands gone, but how sad that he should have to suffer so long without medical care or rather surgical care. The other man, of whom I spoke having been lost in the mountains, is still missing and doubtless is frozen to death. The Catholic priest who lives just above Ougavig is said to have frozen his feet and had a part of one amputated. We do not know just the truth of this story as it is only the report of natives who are often mistaken in their ideas. The Russian priest is said to have frosted his feet or hands also. I am afraid we will hear more stories of such cases. We never knew it to be so cold as it was during the last cold spell.

Herman's dogs are all sore footed, but must start out again tomorrow as Herman has a call to Ougavig to see Mr. Helmich who is sick, and also to baptize several babies lately born in the village. We are daily looking for the in-coming mail. The third out-going mail will soon be due here, and the first one from outside not yet here. We are all anxious to hear whether or not Mr. Carter is safe and well, as he was on his way to Nushagak with the mail during that terrible cold spell. I am glad that Herman has no long trips before him this Winter, or at least none that we know of. This is a hard country to travel in. Whether in Summer or Winter one is always so much exposed to all kinds of weather, the villages are so far apart, and such miserable places to stay in, at any rate.

Sunday, February 9, 1902

Herman left for Ougavig yesterday morning about ten o'clock returning again in the evening at about seven. I was worried when Mr. Weinlick ran in to say that the doctor was coming, lest they had met with accident,

---

96. Forty Fort and Kingston are neighboring communities in Pennsylvania near Wilkes-Barre where Ella was born and raised (Ella Romig's application to the Daughters of the American Revolution, DAR Headquarters, Washington, D.C.).

but this was not the case. Herman had met a messenger from Ougavig saying that Mr. Helmich was much improved and received two letters, one from a miner at Ougavig and one from the Catholic Priest, both victims of the cold weather, asking Herman to come to amputate a toe. Herman will start again tomorrow, (having returned for his instruments). After operating [on] the man at Ougavig, [Herman] will then go to the Holy Cross Mission on the Yukon where Father Robert is at present having gone there about Christmas time. This will mean another long hard trip for Herman, and his poor dogs are now tired out.

Many of the dogs about here are going mad. Queena, the mother of our team, is at Akiachak now, where Herman left her yesterday, mad. She will no doubt die. I am so sorry, she is a very good as well as a pretty creature. Raising dogs is, of late, very discouraging. We lost three of our very best young dogs last Summer.

Tuesday, February 11, 1902

Your letters written October the ninth were received yesterday with the first incoming mail. There are still two mails from the outside, and I do hope I will get some more home news. I have heard so little of late. Two white men, one from Sitka and the other from the coast somewhere near, brought the mail through. A Mr. Shaw and Mr. Donaldson. We were very glad when they came as we had been long looking for the mail. Herman had left early yesterday morning, but the mail carrier from here to Anvik runs past Ougavig so I sent Herman's mail with him.

I have had such a time today looking for my glasses. After looking last evening and all day, I finally found them behind Herman's typewriter where the children must have put them. My poor eyes, how troublesome they are. My glasses are very little good, but better than not at all, for without them I can neither read, write nor sew.

The days are growing so much longer. How nice it is to have a little more day-light. Robert said tonight, "It is dark now, mama, I want to go to bed." I sincerely hope that he and Margaret will go to bed before dark when the days are longest, for a short day of their pranks is often too long for me. I send Robert to school every day but there is still enough time for him and Margaret to spat. They have been going too far for me of late. I was obliged to spank Margaret last night for her naughtiness. And to-night also. It seemed to amuse her brother tonight for he giggled but was somewhat surprised when I treated him likewise for his fun. Anyway he has needed a little reminder for some time on general principles. I often feel that the care of the children is almost too much. Herman is gone so much of the time. If only his duty would not take him from home so much.

George's wife and David's, Mary and Fannie, are staying with me while George and David are away. They are both very nice girls and a great deal of company for me. I can never grow accustomed to Herman's being away. I always miss him so much, and especially the nights. I never like to be alone with the children.

February 14, 1902

Mrs. Stecker, the children and myself were all over to Mrs. Weinlick's for dinner today, this being Mr. W's thirty-first birthday.

Monday, Feburary 17, 1902

The mail arrived from St. Michael yesterday and left today for Nushagak and Katmai.

Friday, February 21, 1902

Herman came home yesterday having been gone ten days having traveled over four hundred miles in all. When he reached Ougavig on the eleventh he amputated a toe for a Mr. Edwards of whom I spoke before. He also baptized three babes and buried two while there. The poor little native babies, so few live very long. Where will our future generation come from? When Herman reached the Holy Cross Mission, he found Father Robert in a very critical condition and operated at once. He may have died in a short time from blood poison had he been left much longer without proper attention. Just think, a little thing like a toe causing so much suffering and loss of life. The priest was somewhat improved when Herman left him, but still not out of danger. The Fathers and Sisters treated him royally while there, and were so grateful for his coming so promptly to their aid [that] one day before leaving they had an entertainment for him. They have a very fine school there, and Herman says some very bright as well as pleasing children. If some or all of the other churches were as thorough in their efforts to win and train the young as are the Catholics it might be better for them and much better for the people as well. Herman also had a call to go to see Mr. Bel'kov's son who is very sick of typhoid fever and may die. So you can see that Herman's last trip was a very busy one. Poor boy, he is tired too and needs and must take a good rest before starting out again.

Elizabeth walks all around today. She falls often, but how very happy she seems over her success. She is a very dear happy little mortal anyway. Margaret has also had a happy day out riding. Mr. Shaw, the mail agent who is here, had her and Annie Weinlick out sleigh riding today behind one of his dogs and such fun it was for them. Herman had Robert and me out for a drive this afternoon, and I think we were as well pleased as the rest of the children were. Robert is a great boy. He is thoroughly enjoying this fine weather. I am sure he never enjoyed anything as much as the sport he has with the little sleigh Herman made for him last Fall.

March 5, 1902

Mr. Stecker arrived at home today after having been gone over six weeks to Nushagak and reports a very hard trip. We all thought that he would bring the mail but it was not in yet when he left Carmel so we still have this to look forward to.

Herman is over the tundra; has gone to give communion to some new converts who are to join our church. Mr. Shaw, the U.S. mail agent, is with him. I expected them home today as they expected to stay only one night, but now I look for them tomorrow. I will be glad when they are home or rather when Herman is here. I am tired of being so much alone, and then Margaret is sick. She had grippe I think. Poor little girl, she is so thin. She has not been well for a long time, has no appetite and cries for every little thing, and she used to be such a bright happy little girl. Elizabeth runs around from morning till night. She is so very proud of her new accomplishment, that of walking. She is so mischievous too. Today she reached up to my full ink well upsetting its contents down her sleeve and down the same time to her boots. Her little hands and side, as well as her shirt were well blued. After she was washed and newly dressed she upset a pan of lard over herself and the floor, afterwards sitting down in it. Now that George is home again and Mary gone to him I am quite alone. I will miss Mary very much [as] she was very good to the children.

Sunday, March 16, 1902

Herman left for the Yukon River a week ago this morning to see young Mr. Bel'kov who was very low when Herman was sent for, but from a note from Herman written at Akiachak last Wednesday, we were glad to learn that Mr. B. is or was improving when Herman left him. Herman and Mr. Brown, who accompanied him to the Russian Mission, are now out deer hunting, having been all ready for the hunt when the messenger came from Mr. Bel'kov. I do hope that they will get some deer or even one, for cooking is getting to be a pretty hard task. We are so tired of canned stuff, in fact I have been tired of it all Winter, even the fruit tastes so "cannie" to me. I think that if Margaret could have more fresh fruits and vegetables, eggs and meats, she would be better. She is much better now of her cold but looks so pale and thin. My poor little Margaret, she is as much trouble as baby Beth and that is enough too for baby is very troublesome; she is teething. Robert talks so much English of late as well as does Margaret. Robert ran in the other day to tell me that Mr. Weinlick's dog, Bob, had run away breaking Annie's sleigh. He said, "Mama! Mama! harness broke the sled Bob!" I wanted to laugh, but his lordship's feelings are so easily hurt. If we would laugh at him he would not try to talk English, and we are very anxious for him to learn it. He is learning to say grace at meals, and has it almost learned. He will say it sometimes when Herman is gone. Baby Beth talks some, more than Robert or Margaret at her age, and is the fattest cutest baby of all. Herman often says, "Oh, if she were a boy would she not be a gem," but I am perfectly satisfied that she is a girl. She will say "yes" to everything we ask her, and sometimes the folks ask very funny things then they all laugh, baby too. They make such a monkey of her. Always she is a great favorite with all the natives. She pounds on a pan, sings and dances like a good fellow.

April 1, 1902

Herman returned from his hunt nearly two weeks since, having been unsuccessful. It was very stormy while he was away, and as there were many snow storms the roads were very heavy. Both Mr. B. and Herman were glad to get home even if they had no deer, for they had a hard trip, and came in just in time to escape a very severe snow and wind storm. There has never been so much snow since we are here. There are great high banks all around our house. All during Easter week the wind blew so hard that we could scarcely go from our houses to chapel without being nearly blown breathless in from our feet. And, as Margaret says, it was "snoozing" all the time. It is great fun for her to stand at the window and watch it snow, she often says, "Mama it is snoozing again."

The Romig children enjoy a sled ride. Left to right: Robert, Elizabeth,
Margaret, Nellie (one of Ella's domestic helpers) and Rover, the family pet.
(Courtesy, Alaska and Polar Regions Department, University of Alaska Fairbanks
Joseph Romig Collection, acc. #90-043-875aN)

We are all ready to go to the deer herd up in the mountains with Herman,
but the deep snow makes it impossible to travel, so we must wait until the
roads are better. Robert and Margaret are making great preparations to go
to the mountains. They get their bags filled with popcorn, sugar, cakes
and sweet chocolate, have two or three scraps over them, then eat the
contents, often which they want then refilled. Margaret likes the young
Lapland girl so much and talks of her so much now that we are all going
to visit them.

April 7, 1902

Well, here we are, still at Bethel. Mr. Weinlick left last Thursday for
the mountains with Herman's team. It just snowed and snowed continu-

ally, and the roads were too heavy for a man to travel alone, much less for a woman with three little ones. I was much disappointed, and it was not easy to say yes to staying at home, for I was very anxious to go to the mountains and to see our herd of reindeer again. But how thankful I have been everyday since Mr. Weinlick left that we are all at home and in a warm house. Friday, Saturday and Sunday it blew a perfect gale and it has been so very cold, the coldest weather we have had this Winter. At least we have felt it the most. Both Friday and Saturday night we were snowed in. At the kitchen door the snow was half way to the top of the door, and at the front door or sitting room door it is just all but to the top. There are some of the prettiest snow drifts around the mission, how I wish you might see them. David's house at the south side is completely covered. We can walk upon the snow over the roof. Herman is going to take pictures from all sides of the mission tomorrow, and one of David's house with me sitting on its roof. The snow is packed so solid too, we walk over the highest drifts and scarcely leave a print of our feet. We melt all of our wash water. It is fun to go out and bring a large piece of drifted snow in to melt, and it is so heavy too, every piece counts a great deal toward adding to the water supply. I brought in pieces yesterday just as large as I could carry. All this snow means very high water this Spring. Mr. Helmich's folks may have to sit on their house top or go across the river when the ice leaves, for a very high water always goes in their house.

We will soon look for the geese. Herman expects to eat geese in two weeks. I will eat them when they come. But I do hope that may be soon, for when the geese come they bring Spring, and we are so tired of this extremely cold Winter.

Saturday, April 12, 1902

It seems to be getting a little warmer, and yesterday and today have been lovely days. Mr. and Mrs. Stecker left yesterday for Ougavig. Mr. Stecker will help Mr. Helmich repair the *Swan*.[97] How pretty and green everything must look by this time at home, while here we see nothing save high banks of snow all around us. We can scarcely believe that in another month we will begin to look for the breaking up of the ice, and in two months more the boats will leave for the coast. How time does fly.

---

97. The *Swan* was the mission's boat built by Benjamin Helmich in 1894 (Schwalbe 1985, 47–8).

The Romig home at Bethel after an April snow storm in 1902.
(Courtesy, Alaska and Polar Regions Department, University of Alaska Fairbanks,
Joseph Romig Collection, acc. #90-043-921aN)

Thursday, April 17, 1902

Planted my seeds this A.M. I am not going to work so hard in the garden this year, it always means a big effort and very unsatisfactory results. I sowed cabbage, celery, a few rutabagas and a few pansy seeds. Herman sowed the hot-bed this afternoon. We have a fine large new hot-bed and look for good results. We ate dinner at Mrs. Weinlick's, had a fine venison roast to which we did ample justice. I am in [the] dress making business at present. Mrs. Fredericks, the Yukon trader's wife, sent me a new dress at Christmas, and I am just finishing it. I am going to send you a sample of it, and then have my picture taken in it so you can then imagine just how I look in one dress.

Friday, April 18, 1902

Mr. and Mrs. Stecker returned today from Ougavig having had a very pleasant time. Mrs. S. brought all of the children a box of cakes and nuts and some undershirts for Robert and Margaret; a new apron for baby

Beth. Mrs. S. is such a dear kind motherly woman, and I love her very much. How often she makes the little hearts happy.

Saturday, April 19, 1902

We were all out today for a little picnic. Herman made his goose nest. We will all go out with him next week if the geese come. The snow was up to my waist, [and] we had to walk on snow shoes when off of the trail.

April 19, 1902[98]

DEAR FATHER:

I will steal a few lines of space in Ella's journal while she is out. We were off camping, and I was making a shelter in which to shoot geese. We were in the same place as last year, and you can imagine how it looks from the pictures of last year. This is a season of outing[s] and rest after the winter of work and cold, and I greatly enjoy being with my family when there is no strain of work, or as Ella would say, having my family with me.

We sometimes have a dialogue as to whether she would enjoy my company in the house or in the tent best, for it is quite a job to get off camping, but I tell her as her physician I prescribe an outing for her and the children, and she must go, and most pleasing are the results of these outings even if it is some trouble, for none can appreciate better than I the good it does her and the little ones, and she says she most heartily accords with me when once she gets away from the house.

I have a very happy home, and all it lacks is the visits to or from those we call father, sister or brother; Grandpa, Aunt or Uncle, as the case may be.

I often tell Ella I wish you could come to see us and our little ones, and I wonder if you think of us as happy in this far away land. For happiness is truly where a contented heart is, and I would now as before thank you for the healthy sweet pure wife you gave me, and it is my desire to ever be worthy of her.

The winter has taken me much from home on my duties, professional and missionary, and I am now happy that spring has come. A request though not a call would still take me 80 miles up the river, but this can be postponed. I said when coming from my last trip that if another was to be

---

98. This journal entry was made by Herman.

made Ella and the children must go along. Ella says she is tired of being a Grass-widow so much so I told her I would not travel more this spring without taking her.

Well I have stolen about as much space as is good for one time.

My love to all the family.

Herman

P.S. Ella says, "Trying to taffy up my poor old gray-haired father-in-law" about what I wrote of her, but you have it on paper from me and she has many pages to tell her story as to whether or no it is so. She is like the natives, bashful for me to brag about her, but I have reasons to be proud of her. *JHR*

Monday, April 21, 1902

Three geese arrived at Bethel at 10:20 A.M. today. So we are off on a lark tomorrow. Herman takes tents and some of our things today while I bake pies, cookies & crullers.

Tuesday, April 22, 1902

"The mighty hunter's camp." Here we are happy, but very tired. Herman shot his first goose just over our tent just before supper. Had an ugly trip down sometimes in the water up to the bed of the sleigh one time. I got in up to my knees. When the ice raises traveling will be better which I trust may be before we return home.

Wednesday, April 23, 1902

Mr. and Mrs. Stecker arrived today, so it seems more like a picnic now and not so lonely. It has been quite a pleasant day, although cold. The geese seem to be frozen up or else they are passing us by, as no one has shot a goose yet today.

Saturday, April 26, 1902

Mr. and Mrs. S. started home this morning but when just a short distance from camp they ran, or tried to cross over tide ice, and broke through

Mr. S. getting in to his waist, and in attempting to get out fell down getting a thorough wetting, so they had to come back to dry his clothes. Started again this afternoon. Mrs. S. was thoroughly frightened, and I am afraid this will end her camping for which I am sorry for it will be so lonely now. But the miserable weather keeps the geese away and Herman in the tent much of the time. We are all, especially the children, enjoying our outing very much and will be sorry to return home again.

Wednesday, April 30, 1902

Back at Bethel again, returned today. We were loath to give up our picnic but the wind is in the east raining much of the time, so [we] thought it best to return on good roads. With the exception of our second day out, and last Monday (our only sunny day), we had miserable weather and did not get enough geese to eat. But not-with-standing we are all much, *very much*, benefited by our outing.

We are married six years today. I have thought much all day of six years ago tonight when I saw many of my friends for the last time for years; of my dear mother whom I shall never see again in this life. And I have thought not a little of all the blessings God has bestowed upon me. He has given me the kindest of husbands, almost perfect health, three perfectly formed healthy little ones and a warm comfortable home. Truly God is good and kind, and how happy I am to be one of His children. We were thinking of having a dinner tonight and ask our friends to dine with us, but having no geese to roast and being away we had to give it up.

Elizabeth is so happy tonight, she fairly floats on air, singing, yelling or dancing as the notion takes her. Our baby surely is a sweet, fat, cunning, smart girl. She talks so much, and is so independent already, and a picture of Robert.

Sunday, May 11, 1902

The water is raising very rapidly. The ice has raised and has broken in large pieces in our Bethel Creek but it does not look like leaving yet. The yard is nearly clear of snow, one can hardly realize that a month ago was so cold and nothing but high snow drifts. The drift back of our house is still quite high, for which I am very thankful as it furnishes us with good water for washing and household use. The men repaired the old scow and took her up in the creek back of the trading post where she will be free from ice. We are sleeping in our tent out on the bank. The children all like it so, and I am thoroughly disgusted with and tired of my dirty house and find it such a relief to get out of it for a little while. We are all to dine with Mr. and Mrs. Stecker today.

Monday, May 12, 1902

The ice broke up in places today. We look for it to run at any time. Very high water, cold and disagreeable.

Tuesday, May 13, 1902

The ice has been running at different times all day; at present there is a jam somewhere. Since noon the water has raised about five feet. The natives are all afraid of very high water; it is now nearly up to some of the natives' dwelling places. We have never seen it so high. I have felt somewhat sad all day at seeing the ice leave. It seems like losing an old friend, for I like the Winters here better than the Summers, although they do sometimes get pretty long. I will be glad when day breaks again to see if everything is all right. Hope to see the river almost clear of ice. I will have a time from now on until Winter again watching the children. They always want to be near the water. I will be so glad when our mission is fenced in, for really I get tired running to the bank to look after the children.

Wednesday, May 14, 1902

The ice was running in the main channel this morning when [I] awoke and about 2:00 P.M. it started in our creek. We were all out to see it leave. Now begins a long Summer of waiting and watching for our home mail and provisions, and how tiresome this wait grows. I do wonder if we must wait as ever, till we are too disgusted and discouraged to enjoy the things when they do come.

Friday, May 16, 1902

We were out today for our first boat ride. We went up the creek and back of the trading post nearly down to the mission again over growing [grass] that will soon be dry until next Spring's high water. The water is still very high. The little island in front of the mission is still covered. It seems like one wide river now. The river is almost clear of ice. Now and then we see a stray piece floating down stream. The natives, or many of them, are out gathering logs. David brought in quite a large raft[ful] today and has gone for more. Christian found two goose eggs yesterday and gave them to me. These are the first of the season. I set my cabbage plants out in the hot-bed tonight and very sickly looking ones they are too. I hope they will pick up now. So many of them have died off at the root. Also sowed some "Hanson" lettuce in my hot-bed and will sow radish seeds tomorrow. We are looking and longing for the smelts to run. These always come as soon as the ice leaves. How I will miss my patient, kind and faithful Christian and Nellie when they go fishing. The children love them so much as does their mother, and especially Elizabeth. Nellie is so devoted to her as she, baby, is Nellie's mother. But then she has so many relatives, she being the first babe born after so many of our poor people died. She is Nellie's mother, David's brother and son, and Bessie's baby. Oh, I could not tell you what all she is to the people who all love her, for she really is a fat, happy lovable girl. She sings and plays all day long with her eye on the stair door to sneak up to her papa, or on the outside door to run away visiting. As soon as she gets out she starts for Weinlick's home. One day we missed her and after looking over the mission, we finally found her over in Mrs. W.'s bedroom.

May 24, 1902

A messenger from Ougavig arrived last night for Herman to go to Mr. Helmich who is quite sick again, so Herman left for Ougavig this morning. Poor Mr. H. He seems to be completely worn out, and I do hope he will go out to the states as Herman and Mr. Stecker strongly urge him to do. Herman wanted me to go with him but the other missionaries did not seem to think it necessary. Herman will have to fix up the *Swan* also which is in a very poor condition having had a hole put through her by the ice, and then she is in the trees instead of the water, as Mr. Helmich was sick during high water time.

We were all on a picnic last Tuesday. [We] went down to the high banks just below Napaskiak, a place Herman has so long wanted to take us to. The bank at one place is probably seventy feet high, and from its top we had a lovely view. We had quite a wetting just before we reached our picnic ground, but had a lovely day and pleasant trip home sailing all the way.

Left to right: Rosa and Joseph Weinlick, and Ella and Herman Romig.
Children are unidentified.
(Courtesy, Alaska and Polar Regions Department, University of Alaska Fairbanks,
Joseph Romig Collection, acc. #90-043-865aN)

Sunday, May 25, 1902

Mr. Joaquin arrived today from up river on their little steamer.[99] Mr. Lind will not come down this Spring. They left Ougavig this morning. Mr. Helmich seems to be somewhat improved. Passed Herman at Akiak about noon.

Sunday, June 1, 1902

Herman's crew returned this A.M. Herman will come with Mr. and Mrs. Helmich who are going to the states this year. I am very glad that Mr. and Mrs. H. have decided to go down as Mr. H. is very poorly. We are all very sorry to lose such good missionaries. I have always liked Mrs. H. very much. It seems very hard to give her up but, I trust they may be able to return again to the work. They will probably go to Mrs. Helmich's old

---

99. Frank Joaquin was one of three traders who organized Joaquin, Twitchell, & Fowler, a Bethel trading company (Oswalt 1963, 47).

home at first in Ohio. I hope Sadie will write to Mrs. H., and I am sure you would enjoy seeing and talking with both Mr. and Mrs. Helmich as they will come from our home and can tell you so much more than I could write. If any of you should write them, [their] address [will be]: Gnadenhutten, Tuscarawas Co., Ohio: care of Mrs. Jacob Lichty.

Mr. Joaquin and party will leave tomorrow or Tuesday for the coast, so I will close your journal to send with them as the boat might accidentally come in early for once, and I want you to get my feeble effort at journal writing. It has given me a great deal of pleasure to write it, although it has been hard to find time often to write. My children, my husband, my house and my natives just about fill all of my time it seems.

Baby Beth is quite sick. I think she has chicken pox. She was very feverish and flighty last Friday. I was quite worried. I never like to be alone at such times, but it so happens often. Robert is getting it too, and Margaret of course will follow in due time. I hope Herman will soon come home.

I was quite agreeably surprised yesterday when I went out to my hot-bed to see how my plants have picked up. I feel quite encouraged now. After all we may have some garden. We will have a new cabbage patch as the new garden back of Kilbuck's [former] house has been extended back toward the lake, and it is excellent ground.

Mrs. Joaquin will come up to Alaska this Spring and will live up at the post. How nice it will be to have a real live white neighbor woman. But I am afraid she will get very lonely here.

This is such a perfect day, so bright and sunny. I hope the sun will soon bring our potatoes up. Herman writes that they planted Mrs. H.'s garden. If they go down we will have their potatoes too. The Ougavig soil is excellent, but the potatoes are always so sweet and watery up here, I don't care very much for them. We are getting plenty of eggs now.

It is hard for Robert to stay indoors, such nice weather, but he enjoys watching our two sparrows who returned to their nest this morning, up in our porch. I often wondered if they would come back. We enjoyed them so much last Summer watching their nest building, their laying the eggs, later the little open mouths over the nest for food, and then learning to fly. How we missed them when they left us. Robert says they are whistling all the time today.

As space is almost gone, I will have to close with lots of love from us all to all of you. Your affectionate daughter.

Ella

chapter 4

*June 9, 1902 to
November 23, 1902*

To Mr. A. F. Ervin
Forty Fort
Luzerne Co.
Penna.[100]

To my dear father:

Before the season is far spent I will begin your journal, for long continued neglect soon becomes chronic with me. I unfortunately broke my precious glasses today, consequently writing is a very difficult task as I must rest my eyes after every few words, but I can at least make a beginning.

Mr. Stecker left for the coast today on the scow *Bethel Star* with David as captain. As I caught the last glimpse of her, I wondered how long it would be until we see her again. No doubt it will be long enough.

Herman and I set out about one hundred nice hardy cabbage plants, and about thirty rutabagas this afternoon. We have been waiting so long for rain, but as it never rains at this time of the year, we concluded to carry water and get the plants out as they are very large. Mrs. Helmich started for Ougavig this A.M. in Herman's Peterborough canoe to gather up some fur work she had left to be finished. Mr. Helmich, Ernest, and Julia are staying here until she returns when they will leave for the coast to catch our vessel. Mrs. Weinlick, Mrs. Stecker and I will do what we can for her in the way of sewing while she, Mrs. Helmich, is away.

Thursday, May 10, 1902

The sawmill is running today. With all [of the] hands to feed it is hard to find time to sew. It does seem that Mrs. Helmich needs clothes more than we do lumber, but then Mr. Helmich will soon be gone, and as he is the only one who thoroughly understands running the saw, the men want to "make hay while the sun shines."

---

100. A note on the inside cover indicates that this journal was first sent to Herman's father, Reverend Joseph Romig, Ottawa, Franklin Co., Kansas, to be forwarded when read to Ella's father, Mr. A. F. Ervin, Forty Fort, Luzerne Co., Penna.

Wednesday, May 11, 1902

My egg trader came in today with a large wash tub full of eggs, so here is another hindrance in [the] way of sewing. I am afraid Mrs. Helmich will think we don't want to help her. It seems there is no end to a woman's work. How the work does pile up. One is never done. I will have to make more noodles or my eggs will spoil. Oh, if only the boat waits a little longer until we are ready for it, and have a chance to take a few good full breaths.

Saturday, May 14, 1902

I ran over to Mrs. Weinlick's this afternoon for a little while. We sat there sewing when Mr. Weinlick came to say that he thought the Peterborough was coming. Just then he looked down the creek and saw a *"Kyak"* (one holed skin boat) and said, just in fun, "Here comes the mail." (They always send the mail in a *kyak*, so naturally we are always on the look-out for one). Just as he said this I thought, would we not be surprised if such were the case! Mr. W. then went out and soon came running up to say, "The boat is in!" Truly we were surprised, and are not at all pleased for we did want a little rest before our goods came. But then we are never suited. When the boat comes late, it is too late, and when it comes early, it is too early. I pity Mrs. Helmich so for she is tired from the trip, and must now rush to get ready to leave tomorrow morning.

Sunday, May 15, 1902

Mr. and Mrs. Helmich left on the *Swan* this morning about ten o'clock, a fair wind in their favor. Before they left we all gathered in Mr. Weinlick's house and had prayers and sang "Blest be the tie that binds, Our hearts in Christian love." How nice it is for them that they get out so early. They may be at home in six more weeks. We will soon begin to look for the steamer and our mail. Our mail did not come, only word from Mr. Ryfkogle that "the boat is in the Bay." The steamer had not gone out yet owing to rough weather. The natives who brought the message had been aboard the *Kodiak* and brought a letter from Mr. Hinz to Mr. Stecker.[101]

---

101. Reverend John L. Hinz, D. D. and his wife, Maria J. W. Henzel, served in the Kuskokwim region from 1902–1914 and 1920–1924. Reverend Hinz was noted for translating hymns and parts of the Bible into the Yup'ik language (Schwalbe 1985, 88–89 and 300).

A Bethel gathering in the Romig home.
Left to right standing: Reverend Joseph Weinlick, Reverend John L. Hinz,
Reverend G. Adolph Stecker, and Bethel trader Frank Joaquin.
Left to right seated: Rosa Stolz Weinlick, Maria J. W. Henzel Hinz,
Franziska Pitschmann Stecker, Ella Mae Ervin Romig, and Mrs. Joaquin.
(Courtesy, Alaska and Polar Regions Department, University of Alaska Fairbanks,
Joseph Romig Collection, acc. #90-043-947N)

Wednesday, May 18, 1902

Mr. and Mrs. Joaquin arrived at Bethel this afternoon on the little steamer, and are staying with us until their house can be made somewhat more agreeable. It seems very nice to think of having a white neighbor, but Mrs. J., I fear, will get very homesick up here where as she says, "Only silence can be heard." But I am sure we will do all we can to make it pleasant for her.

Thursday, May 19, 1902

A native woman who froze both feet early in April was brought here for Herman to care for. In all my hospital experience I never saw anything as offensive as her two feet. I would not try to describe them to you, it was just all that I could do to help Herman clean what was left of them up and bandage them. Tomorrow Herman will amputate both feet. The poor woman, how much she has suffered. Mr. Julius Jensen, the young man who brought her here, found her at the Greek Mission about one hundred and twenty miles up river, lying out on the bank, her feet full of worms, starving, and the mosquitoes torturing her. Such is the work done by the Greek priests and their followers.

Friday, May 20, 1902

Herman amputated our patient's both feet this morning. Mrs. Joaquin, Mrs. Stecker, and Mr. Weinlick helped with the operation while I gave ether. The patient is doing very well. I pity her so much, but she will not miss her feet as much as she would her hands.

Sunday, May 21, [sic] 1902[102]

Mr. Stecker sent word last night that the *Swan* was near Bethel, but the wind had gone down, and wished someone to come for Mr. and Mrs. Hinz and their three little ones. They arrived here about midnight in a small boat. How glad Mrs. Hinz must be to have her feet on solid ground again with her three babies, for babies they are. The oldest is not three years old yet. Mr. and Mrs. Joaquin went up to the trading post to live yesterday afternoon. We have never had so many mosquitoes since our first year. They drive us about mad. The poor children are miserable. Margaret cries about half of her time over the "hateful mosquitoes" as she calls them.

Tuesday, July 1, 1902

Our goods are nearly all in and housed before the "Fourth." It all seems like a dream; too good to be true. We have one more boat load to come,

---

102. Sunday would have been the 22nd of May 1902.

and as the wind is fair [we] are looking daily for it. Natives from all directions are coming to trade. We are buying our furs and boot material for the Winter. Oh, how tiresome this everlasting trading gets. How nice it would be to go in a store and buy hats, shoes and coats again. First we have to buy the skins, then have someone clean them, then look up someone to do the sewing. When all this is done for three little folks and ourselves it is no small task.

July 13, 1902

Much has happened to record since I last wrote. One great event of course was the American's glorious fourth. I always feel glad that I am a free born American, but somehow I always prefer to have our quiet Alaska Fourth than the noisy ones you have at home. Our last Fourth was as any other day, with the exception of a few rifle shots fired by some of our best "Americans," and then of course it was a holiday, [and] we did no work. During the afternoon we all had coffee and cake over at Mr. Stecker's. Both Herman and Elizabeth have been quite sick for over a week. Herman had a very severe attack (not necessarily so severe, but very annoying) of tonsillitis. Threes days ago he was very much distressed. He could neither eat nor rest, and wanted me to try to lance his tonsil, [but] this I was afraid to do. Then he tried to do it himself, but did not succeed. Finally, after I had poulticed it all day, it broke during the evening. After this he was a little better, but yesterday was almost as uncomfortable as before and [I] had to resort to the poulticing. Today he seems almost as well as ever. I do hope it may last for it does not seem right for Herman to be sick. He has always been so well. Elizabeth is teething and has had grippe. [She] was very sick for some days [but] she seems much better today for she is asleep now and has been for about five hours.

Two great events have taken place in the past week. Little Martha Hinz was three years old on the eighth. We sisters and the children were all over to drink chocolate and eat of her birthday cake. Then on the tenth was Brother Stecker's birthday. We all took dinner with him to honor the occasion, only Herman who especially enjoys big dinners, was at home suffering, for this was his worst day.

Sallie, who had gone over to Nushagak to marry a white man (Tonie Guinther) returned on the second of this month having been gone for over a year. She says Mr. Guinther was too big and ugly. She would have nothing to do with him. Bessie, Sallie's daughter, is helping me now while

Jessie is on the Yukon steamers working. I am so glad for her help for she is an excellent servant and a very good natured girl. So many down river natives are here trading; nearly all of whom are heathen. One party brought a sick man to be treated. He has consumption, the itch and other serious troubles. His friends said they had done all for him that they could and now they gave him to Herman. If he could make a *Yuk* (a person) out of him, he would belong to him, (Herman). I do hope Herman can partly restore him for it may mean much for God's own cause. It seems such a pity that we have no missions save one down river, for there are so many souls to be won for Christ. Bethel *is* a center. Natives and whites pass through here going north, south, east or west. We see more here than we could at any other place, but one or two sermons a year can do little toward luring an old case-hardened heathen from his old ways.

July 14, 1902

The men are all working in the mill trying to fix up a planer to finish lumber for a house, or part of the new schoolhouse, for Mr. Hinz to live in. Such a time we do have trying to fix up the miserable old sheds to live in, and then nearly freeze to death. *We* are going to Ougavig until after Christmas, *there* is a warm log house in among the trees [where] we will be comfortable for awhile at least.

July 21, 1902

Herman and Elizabeth [are] quite well again, and it is truly good to have them so. We are having such perfectly lovely weather, so bright and sunny, and *no* mosquitoes to torture us; they seem to have flown. During the past three weeks we have had several very good showers, and our garden shows its full appreciation of them. We have fine lettuce and radishes, cabbage beginning to head, and Herman has some potatoes and a few hills of beans all doing fine. Potatoes all in blossom. Koltchoff, our old friend, arrived from Nushagak two days ago, having been down to Juneau since he left here in March. Tomorrow he will start for St. Michael. He is trying to get part of the mid-Winter mail run from Katmai to St. Michael. The up river natives are bringing plenty of wood. From the seventeenth until this morning we had quite a little Ougavig colony down on the beach below the mill. Mary and McKar, two old servants of ours. Lumpka's brother and sister, the squint eyed trader, his daughter and husband, and her husband's brother and wife were all here.

July 24, 1902

Mr. Lind's party left for up river this afternoon on the little steamer. Margaret was nearly frightened out of her wits when they blew the whistle. Robert says he is no longer afraid of the steamboat, (he was very much so last Summer) but I take notice that he is always scarce when the steamer is nearing the mission. Robert and Margaret talk so much English of late, and it sounds so queer to me. Margaret says we are going to the "old vissage" on a picnic. She means "old village." We have been trying all week to go out camping one night. On Tuesday they sawed; yesterday we made out our requisition; today it had to be copied on Herman's typewriter to send out with a Mr. Bush who is going to the Yukon; then we had callers until six o'clock, and so it goes. What tomorrow will bring forth remains to be seen. Herman's down river patient died night before last after much suffering. We all feel sad that he should have to die in heathen darkness. I often wonder how the heathen fare after this life. Our true just God will not judge the ignorant sinner as He will those who sin in full knowledge of our crucified Savior, but what becomes of them after death?

July 25, 1902

The men have been working all day on the new unfinished school room. They will finish it now, [and] make three rooms out of it for Mr. Hinz's family this Winter. They have put white drill on the ceiling and are finishing boards for the sides. Surely this is getting the cart before the horse, for it ought to be just the other way according to my notion, the ceilings are so hard to paper. My kitchen is all boarded, and it gets awfully tiresome looking at the same old color. It is four years since it was painted owing to scarcity of paint.

We are getting so many fine blueberries this Summer, and enjoy them very much. Mollie, one of my good friends, brought me a large panfull of such delicious large ones tonight. Even Elizabeth stands beside me when I pick them over with her little hands out telling me to hurry and give her some too.

Saturday, July 26, 1902

Robert earned his first money today. He helped carry boards to be finished down in the mill for awhile, and Mr. Weinlick gave him ten cents. I put it with his other money to bank when we go down. Last week he carried wood from the mill to our yard to be split. Some he wheeled up on the wheelbarrow. He told me once that he had brought "two big fellows" up at one time, and sure enough he had. Robert has many friends among the whites and natives. He is such an old fashioned little man. When he speaks of his papa he generally calls him "the doctor" either in English or native. "Yung-Cha-Wista."[103]

August 15, 1902

Yesterday afternoon we were agreeably surprised when a native who had accompanied a Mr. Bosh to the Yukon returned bringing quite a bundle of letters for us all. These were the first letters, save one or two stray ones now and then, that we have received this summer. No doubt they came too late for our vessel as it left San Francisco unusually early. This is a rainy day, so everyone is writing letters. I want to write some too but as it is a long time since I wrote in your journal I will write a little here first. The men have been sawing lumber and firewood for over a week. There is a pile of firewood between Mr. Stecker's house and the mill several feet high, long and wide. I want Herman to take a picture of it so you can see how much wood it takes to keep us halfway comfortable in Wintertime in these miserable houses, *"so called."* Two weeks tomorrow, August second, Herman, the children, Mr. and Mrs. Joaquin, a number of natives and myself left for the mountain village to marry David to the "Mountain Boy's" daughter. We arrived there the following day, Sunday the third, and Herman married them about nine o'clock P.M. It made my heart ache to see the bride-elect bow and cross herself to some picture on the wall, for she is a Greek which is almost nothing here in Alaska. The Greek Priests are such wretched specimens of Christians and teach their members next to nothing. While she and her parents are willing that she shall become a Moravian, yet I am unhappy that our own David, so soon after the death of his dear little wife, Fannie, should marry a Greek, whose father tried to kill John [Kilbuck] some years ago. At the time, his brother, "Hooker" by name, was ill and delirious. Some of the natives said that the missionary's teaching had put the devil in him, so they sent for John with one of their teams, and then this "Mountain Boy," after telling John what he thought, was going to kill him and would have done so had it not been

---

103. The Eskimos' favorite name for Herman was "Young-cha-wista" which meant "person-working-for-others," or doctor (Anderson 1940, 18).

for a native who befriended him and helped him home. Of course this is all of the past, and the man claims to be one of our best friends and very sorry for what he did. But still he had never belonged to us since, and I am very sorry that one of our *very best* helpers has married into his family, but we can only pray for the best.

Ougavig, September 14, 1902

We are in a new field of labor since September third, (Herman's birthday) having come up from Bethel on Mr. Lind's steamer. We were two days and one night on the way, and were very glad to be spared the long trip up on a row or sailing boat. Camping on a muddy shore in the rain sometimes, no doubt, as this is the rainy season. Just a week before we started up here, we arrived at Bethel from a very unsatisfactory trip down river to stake out a mission site and some cannery sites for the mission. We had very ugly stormy weather. The third day out we were run on a sand bar in a gale where we were for two nights and one day. After very hard work, we finally got off and instead of going farther down to stake claims we all agreed it best to start for home, as many times we were afraid of being wrecked in our top-heavy ill-proportioned *Swan*. Several times on our way home we were nearly tipped over. I assure you I was glad when I reached Bethel for many such experiences would soon make me gray. After we reached home Herman had to help saw for Mr. Lind, who had come down for lumber to finish his new house, while I straightened up the house and got our things ready to come up-river. We cleaned and papered the bed and sitting rooms and tried to leave the whole house in a livable condition for when we should return after Christmas. But we did not find as clean a house here as we left at Bethel I can assure you. We had to paper and clean house here too. We are about through now, and I feel that I have done my share of cleaning for one season.

We have been having very bad weather for the past two days; south storms and very high water. There are so many nice young babies here, but when I look at them I wonder how long they will be here. Nearly all of the babies born within the past three years have died. This is such a miserable diseased class of people, and the epidemic of nineteen hundred has wracked them so much. Day before yesterday one of the nicest babies died. He took cold while teething, and like all of the poor native babies just faded away. Herman lanced a very ugly abscess on a baby's neck today. Poor little fellow, he looks so pale and sick, I do hope he will get well.

September 15, 1902

Herman and I were out for quite a long walk this afternoon in the rain thinking we might find some trace of Rover who has been gone for two days, and we feel worried as he is a very valuable dog and Herman's leader. But we were not successful. I hope nothing has happened to him. We have just heard that another baby is dead. He had such ugly sores on his little arms and shoulders when we first came, but seemed better when his parents started down the river to their Fall fishing place. His mother was the wife of blind Nicholi of this place, a very pitiful case who died two years ago. Soon after his death she became the wife of a young man from Akiachak whom we call Fattie. He has not been living with her for nearly a year. It was only a week ago he came back to her on account of his child. I hope he will not leave her again for she is so helpless with three other children to feed.

(Later) Rover returned tonight while we were at supper, nearly worn out and so poor! We think he must have gone hunting rabbits and got lost. I can assure you we were glad to see him. I treated him like a prince; fed him on duck and rice soup. I made, with Christian's help, about ⅔ of a half-barrel of sauerkraut from the cabbage the rabbits had nearly destroyed. Herman is working on a new desk for me. The work shop is just a few steps from the kitchen, and I often run out to visit Herman while he works. He already complains of loneliness but for me the novelty has not yet worn off. I like it very much back here amidst the trees.

September 16, 1902

Have been working the greater part of the day on mittens for our school boys. Minnie's sister, who made all of their boots last Winter, helped me, and we finished six pairs. Tomorrow we will make six more pairs. We are expecting Mr. Koltchoff back from St. Michael and will ask him to take them to Bethel. If Mr. K. does not come, we will have [to] send someone down with some things. Herman has my desk almost finished and it [is] so pretty. I think he must take a picture of it for you. He also has a cart being made with which to haul water; the boys have to go so far for water. Then we want to fill in around the kitchen with gravel. It is the very dirtiest muddiest hole imaginable. The rainy season is almost past or we would have to send to Bethel for lumber to fix the roof. When it rains the

Left to right: Ella, Bessie, and Nellie clean geese, spring 1901.
Margaret's blurred image is seen in the foreground.
(Courtesy, Alaska and Polar Regions Department, University of Alaska Fairbanks,
Joseph Romig Collection, acc. #90-043-893aN)

roof leaks almost in every part of our bedroom. How you would laugh to hear Margaret talking English. She speaks it nearly altogether now. Last night she called me out to see the moonlight. When I went out to look she said, "Yes, and Mrs. Stecker down at Bethel in her dirty house sees it too." Now Mrs. Stecker is perfection in neatness. I guess Miss Margaret has heard me say something about this dirty house, no doubt she did, for dirty was the name for it when we first came.

September 17, 1902

Finished the mittens before dinner, and I am sure they will make the boys happy with their mink trimmings. Christian and Millie's brother Fritz, and Evan, Minnie's sister's step-son, were out hunting today and brought in twelve geese, five grouse, four rabbits and one duck.

The flies nearly drive us wild up here. They torment Herman *so* every night. They do not often bite me but they get in my clothes and crawl around until they give me the fidgets. Elizabeth is such a cute saucy young-ster. I am often surprised to hear her talk; she talks nearly everything. This morning she came in bed with me for a few minutes and then said in native, "I want to get up," then ran over to the stove pipe and called, "Come Nellie," and Nellie came too. Our faithful Nellie and Christian are with us again. Herman finished my desk today and it is a beauty too. He is working on his cart now. Elizabeth is scratching her neck and says, "Bugs." The poor little chick, how the flies do worry her.

September 18, 1902

Christian, Evan and another boy left for Bethel about noon in Herman's Peterborough canoe and expect to reach Bethel tomorrow evening by going nearly all night. They had quite a load: one-half barrel about two thirds or more full of sauerkraut; about a fourth-barrel of pork; a cracker box of canned stuff; the mittens and other things from the store; one large box of soap; some carpenter tools and dishes; and a bag of Lynx skins. Sumpka's brother, a quite feeble old man with one hand partly paralyzed, came up this morning and said he would get wood for us, that it seemed as though he and us were about all that would be left (the people [are] all nearly all gone to their Fall fishing and trapping) and accordingly set to work. He carried wood nearly all morning from the beach on his poor weak old back and then sawed and split it and seemed so glad to do it. It was with a great deal of pleasure that we asked him to come in and drink tea, the one great treat especially to the older folks here. He started home before supper, but I ran out to call him back, and how he did enjoy his goose stew. I am going to make some under clothes to keep his poor body warm this Winter. He, by name Evegan, and the one we call the "squint eyed trader," are two quite old men in the village.

Nellie has taught Elizabeth to call the old women "grandma," and how pleased they all are. Jerry's mother was so pleased tonight when she called her grandma and had her say it over as often as the little chick would. We were only about ten in chapel tonight. We will have chapel very seldom now until the folks come back. David and the "thumbless trader" went deer hunting yesterday. How good it would be to taste deer meat. The geese are too fat to be good. David and Anna are living in a little room between the chapel and our sitting room. David is such a good Christian man and such a thorough and reliable help in every way. We would be lost without him.

September 25, 1902

The children have all been sick of grippe during the past week. First Margaret, then when she began to improve Elizabeth began one day and Robert the following. Robert was very sick one night while Herman watched beside him [all] night dosing him with medicine to keep his fever down and from going into convulsions. I did the same with Elizabeth, dear little soul. She has been so ill and still is, while Robert and Margie (as baby calls her) are quite like themselves again. We have walked the floor almost night and day for the past three days, and are not very well ourselves, so we feel pretty tired. This morning Herman gave baby chloroform and lanced her second stomach tooth that seemed to worry her most. Tonight she seems to be resting more quietly. I do hope she will improve now for she is growing very weak from suffering so much and from high fever. We have been so glad for the wood Sumpka's brother cut, for with Christian gone and the little ones all down, I am afraid we would have run low. The faithful old fellow came up again this morning and wanted to help us, so Herman told him that we would be glad for him to help if he felt able. I am so glad that he is spared this sickness for it goes hard with the old folks up here. One of our natives returned from the Yukon today, and says the natives are all sick but not seriously. I sincerely hope we may be spared another severe epidemic of this awful grippe. Margaret says she is "a sick little girl." Last night she said if I would give her my brush and comb she "would comb her hair very nicely." Tonight when I went down to supper she said, "I am getting very sleepy mama." It is only such a short time since she began to speak English, so it all sounds very funny to me. Christian and the boys returned tonight. All are well at Bethel, and there are eighteen boys in school and some still to come. The folks are all coughing, the house seems somewhat like a hospital now. Our good kind faithful Nellie has been quite sick all day but is better tonight.

September 26, 1902

Baby rested very well all night, with the exception of three quite hard spells of coughing, and seems better today, though very weak and how pale and sick the dear little tot looks. Sometimes she forgets herself for a few minutes and tries to sing, but it is a very weak effort. She is the very happiest little mortal to be found when well. The house seems lost without her happy prattle. Margaret is improving right along, but Robert complains some of his ear "singing" as he calls it. Both baby and Margaret have had earaches. I hope Robert may be spared that.

September 27, 1902

Robert cried all of yesterday afternoon with earache. Poor little fellow, he just tossed from one side of the bed to the other, [but] nothing that we did seemed to relieve him. His papa tried everything that he thought would relieve him, but the more he did the more Robert thought him to blame. The best remedy seemed to be mama. He wanted me to be down with him or rock him all the while until about nine o'clock when he fell asleep and slept all night. This morning when he awoke his eyelids were red and swollen from crying, but the ache is better. Only at times does he complain of sharp shooting pains through his ear and head. His ear has been running all day. Elizabeth is better but oh, so mean, she is really wicked, she looks so mad, scratches me, slaps me and tries to tear my eyes out. I do all in my power to keep her quiet and her fever down, but find it a very hard task, as I am feeling miserable myself from loss of sleep and a very bad cold. Elizabeth's appetite is very poor. I almost have to force her to eat. The natives, I am very happy to say, have the grippe in a light form. The thumbless trader's wife's little girl, (the one whom they always called Ernest Helmich's wife) is very sick. But the others are sick a few days with pains in their chests and have a cough (of course this people are always coughing) and then begin to improve. Some natives from Tuluksak arrived today and say all are well at that place.

Sunday, September 28, 1902

Just a week ago tonight we began our night and day walking and worrying, and tonight for the first [time] everything thus far is quiet. The little folks are all sleeping naturally, and I trust they may continue in their good work. The discharge from Rob's ear grows less, and he is almost free from pain. I never like the children's ears to trouble them. Earache is not only distressing, but inflammation of the middle ear often leaves serious results. Elizabeth, though very weak, is improving. By tugging away I have managed to get about one-half cup of beef tea, one cup of milk and a small dish of cracker soup down her during the day. She has been somewhat better natured all day for which I have been thankful. Margaret is about well excepting the cough peculiar to grippe. Only when I ask her to do something that she does not quite favor she says, "I am a sick girlie."

The trader, his wife, and Sumpka's sister drank tea here today, or I guess you would say ate dinner. They had the little girl with them, but she is a *very very* sick child. The little baby whom Herman baptized the first Sunday we were here, (Moses) and a grandson of the squint-eyed trader, is also very sick. Had two services today. I could not go on account of the children. Attendance very small. It seems almost foolish to have services when nearly *all* of the folks are away. Herman is reading *David Harmen* and evidently enjoying it. I read it some time ago and thoroughly enjoyed it. David Harmen is such an original character, so quaint and funny. Some parts of the story may be considered illiterate by some goody good folks, but I truly enjoyed it all through and laughed more than I have in a long time over some of David's dry, quaint sayings. I am sure you would enjoy [it] too.

September 29, 1902

The baby and Margaret are improving right along, but my darling boy looks very badly and has no appetite. Tonight he is moaning in his sleep as if in pain. There seems to be a kind of colic that is present in this attack of grippe. Baby too had two very severe spells during her sickness. Herman has been working all day on his wagon, David helping him. Christian has been very sick all day, high fever and pain in chest. It just rains, rains, rains, and the mud around our back door is almost ankle deep. One scarcely feels like sticking one's nose out of doors considering the disagreeable weather overhead and the dirt underfoot. Andrew, a native who left some time ago for his Fall fishing home, came today with fish to trade and reports his baby worse. Herman lanced an abscess on his neck some time ago. The father and mother love their little Joe very much, especially the mother who never had but one child before, and that one died some time ago. The father of this first one was the Ougavig helper and trader for Mr. Lind for several years. Some time ago, about three years, he and the "squint eyed trader," his brother, dealt out a great many very valuable things which they had been saving for a long time in honor of their dead. This is a heathen custom and against the rules of the church. The missionaries were obliged to put the helper under discipline for his sin. Soon after this he died.

September 30, 1902

We have just heard that the "Bad boy's" baby, Moses, died this A.M. These poor weakly diseased little human beings. Herman just came to the door to say that Andrew's baby died last night. Oh, how sad! Where is our future Kuskokwim Indian to come from at this rate? Robert, after moaning all night and crying part of the time from pain in his stomach and abdomen, is somewhat feverish, and very weak. He really ought to be in bed but he won't hear to this. Elizabeth is downstairs fighting with Fritz whom she calls Dick. Mean is no name for our little tot. She can't do anything mean enough. She has it in for poor Margaret's curls, how she does pull them. Oh, how glad we will all be to see cold weather and have this everlasting rain stop. I think we will all feel better.

Evening. The two little bodies have been laid to rest already. This always seems cold and unfeeling to bury their dead before they are cold, but it is a custom of this people to bury their dead and give or bury all of their belongings just as soon as they can after they are gone. How very sad it is to see all of the little ones go. Four from this village have died in less than a month. At this rate the Eskimo of this river will soon be of the past. This village that some time ago numbered around three hundred has only about sixty now. In walking from the house down to the village, unless you keep to the path, you can stumble over graves nearly anywhere. How gloomy it makes one feel to see the people all go, and so very few babies left to fill their places.

October 2, 1902

How time flies! Tomorrow we are here a month, and most of that time we have spent indoors. Rain! rain! Will it ever cease? I think of Longfellow's poem very often these days, for surely the days are "cold and dark and dreary. It rains and the wind is never weary." But now that the little folks and the natives are improving, one need not feel quite so gloomy, even though the weather can scarcely cheer one.

Herman's ears troubled him some yesterday so he spent the day with David working on the Marriage ceremony which they are trying to translate. Today they are working on the wonderful cart. Nellie and Anna washed some clothes yesterday, as we were about out of clean clothes not having washed for two weeks, but drying clothes indoors is not very satisfactory, and the few we hung out were partly blown down this morning.

I am sitting at the southwest bedroom window writing on the desk made and used by our poor unfortunate Bro. Weber. And as I write and look out upon the trees, for trees are all that one can see, save a sled rack, a little ice house made of sod, and our clothes line full of clothes, I wonder how often our poor Bro. and Sr. have done likewise. Mrs. Weber was in very poor health during the last years and spent most of her time up in this room. Herman says the room is much as it was then. The little round table in the center on which they frequently served tea in the evening before retiring; Freddie's and Christie's little bed made by their father; the picture of the three Graces, Faith, Hope and Charity over the bed. Every time I look at it I think how many many times eyes that are closed forever on earthly pictures looked at this same lovely picture. But enough of this, it gives me the blues to dwell on the past for it does seem that everything that belonged to Ougavig is passing away. I am making six more pairs of mittens for our school boys and must [get] to work or I will lose all the gold of the morning hours.

(Evening) I must jot down the fact that since about nine A.M. the sun has been shining and a more perfect day can not be imagined. The men were out hunting and brought in six rabbits and two spruce grouse.

October 3, 1902

Another gloomy dark rainy day. Nellie went to pick cranberries, and I had the work all to do, and good for me it was to have been busy or I should have had the blues. Robert spent most of the day with Herman in the shop and seems better for it. The wagon is about to be completed. Herman is going to read to me awhile now so [I] will stop writing. My eyes are troubling me so much again. All of yesterday and today I have been miserable from headache and pain through my eyes. Oh, how good it will be to get out next year for so many reasons. We know our church board will object to our going, but if they will not pay our fare we can work for it. "There is always a way, where there's a will," and we *"Will"* go down next year.

Sunday, October 5, 1902

We were asked down to dinner at the trader's today. We enjoyed the tea drinking very much and always thoroughly appreciate the kind feeling, or rather the thoughtfulness, in asking a missionary to eat with them. The trader always has butter for us, and his wife makes such excellent baking powder bread. We were very much amused at the pranks of a tame fox the traders have. They brought him in the house while we were there, and how he did frisk around. You can pick him up and pet him like a kitten. Waska says that after Christmas they will visit Bethel, and if they are asked to spend Christmas there this year they will not go, "not a bit of it." They had their hearts broken last year. (Last year they were asked to stay at home). Waska is Neck's brother. Very good attendance at church this morning as well as at the evening service. David interprets so well and adds so much to the services; we would be lost without his valuable help. Nothing that I can write today can be of interest for my head is bursting. Oh, I feel that I shall go mad if I can not find relief.

October 6, 1902

The wagon is completed at last. I tell Herman that I think it deserves a place in history as it is the first wagon on the Kuskokwim. This wonderful piece of workmanship possesses two large back wheels with spokes, while the two smaller front wheels are regular chariot wheels made of solid wood. We will photograph it so that an illustration can be had when it goes down on the books of time as the first of its kind on this river. Fritz brought in a live rabbit tonight, and the children are wild with delight. We will keep it for them [as] it will be interesting for them to watch him change his brown Summer coat for a white Winter one. Of course we will call him Bunny. If the weather permits we will go berrying tomorrow. Surely it will be queer if the weather ever permits us to stick our noses out of doors. We have had to bring all of our cabbage from the root cellar to the shop, as the cellar roof leaked and wet the vegetables. We found the cabbage badly rotted and some of the heads eaten through by the mice. There are plenty of mice here to keep us company. We have several pets who come up through the cracks in the floor for their food. It surprises me to see how bold they are to come up and run all around the floor while we are sitting near them. We are glad for any friendly live thing up here in the woods. This is a very lonely place but, I am daily thankful for a quiet rest. Really, at Bethel one never knows what it is to rest. Someone or ones who have plenty of wants are always coming and going there.

Well, I must jot down a very rare occurrence. Johnnie got two well-deserved spankings this morning for clubbing his step-mother. First, I shook him up and brought him in with me, but he waited his chance, ran out picked up a large club and started again, then Herman spanked him.

Soon after this David appeared on the scene, then he took him home and after removing his trousers he gave him another dose. The treatment had an excellent result for after he had cried awhile, he has been "as good as pie" ever since. He and Robert chopped wood for us all afternoon. Johnnie is a nice little fellow, but often took such bad spells when his own dear mother was alive when he would try to hurt her in some way. Such a little monkey! And not yet seven years old.

October 9, 1902

We have had a nice little outing since I last wrote. The day before yesterday was a lovely one, so we all planned to go for berries. One boat load of villagers started on ahead of us, and we tried to follow but when it seemed to us that they were headed for the Yukon we turned around and dropped down the river to an island with such a nice long gravel beach. Here we pitched our tent, and while the men went hunting Nellie, Martha and I cooked while the children enjoyed gathering stones and throwing them in the water. Early yesterday afternoon the clouds looked very much like rain so we concluded it would be best to come home. After taking us across the creek, Christian and Fritz rowed nearly up to the village while we walked through the trees and enjoyed it very much, although Robert and Margaret got very tired before we reached the Peterborough. We arrived at home just in the nick of time as it began to rain as soon [as] we got here and has been raining ever since. The natives got in this afternoon and report a wet time. Herman and I went up and down the beach for a walk this afternoon, and Herman shot four rabbits. I must say that I am very tired of rabbits. The squint-eyed trader (now don't think this a lack of respect; everybody calls him this) was up to visit us this afternoon. He enjoys looking at the magazines more than anyone I know. He seemed so pleased when I asked him to stay to supper. Poor old man! He is much alone now and growing feeble, "his race is nearly run," and yet he claims to be much in love with Minnie's sister, and wants to marry.

October 10, 1902

This is your birthday, or is yours on the ninth? I cannot remember whether yours or Mama's, only that they always come one day apart. And Ed's too has past. If God is willing we will have many happy birthdays next year. How nice it will be to be home again, and enjoy with you all, our birthdays and Christmas. When we first came seven years ago, how long seven years looked then, and many times since then how gladly we would have gone home for awhile could we have done so. Especially after poor mama died we wished so much to be with you to help cheer your lonely hours, but even that we could not do. Now that the seven years are almost past, after all, how quickly they have flown. It will be hard to leave our Eskimos who grow more dear as the time comes to part with them. They have so little to make them happy or comfortable. They all seem very sorry that we are going, and want us to promise to come back to them again.

Herman has [a] toothache and says that I must pull his tooth. I don't feel that dentistry is in my line of business, but if it comes to the point I can try at least. One must be ready to do any and everything up here. Raining still.

October 11, 1902

Herman had [a] toothache all night and said this morning that I must try to pull the offender. So I did try, and I can assure you we were both glad when the tooth came out with the first effort, although Herman said I just about pulled his head off too. I guess I did not handle the forceps just the proper way, but the tooth, roots and all came out, and as this was the desired object, what more need one expect? However, there are other duties I would prefer to tooth pulling.

Well, "and it still rains." I am not going to give this abominable word, rain, any more space in your journal. Certainly this is trying weather. With the exception of about three days, we have not had a peep at the sky since we came here. Herman is having a time to put "his boy" to sleep, so I will go now to his relief. Elizabeth sometimes says she is "papa's boy." Sometimes "papa's monkey." We often wonder how long she will be willing to be a monkey. A year ago today we arrived at this place for our six week stay. We enjoyed that visit very much. I especially, as we women so seldom get away from home. Time goes much faster this year though for we have our little ones with us and have not to worry about them.

October 12, 1902

We had quite a fall of snow during the night, as the ground was covered this morning when we awoke. And the sun is really shining brightly this morning.

October 13, 1902

This has been the stormiest day we have had yet. Ugh! Such a cold, raw wind blowing, it makes one shiver to hear it. David and Anna started for Bethel this morning when it seemed for awhile that it was getting better. But soon after they left it grew much worse than it was before, and the water is so rough. I feel worried about them, but they are doubtless somewhere in a sheltered camp. We will be more lonesome now that [the] Davids are gone. But Herman really does not need him now, and as we have only our own provisions we did not feel that we could supply him, so we thought it best for him to go down home. Nellie tried to wash today but as usual it was a very unsatisfactory wash-day. We have not had one nice day to wash and dry clothes since we arrived at this forsaken hole. The children all have colds again. Margaret was quite croupy last night. This must be the worst place on earth for taking cold. It is just cough, cough, cough! How tired I get hearing it. Sometimes it is very difficult to hold chapel, I imagine, for everybody seems to cough when there is a spell. I am sure I should get rattled were I to try to conduct a service at such a time. We put a little stove up in the bedroom this morning. This is a thing Helmichs never had. They seemed to think it a crime to be cozy and warm. Anything but comfort and ease would suit them. But then everyone to his own notion. For me, I like to be as comfortable as I can be under the circumstances.

October 14, 1902

We had our first snow storm this afternoon. It snowed lively the greater part of the afternoon, and tonight the ground is covered, as well as the trees and a cold bleak wind has been blowing all day and has grown worse tonight. Our bedroom is uncomfortably cold without a fire. Nellie is in her glee over the first ice-cream of the season. As for me I think I should prefer something more warming. But then the native ice-cream is not like ours, and is probably more warming than otherwise. [It is] made of seal oil, tallow and berries. This is all mixed up with snow and really *looks* very pretty, but as for taste it makes me sick to think of it. I have honestly tried to eat a little at different times out of courtesy, but have failed utterly to appreciate it. Margaret says she is tired for ice-cream too. She always says "tired" for "hungry."

Thursday, October 16, 1902

Truly, this is thoroughly disgusting weather, such a dismal, gray black ugly sky. I must confess homesickness. The children are very tired of the house and beg to go out to the shop where Herman is working on a new sleigh, but it is too damp and cold for them out there. And how they do spat and fight. Now and then I am obliged to take a hand in their battles also. I just told Margaret that she is a good little girl when by herself, but she says she is not by herself but by her mama. She is still very "tired" for ice-cream and asks why I never make any.

Friday, October 17, 1902

A real respectable Fall day. I believe the sun has half a mind to shine and I, for one, feel like a different creature. Only I had a very unsatisfactory breakfast of dried fruit, stewed of course, mush and coffee. I am not unlike the natives, who are always hungry if they have not eaten meat of some kind for their last meal. Yes, there comes the sun, full and strong, and the sky is nearly all blue. I trust the few floating white clouds may mean no mischief. My mind dwells on home and you all so much now that we are really going down next Spring, that I dream of home or Philadelphia nearly every night. And often my dreams are so vivid and real that I feel in the morning almost as though I had been home again for a short time.

We had quite a laugh on Robert this morning. He is a very proud little fellow and likes his clothing just so. Last week I cut a long pair of stockings down, something after the manner of the way stockinet is used. Just swing it over the toe, and let the foot form itself. Robert has worn these for nearly a week, and this morning for the first [time], noticed their queer make up. After examining them closely, he was most thoroughly disgusted and declared he would wear them no more. We could not help laughing at the expression of disgust written upon his face, although we helped him to put the stockings on again. Yesterday he came to me and said, "I don't want a knife any more. See, I am always cutting my fingers; I'm just going to put it on the shelf over there." This morning we found the knife on the shelf with the large blade broken half off. You will never get Master Robert to willingly carry a crippled knife. I am going to make him a new pair of pants today, and when he asked me to put two hip pockets in like papa's I had to promise that I would, for he has had enough to try him for one day. He is in his element now, for he has gone out to visit with papa.

Margaret and Elizabeth are fighting pretty lively down stairs and from the sound are more than Nellie can manage, so I must go to her rescue. The sun really is still out.

Saturday, October18, 1902

Fritz came in last night from hunting, and said a boat was coming from down river, and from her sail, a large one. How glad we were at the thought, that doubtless we would hear from Bethel, and see a white face. Herman went down to the shore to see whom it might be, but soon returned to say that the boat had passed at the farther side of the river. I must confess that I was very much disappointed, for I had already imagined myself reading letters from Bethel. This morning while we were getting breakfast some-one knocked at the door. I opened it to find a Mr. Barry of the boat of last night who had passed, not knowing, and had come down this morning with a package from Bethel containing six lead pencils and a note from the trader at Nushagak. Not a word from Bethel, but I dare say that they are all alive or would have written at least to say so. Mr. Barry had a cup of coffee, then left as they are in a hurry to get as far up the river as possible before freezing. Herman went down to the shore with him, and to see his partner who turned out to be his son, a boy of about sixteen. I think of the poor boy so much, up here in this weird, wild, forsaken country. He has his father of course, but he has not his mother. I just feel like doing some-thing for him, or sending him something nice, but they are too far away now. Robert's pants are nearly finished and have four pockets. Christian asked him yesterday for his knife. Rob said, "Too bad, but my knife is very dull." The river has been very high three times in the last few weeks, it is going down, for the last time, I trust, for truly we will hail with joy freez-ing up time. Just here, I might say, the sun did not hurt himself at shining yesterday, and today is anything but clear.

Friday, October 24, 1902

Since Tuesday we have been having Winter. The boys brought ice in the water barrel this morning an inch and a half thick. The ice has been running all day yesterday and today. I never saw a more beautiful Alaskan Winter picture than this morning proved to be. A heavy snow had fallen during the night, and everything was white. Our house, as I have said before, is among the spruce and pine trees, and these all heavily laden with snow. The sled rack, the ice and fish houses, and shop all in their Winter dress, with the faintest ray of sun shining upon them looked grand to us at least, who for nearly two months have known only mud and rain. The children are in their glee. The first thing yesterday morning they had to have ice-cream made of snow and milk. Baby claps her little hands and fairly yells with delight at the falling snow. The natives too are nonetheless happy. The few that are here can be seen running from one barabara to another treating one another to ice-cream. Nor am I missed. They all bring a dishful to me, and though I cannot eat it, I do appreciate their thoughtfulness. I had Nellie make a large panfull for me yesterday, and gave her apples and sugar to add to the cranberries, (the natives think these fine) and then treated my friends in the village. The trader's wife has just about kept us in fresh fish. Every time they come from the trap they remember us generously, and we are *all* very glad for a change from rabbits.

We had our first sleigh ride yesterday down to the beach and back. Robert and Fritz are hauling wood from the bank. A happier boy can no where be found than my Rob who spends all of his time working with his papa or Christian and Fritz. I scarcely see him from one meal till the next, unless he cuts his fingers, then he runs to Mama for surgical care.

Sunday, October 26, 1902[104]

Dear Father, as Ella is not well today, I will add a line or two to her journal. She may write herself but then it won't matter if we both write. She is reading at this particular time, and so I will write. Day before yesterday she began to have colicky pains and cramps, and was worse yesterday, and I have forbidden her to get up today but she talks of dressing after while. I feared she might be getting appendicitis and for this reason have been cautious of her. She says she did not at any time think of that until I mentioned it. I have been through the mill having had a good many attacks before I was operated [on], and so my over caution on this subject, and then too at this remote place alone I could do very little if I had a bad case of appendicitis to deal with, for we are all alone until we return to Bethel the latter part of November or at the longest until after Xmas. Ella has not been sick since we were married, only when she has her babies, and for her to be ill is a great worry to me. I slept far less than she did last night for her health is of the greatest importance to me. Her

---

104. This date's journal entry was made by Herman.

symptoms are more those of inflammation of the stomach and bowels probably due to acute indigestion, but to me a strict watch for appendicitis cannot be overlooked.

Oh, how we would enjoy a visit from you or some of our relatives. How long has our stay been. In the Spring is our time up and we are determined to return, but we scarcely can hope for the consent of the Board. They are very loath to see us leave the work and very unbending in their rules as well as their reasons for what they do.

This is a hard country, and we will be glad for a rest at home. I would not consent to take charge of this work up here unless we return to Bethel when I must begin to travel; for I will not go and leave my family alone in such a land even if others have done so. And then there are many risks to such road work and it is best for my family to be at the main station. I often tell Ella that it is better to have a home without a father than for the mother to be gone. So it is best that the risks are mostly on my side when traveling. At any rate I want the best for my wife and babies and the best of this land is little enough I may say.

I must soon go and keep service. There are but few people here and as Ella cannot go today we will have poor singing. Some times it would be worth your while to hear my interpreters and myself along with the natives singing the translated songs. A native is always slow and cautious when he should keep time and as a rule the quarter notes are sung as half or full notes and he comes along as if carrying a heavy load and though late and out of breath not discouraged by the job. I well remember at one meeting when one of the young missionaries was helping he announced a piece that was rather high and as all had colds it was a task. Only one old native whose voice was cracked by his cold of which he was recovering could reach the high part of the chorus, the others and the missionaries (men only present it was an evening chapel and no sisters went) fell off one by one until this old fellow had to scale the high part of the chorus by himself. The situation got so funny that I had to hold my book up and laugh during each chorus. Finally after two stanzas and the choruses the missionary thought that would do and so stood up to read, but that never phased the natives. There was one verse yet and as half seemed to have their eyes shut, they waded in for the last round. One with the cracked voice and another bellowing like a bull at times for his voice was more like the bellowing of a bull than anything else, and he would only sing parts of each verse. Well, the missionary did the only thing left to do. He sat down until the singing was over and then got up and read the lesson. I myself was so amused and almost beyond controlling myself. I will confess, I laughed so hard that I thought I would burst trying to hold in from an outright laugh. After the singing, I straightened up my face and looked around at one of the chief singers. He saw I had been laughing and his smile of satisfaction was something to be remembered, for he thought they had accomplished something almost beyond the *Kass'aq* or whites, for had they not sung a *Kass'aq* tune and stayed with it when the whites could not? So it looks that today with the few people we will have a hard time to sing.

I will close for this morning.

Your Affectionate Son,

J. H. Romig

Evening

Service went off quite well today. Bob and Margaret promised to help sing but forgot [their] parts, and I had to make Margaret come up and sit beside me as she could not remain still anywhere else. Just now they have just said their evening prayers. They often forget what to say or what they have said. Last night Margaret said part of a table grace to begin her prayer, and today they both tried to follow me when I said grace and when done announced that they had also prayed with me. The baby also gets religious spells, and today amused Ella and myself not a little by lying down and singing, and then raising up and extending her arms to pronounce the Benediction.

I am sure you would be much amused at their capers, but you could get along with only a short amount of the same for they are lively and certainly full of mischief that keeps one ever alert that they do not some damage. Ella seems better tonight, and my heart is lighter. It seems I suffer most when she is ill. Other people I can attend in sickness, but when she or the babes are sick my heart is gone. I give them all the care I know but my interest is so great that I can't help but worry when the same if others were ill I would feel no occasion to worry. The snow is falling heavy this evening, and winter seems to come on a pace which we can but welcome as we have had a wet and disagreeable Fall. As I sat down to post-up the mission journal, I will not write long at this time.

Affectionately,

J. H. Romig

October 31, 1902

MY DEAR FATHER:

I have been up the greater part of today, but feel very weak and tired. Just what was the matter with me, I am sure I cannot say. While I did not suffer very much, I was ill. Herman says that it is not how sick I was, but how sick I might have been. I know now that he thought I had appendicitis, and of course no one need tell me how serious it might have been. My dear loving Herman was much worried I could see, and he was the more to be pitied. I do not know which saved or relieved me of my ailment, Herman's medicine, his faithful care or his ardent prayers. But we truly feel that God has wonderfully cared and watched over for us during this past week. Herman told me today that as soon as the creeks were half-safe enough, he sent two boys up the River for Mr. Barry, (the white man who passed here in a boat some time ago) to come down as soon as possible thinking that, should I grow worse he, Herman, would not be alone if an operation should become necessary. I am worried lest the two messengers, or they and Mr. Barry, come to trouble in their efforts for my welfare. But the God of our comfort, and of ice and water can care for them too. Oh, how blessed it is that we have such a loving Father who never turns a deaf ear to our prayers. Who, even when we least think of Him, so tenderly cares for us. I think of Herman walking down to the beach during the days of my sickness to see each time the ice running and grinding like a freight train down stream. And I can imagine how his heart must have sunk within him when he thought of all that might happen to me, and he all alone back here in the trees. My poor boy, I am so glad for his sake that I am better. I never want for anything when I am ill, he takes the best of care of me. One morning last week he brought my breakfast to me, and then threw his arms around me and cried great manly tears because he could bring me nothing good. How sweet that breakfast of a roll, coffee, and rabbit stew was. Nothing ever tasted better to me. I often thank God for one of the truest, kindest and most loving of husbands. I hope I may be spared another attack of appendicitis (if such it was). But I do not complain, each of these little trials but bring us nearer our Savior, makes us to feel how helpless we are in His hands, and makes us stronger for the greater trials, of which we must expect a share.

Saturday, November 1, 1902

Mr. Barry and the two native boys arrived about 9:30 last night having walked about twenty-three miles from eight o'clock yesterday morning, and says he would have come even had the distance been far greater. I am sorry to be the cause of so hard, as well as so perilous a trip, for many times in crossing the creeks or parts of the river they were in danger of being drowned. He will stay now until traveling is good when Herman *will* send him back with our team. We will not soon forget so great a kindness and from a stranger too. I for one will not let an opportunity to do him a kindness pass. Mr. Barry will get birch for a sled while here, put it up to dry, and then when he and his son have gotten ready for the Winter they will come here to make the sled.

I am getting stronger, but slowly; have been practicing on the typewriter today for just a little while and feel very tired. It is steadily growing colder. I think it must be very cold out of doors as the bedroom is uncomfortably cold without a fire this afternoon.

Thursday, November 6, 1902

This is Margaret's fourth birthday, and a very happy one it has been. Her presents, a little sled, (the exact pattern of her papa's,) and a new dress from me, together with a nice breakfast, the table having on it her birthday cake with four lighted candles on it, were complete surprises to her this morning. Herman asked her last night why she had not had her birthday celebration yet, (she knew that it would occur at Ougavig) and she turned to me to know the reason why the happy time had not yet arrived. I had a great time yesterday trying to finish her dress, she kept running in every few minutes. I tried the lining on her twice and I am sure she saw the dress, but she never smelled the mouse. We wanted to take a picture of her, but the light has not been good enough for an exposure today. Just here I may record the fact that it is raining. This is the queerest Fall that we ever had, no real cold weather yet, and today has been just like a Spring day. It looks as though the ice might run out again. Mr. Barry started home yesterday with the trader from here, who is going up to Mr. Lind's place. Christian took Mr. B. nearly home with Herman's team. We were very glad to see the team return in the evening and to hear that all, as far as they went, had been well, for the ice cannot be safe. I always think that the natives venture too far, they always walk over ice much sooner than I would care to venture out on it. Herman has been painting his sleds today; they will soon be completed and I am sure he will be glad when he can call them done. Herman and Mr. Barry were out on Monday for wood for a sled for Mr. B.; he and his son will come down in a short time to make the sled here, where we have a large shop and good tools.

Friday, November 7, 1902

Nellie has been sick all day, thus leaving me alone with the work. I wanted so much to finish a dress I had begun, but could find but little time for sewing today, so I sewed all evening. Robert stayed down stairs with me. Herman stayed down long enough to play two or three rounds of dominoes with us. This was the first time Robert ever played, and he thought it great fun. After Herman left us, and I had begun to sew, Robert amused himself by trying to fit some paste board cuts of different figures together. One was a soldier boy, another a saddle horse and the third a cow. I was really surprised to see how well he got along. Of course he bothered me to help him sometimes, but not often. When we came up to bed Herman was sound asleep, and Robert pointed at him and said, "He is hokes pokes." This is a phrase one of the white men uses when his dogs are tired out, and Robert has often heard his papa tell of the first time he heard him use it. It amused Herman so much, he had never heard it before, and now all of the children down to baby use it frequently. I think Robert was in the same state as his papa for he was asleep almost as soon as his head touched his pillow. It has rained much of the day, and has been warmer. This is much like a states Fall. Herman says that we will go to Bethel in a boat if the ice leaves. As for me, I am in no hurry to leave a warm log house and plenty of game for a barn and no game. Christian brought in four live rabbits day before yesterday. The rabbits seem so tame this year, and so many are very poor. There are so many that we believe that some are hungry. The brush all along the creek are about all eaten bare.

Sunday, November 16, 1902

Herman has been trying to write to the Bethel folks, but Elizabeth bothered him so, he finally gave it up and took her out sleigh riding in Margaret's new sled. I wish you might see her, she is a picture of content as she sits all bundled up in furs, pulled to and from the village. We are having such fine weather, not at all like other years, and how the children enjoy it. They spend much of the time out of doors even to baby. I am very glad too to be able to enjoy the mild weather too, for this I can as I am entirely well again, save indigestion some of the time, and then I am losing in flesh too, but I can scarcely expect to gain when my food does not agree with me. Oh, how glad I will be to have my teeth and eyes attended to! How can one's stomach be expected to do good work [when] two such important functions are pulling against it. I hope with all my heart that I may be spared another attack of appendicitis, if such it was, for I can ill afford to be sick, especially here in this remote corner of the world. We are going to Bethel as soon as we can trust the roads, but that is scarcely yet. Such a queer Winter! But as John [Kilbuck] used to say, each season must have its turn. It must rain just so much in Summer; it must be cold just so long in Winter; and the wild winds have time to spend their fury so no doubt cold Winter weather is yet to come, and I dare say, it will be a long one.

The natives are all in now from their Fall fishing and hunting. The chapel was nearly filled this morning, and for the past few nights we have had a good attendance at evening chapel. Before this the people seemed careless about coming to chapel, and as they have always seemed to be anxious to have an ordained man, and now that they have one, I just thought I would touch them up a little on their not coming more often to chapel. So I said that we might as well go to Bethel where there is plenty of work to be done, for it seems that here many of the folks do not need a minister as they seldom come to evening chapel, that I thought the doctor had rather preach to less empty seats and more people. I think the few who heard what I said noised it about, for since then we have had a goodly attendance. But even though we must often speak to them about coming to chapel, yet I will give them their just dues for I truly believe we Christians in the states would go less frequently to chapel, which is held every night during the Fall, Winter and Spring, than do our Eskimos.

November 16, 1902[105]

DEAR FATHER:

I will add to my former writing a little tonight. The day has been as usual a day of rest from work, and ours to do missionary work in. The Services were well attended today, and we feel sure that some of the people enjoyed the mutterings.

---

105. This date's journal entry was made by Herman.

They are a poor ignorant, peaceable, but lazy folk. Not overly active along any line, and as a rule content with less than they could possess.

I was amused at their singing today. There are no conventional rules. No choirs and no special leaders. One old man is noted for the volume of his voice and can be depended upon to keep the song from dying out, i.e. if noise is music, but they sing for the benefit the song can do, and they sing from the heart, and for my part I think their music comes as near perfection as lots of the stronger and varied sounds heard in many of the Churches at home. So called music from the choir. But in praising the Lord, as well as in praying to Him, it is not the spirit of self that should be first unless it is as a needy sinner, and in this I prefer the songs of the Eskimo to the startling peals of the apparently frightened men and women in front of a pipe organ.

Ella is downstairs just now getting supper, and as she has called I must close until after that extravagant though necessary performance.

The supper is now over, and we have had some time talking and in getting the children to bed. We are very happy again since Ella is well, and hope she may have no more trouble.

I am even preaching to her to not do so much and guard her eating, and we trust and pray that she may remain healed. I must close for tonight. Your affectionate son,

J. H. R.

November 17, 1902

Mr. Barry and his son, Mr. Arthur, arrived today, bringing some states mail but none for us, save a bill for one of Herman's medical journals, and a letter from Mr. J. B. Roberts to "The missionary at Ougavig," who ever that might be. It seems so funny, for we hear from him and his wife nearly every mail. But of course he does not know that we are here. There are two registered packages of photographing supplies for Mr. Stecker, in these I feel an equal interest as he and I sent for them, but I had much rather have a letter. The man who brought the mail from the Yukon to Mr. Barry's place is appointed commissioner for this entire Kuskokwim district. The subject is one of whom we all know, and is not a fit person for the position, but it does seem that the judges of Alaska are scarcely better and only too frequently appoint such specimens. We are daily looking for David who is to come to help with the communion. The trader from here has been absent now over two weeks having started for Kolmakovskiy while the ice was far from safe. I have often felt worried since he left, and even the daring natives are, many of them, beginning now to fear the worst for him. His wife says but little although she looks worried, and I am sure I should too were Herman gone under the same circumstances.

November 18, 1902

The men were all out hunting, but I believe call the hunt a failure. Some strangers arrived from Tuluksak today and brought a lard pail of snaky-fish roe to me from Waska's mother, of which I am especially fond.[106] Waska is one of our nice boys, and his mother is such a dear kind woman. They are a happy family now as Waska and wife have a new baby boy.

This is our first real Winter day, and it is steadily growing colder. Rover and Shang came in this morning from a hunt, the former had the rabbit, and the latter the trap fast to his foot, but I am happy to say the foot was only slightly injured. I was so provoked that I threw that trap out in the garden where the owner afterwards found it, although it really was the dog's fault.

Thursday, November 20, 1902

I just noticed the trader among the folks going in to preparatory service. How good it is to see him, and to know he is not at the bottom of the Kuskokwim. I know his wife is happy, for she was much worried. We have communion this evening. Herman has been with the members since breakfast, and I am sure he must be tired. At this meeting he will admit three new members and baptize one adult, the wife of Jailok, who was at one time, for a little while, in our school. Her name was then Ida. She now wants a new name, and claims to want very much to lead a new life, and certainly there is room for a better one. Herman baptized her Mary.

---

106. Ella is probably referring to what the missionarys called "stinky fish." Schwalbe provides the recipe for this method of fish preservation. "A hole about 18 inches in diameter by two feet deep is dug in the ground. It is lined with grass. Into this is packed the raw fish, usually the small white fish and salmon trout. Some holes are filled with fish heads only. Covered with grass and then turf, they are left to ripen. Months later these small storehouses are opened and the fish eaten with great relish. Although they have a strong and very unpleasant smell, they are considered a real delicacy." The Eskimo word for this treat is *tipmuk* which means, " 'that which has a smell' " (Schwalbe, 1985, 32).

Evening

Communion service is over; it was a very nice quick service, thirty-seven having communed. A week from today, Thanksgiving Day, I hope to be able to prepare for love feast for the people, as we will probably not be here for Christmas, and I want their Thanksgiving as pleasant as possible.

Sunday, November 23, 1902

This is genuine Winter weather. There can be no doubt as to the truth, nor can there be any reason why the ice should not now be safe. But we are very comfortable with our stove in this log house built by a minister, who never knew about carpenter tools before coming here. It is a great pity that all of our houses were not built by non-carpenters. I shiver when I think of our Bethel house. But I must close my journal now for want of space. It is only an apology, and a poor one at that, but is has been written with a great deal of love, and I am sure *you* will enjoy reading it. Affectionately.

Ella

I will begin another journal today lest I grow careless about it through neglecting a beginning. This is one of my greatest faults, "waiting for a better time."

chapter 5

November 23, 1902 to
September 23, 1905

Ougavig, Kuskokwin River, Alaska, November 23, 1902

My dear father:

I have just finished your journal, that is, I have filled a small journal book; so before I get lazy or negligent, I will begin another. We have just been down to the village to have our pictures taken with all of the natives who are all here still. Soon someone or ones will be gone on trips, and as Herman has wanted all Fall to get a picture, he thought best to try it today, although it is very cold. We wanted to go for a ride after the picture taking was over, but were nearly frozen so thought it best to wait until some other time. Elizabeth, however, thought differently on the matter, and expressed her desire so lustily her papa had to take her out awhile. Just now she and Margaret are having prayer meeting downstairs. Mr. Barry and his son, of whom I wrote in my other journal, have finished their sleds. Yesterday they painted the new one and repaired the old one, and now expect to leave soon for up-river.

A native who came here from the Yukon last week claimed that a white man whom he had been with up near Kolmakofskiy, took gold out of the ground and had it exchanged for money. This we believe to be only another story, but wonder how long it will be until some such story will bear truth for we all have great faith in our Kuskokwim. We have been anxiously looking for David for some time now; we are hungry for Bethel news. I hope David is not sick, he is not very strong.

Monday, November 24, 1902

This has been a very cold day, and a high wind has been blowing all day. Christian and Mr. Karr were on the tundra for a load of frozen fish [and] returned just at dusk and report a cold trip. This morning as we were about to eat breakfast, the wife of Nicholi (the most notorious native on the river for cruelty to his wives) came in to say that he had whipped her, and taken her new unfinished parka and gone to the *Kashima*. He has been treating her shamefully at times, as he always has his many other wives. Soon after, we heard that she had gone with her brother, whom we

171

call "Fattie" from Akiachak, without a parka. The native woman then told us how Nicholi had scratched and slapped his wife. This man just needs a good "licking," and I heartily wish that I were a man just long enough to do the job. He has been itching for it seven years, to my knowledge, how long before [that] I know not. John [Kilbuck] gave a "wife-beater" a round-up one time that made a man of him, and I wish John were here to make a man out of Nicholi, if there is any man in him, which I seriously doubt. One cannot pity him with their eyes open.

Tuesday, November 25, 1902

Mr. Barry and his son, Arthur, left this morning, and Ougavig is again the same quiet place. Today little Paul Helmich is a year old. A year ago none of us thought that we would be living here, and Mr. and Mrs. H. [would] be in the states a year hence. How much can happen in a short time. It was only a few weeks after we left here last year that it became perfectly evident that Mr. Helmich was too weak a man for so severe a climate.

We have just finished covering a down comforter. I bought the thing last year from the woman prospector from Togiak, Mrs. MacDonnell, and I may say it was a case of "green goggles," for it [was] absolutely no good. Mrs. Mac was a good sales-woman, (in fact her tongue was in good running order on any subject) and I a green customer, so she naturally got the best of the bargain, for she got four dollars, and I a "holey" comforter. But we had a great deal of fun covering it tonight. We had some native visitors, and one native got at each corner to pull it straight. Herman bossed the job and ran the machine while I pulled from behind to help the feed. We had a good deal of fun, and a very good quilt in a few minutes.

Tomorrow the men are all expected to saw, split, and haul wood for the chapel. We are very busy getting ready for our home going trip. I must confess that when we are all at Bethel again, I will be glad to count that trip over, for it will be no small task with four little folks, but of course we have plenty of servants besides others who are going down at the same time.

Wednesday, November 26, 1902

The men, or some of them, worked at the chapel wood, and are now out hunting for a joint Thanksgiving dinner in the *Kashima*. We all expect to give something toward the dinner, and then eat together. If there is one thing that rejoices Herman's heart more than another, it is some kind of a big meal. Robert worked at the wood all morning, and is now out hunting with his papa. I scarcely ever see the little fellow anymore, save at his meals, he is either in the shop with Herman, or out with Christian and Fritz the greater part of the time. This morning he was looking at some pictures of locomotives, and asked me what they were. I tried to explain their use, and when I told him that they were big steam engines, and would pull the cars in which we would go in next Summer, he wanted to know if they had whistles. Yes, I said, and they make plenty of noise too. Well, he said, "They are no good, and I am not going to ride behind them." Poor little fellow, he will have to get accustomed to whistles when we get in the states. Robert is such a dear old fashioned little man, and such a busy one too. He always helps to get wood for the bedroom stove which is very small, and requires very short wood, then he and Fritz carry it up. They got to fighting over it some time ago, and Herman spanked the both of them, but it did them a great deal of good for they are both better since. We have a nice pile of wood for the chapel, nearly enough to last the Winter through. Herman says that Mr. Nicholi was the first at work this A.M. His wife is still absent.

Thursday, November 27, 1902

Many of the folks gave liberally this morning in chapel, so that every needy person was well remembered. Ougawithiguk gave Eirgure a sled so that he could get wood more easily. Poor old man. He has a large family to provide for and has one hand almost useless from paralysis. He has his sister, an orphan girl, and his second wife's daughter's little girl to care for. I tried to be good to his sister and promised to give her all of my sewing if she would agree to sew at Bethel prices. (Mrs. Helmich has paid these folks such foolishly large prices, and I will not follow her plan) Yes, she said, she would gladly do so, but the last time I paid her she was not satisfied and said Mrs. H. never paid her so little, and I even paid more than I had agreed to. Well, that is the last work I had or will have for her. In the future all favors go to her brother. But back to Thanksgiving. After service we all went to the *Kashima* to eat dinner, and had a pleasant time together. We gave the sugar, tea, bread, some beans and turnips; Nellie gave a dish-panful of ice cream. All of the natives gave what they could, and Mary gave much. Frozen fish, dry salmon and smelts and ice-cream were dealt out so that everybody had plenty, and all were very joyful. Just before service Evan arrived from Bethel bringing letters. Everybody there are, or were, well, but they bring news of a terrible flood on the fifteenth of October, or rather a high tide and south storm. One native, such a nice good boy, deaf and dumb, by name Ianguk, was lost. Many of [the] natives lost their fish that were buried in the ground. The water came up under Mr. Lind's store. They were obliged to take everything out of it. Our boats were landed up high and dry, and will require much hard work in the Spring to get them in the water. Our pier and track to our warehouse were washed away. Mr. Stecker writes that they have not heard of all the damage done below. Some miners whom we know, nearly lost their lives on the same day. Evan brought Foxie and Kieser, two of our dogs. Well, I was so glad to see something alive from Bethel I just hugged them both, but they were just as glad to see us.

I gave out some boots to be soled this morning, among them a pretty pair of deer-skins made by Fannie last year. When I looked at them and thought [of] the soles that she had put on, I cried. The longer Fannie is gone the more I miss her. She was such a nice little woman.

Friday, November 28, 1902

The trader left for Bethel this A.M. and took one of our boxes, but it does not look much like our going very soon, for the weather is very cold and stormy, but as soon as it moderates we will start. I have not felt well all day. I hope I will not get sick again. We are busy getting everything ready for our trip. The children all have warm deer-skin mittens, fur in, warm caps and cloaks and footwear, which are the most important part of all. Herman made a sled which he calls the "prairie schooner" as it is covered with canvas. This he proposes to take Margaret and Elizabeth in. It is made something like a cutter only smaller, just about the size for the babies, and they can be made very warm and comfortable if they will agree to it. I am sure neither one will agree to being very far from me. McKar and another native started this morning for the Yukon to bring our shot which was forgotten in our shipment from San Francisco, and had to be ordered from St. Michael. We are getting so much frozen fish of late. Evan brought a tin of our tallow from Bethel, and before nine A.M. today it was all [gone]. Everyone tried to get here first to get some before it was all gone. The folks have so many berries this year which makes tallow an excellent article for trade. Tallow is used for ice-cream.

Saturday, November 29, 1902

We are about all packed up and ready for our trip, but the weather does not look like starting for it is very cold. Last night the wind blew pretty lively, and we felt the cold very keenly in our bedroom. This morning a cup of water on the table was frozen. When we feel the cold thus at Ougavig we know they are scarcely able to keep warm at Bethel and, I dare say, enough wood was burned there during the night. The children are in their glee in anticipation of our home trip tonight. As we came upstairs to put them to bed, Margaret said, "We will sleep just a little tonight," and when I told her no we would sleep plenty, she said, "I is late already." I guess she is afraid she will not be up in time to see all the packing or else that she will be left behind. Robert wanted to know tonight if his whiskers were growing yet. Well I said I could not see them, but he thought that probably they were starting. He often talks about the time when he will have whiskers like papa, but I tell him that I hope he will have a better crop than his papa when the time comes. Elizabeth has learned a new word today, "somebody." She has been saying it much of the time. Where she heard it I know not. How you would love our baby, she is such a darling child, so busy all day long, she chatters from morn till eve. Sometimes she sings for Nellie to dance, or visa versa. Sometimes she has prayer meetings, but most of her time she spends singing her dirty rag baby to sleep, then she covers her over with her handkerchief, and tells us all to be still for baby is asleep. Unlike Margaret, baby has a splendid appetite and is as thick as long, almost.

Sunday, November 30, 1902[107]

Ella has two letters on the go this evening and so needs help. I have just been writing for [an] hour on the typewriter. I put in a couple of pages more of no value than of special interest, but we have so few things of interest to record up here that we have to fill the space with things of less importance. If we had one of the wireless telegraph machines, we could write and think more along the lines of what is happening down there, but also we can only use the wireless telegraph of imagination to draw on for possible happenings at home, and as we are not given to guessing must confine ourselves to the facts about us, common-place though they may seem.

---

107. This entry made by Herman.

The next topic of interest on the go for us is the going back to Bethel, a little ahead of the time we had planned for, but on account of Ella's recent illness I think it best and so we hope to start soon. The children thought the trip was on already last night, and Bob did up his and Margaret's sleeping bags for the trip. Nothing is of more interest or importance to them than to get ready and go some where. I will be glad to get them home to our own comfortable house (i.e. more comfortable than this one) and where there is more company for them, and I dare say company for us all for I am tired of the trees and this desolate place, where we have had more sickness than in any previous year. And that in three short months. The cold is very intense at this time, and we must wait a few days until a mild spell. I have made two larger road sleds and one sled for Mrs. Romig [Ella] and children, and two little sleds for the little folks and then there is still our larger sled to go and I have only sixteen days to take all. Too few as I drive eleven dogs in my team, but I can pull the whole business when the roads are good with the eleven dogs, so I guess we will get down somehow, but not so rapidly as if we had good teams for each sleigh. The Laps and deer will come for our baggage, and we will travel as light as possible. Bob says "toy chlu." How about it, i.e. my writing, well I will have to close ere he helps.

Herman

December 1, 1902

We are all ready for our trip, but the weather has not given consent for us to leave, for it is still very cold. When we went downstairs this morning some of the natives who are to accompany us were already here, and said, "Oh yes, it is much warmer!" But I think they were so anxious to be gone that their imagination had gotten the best of them, for it was anything but warmer. I am very tired tonight as I have tried to clean up all through the house, and I am sure Nellie must be so too for she has been up since two A.M. and is still at work. She has taken a notion to scrub the dining room and kitchen yet, so that if we should get off tomorrow the house will be clean throughout. Nellie thinks that it would be "agunkytuk" (too bad) to have the *cossacks*, "whites," come here and find a dirty house. Herman, Robert, and I were down to see Minnie's sister's poor little boy who is on the point of death. He has suffered so long and will soon find rest. I have kept him in good tasty food and picture books, in fact any and everything he wanted or that I thought would please him. But he eats nothing now, and has not for four days. The poor little sufferer, how good it will be for him to find relief at last. I hope we may be here to do the last for him.

We do not get so many rabbits now, and miss them very much. The rabbits have been so plentiful, but are now so thin we cannot eat many of them. We believe they are starving for all of the good brush has been eaten bare.

As Robert and I were walking up from the village this afternoon, he asked me to look closely again to see if his whiskers were growing. He thinks they must be just a little out. How anxious he is to be a man. He has a new pair of pants on a waist of the same material of which he is very proud. He says he will be like uncle Stecker now with his vest on. He wanted me to put a watch pocket in too, but as I was very busy and Master Rob has no watch, I did not comply with his wish, so his papa says that sometime when I am away he will put one in.

Bethel, Tuesday, December 9, 1902

Here we are at home again, and I may truly say it is good to be here and have the down-river trip of the past. We left Ougavig a week ago this morning. The first day we reached Tuluksak in the evening, and were received and entertained very kindly. How hungry we all were, and heartily enjoyed the snaky fish Waska's mother gave us. Herman held service in the evening, but I could not go as the children were tired and sleepy so I stayed to put them to bed. On Wednesday morning Herman gave communion, married one couple, and baptized Waska's baby. I named him Edward and held him during baptism. We then started for Akiak. The morning was quite cold, but the roads were good, and we made good time reaching Akiak about one o'clock where we found Mr. Stecker who had arrived about two hours earlier from Akiachak. We were all entertained by Kawagleg and wife, and treated royally. These dear kind people are so good to us always. They gave us their bed again where Robert, Elizabeth and I slept. Herman and Margaret slept on the floor beside us, Bro. Stecker just opposite on the one daughter's bed, Kawagleg near the door, and his wife on the fourth corner bed. So you may see we had a full house. The children thoroughly enjoyed themselves all the way home. Whether in camp or on the road, they were perfectly happy all the time for which I was very glad, for had they been fussy the trip had been much harder. We left Akiak just at daybreak in a snow storm which grew very disagreeable by the time we reached the next village. At Akiachak we took tea with Lonnie and wife. This is always starvation camp. While we are feasted at Akiak we never get much at Lonnie's place. After we had coffee and bread and butter, and the children [were] fed, we started for Bethel in the storm that had grown even worse than it was before dinner. We were on the road but a short time when it began to clear, but the snow had made the roads very rough and our "home run" was a prolonged one, for the sun went down just as we entered our last portage, and it was quite dark when we reached home. But here we found a warm clean house and an excellent meal waiting for us for we were expected to come even before. Mrs. Stecker had Sallie scrub the floors, and everything looked as though we had only just left it for a walk. Then Mrs. Hinz had such a nice dinner for us of fish pudding, roast rabbit, hot slaw, mashed potatoes, coffee, and two kinds of cake. Oh yes, and soup too. I can assure you this meal tasted good to such tired, hungry creatures as we were.

Monday, December 15, 1902

It seems impossible to find time to write. Here it is almost time for the first mail to leave for Nushagak. We are daily looking for it to arrive from St. Michael, and I have just a few letters ready. Company, nothing but company. I wonder that they do not think that we would like some of our own time. I told Nellie this morning that we would put off washing, and I would write all day. Soon I had a caller who took dinner and spent the rest of the day. So it goes. I prefer living at Ougavig where we were alone some of the time.

We have so many new neighbors now. There are two log cabins: one belonging to a Mr. Apple; the other to Mr. Homemeiter and Bloomer. Mr. Homemeiter is the gentlemen who painted such a pretty picture for me to give Herman last Xmas. Later in the Spring he painted one for me, and he is now busy getting one ready for Mr. Weinlick's birthday next Thursday. The missionaries are all glad to have this talented man among us. He is a very fine taxidermist, [and] we are all glad for the specimens he prepares for us. Then he helps to train the boys, or teach them rather, their Christmas pieces. He plays a cornet, and I the organ, and sing what little I can, but this is not much for my throat bothers me so much this Fall. The young Lap boy and Wasilli have been down for provisions, and left again last Saturday. We expect the father, mother, and sister for Christmas. Robert has taken such a notion to Mr. Homemeiter, and is trying very hard to draw and paint like him. Tonight he has been drawing all evening. He has one picture of two hills with trees all over them, [and] he says he will make the house tomorrow. I am really surprised to see how much real taste the little fellow displays in this line. Herman's mother was a very artistic woman, and it may be that Robert will be like her. He looks very much like her picture, and from what Herman says of his mother, he is like her in many ways.

Monday, December 22, 1902

We are very busy getting ready for Christmas. Tonight the school boys are popping and stringing corn, and no doubt they will string it from one end to the other of my house, but then Christmas comes only once in a year. I know Herman's fingers are just itching to make popcorn balls, but here I draw the line. I cannot stand his messing of boiled sugar even for once a year. His last year's work will last for many years. Robert has just gone to bed but not willingly. The dear little boy wants so much to stay up to help, but I want to dress a baby for him, so I told him tomorrow he might have some corn. I am real happy to see him go to bed without making a fuss about it, although his heart is with the corn popping. Today they found the baby I have made for him, and now he is asking whether or not I am going to make her a very nice dress. He is especially anxious that Elizabeth's baby (as he calls her) shall have a very pretty dress. Now you will wonder why I make a doll for my boy. Well he loves dolls just as much as the girls, and whenever he can hide one away until bedtime he will then sneak her to bed with him, and hug her to him and go to sleep. So he shall have one all his own. Herman is as good as nobody caring for a baby, so I am going to encourage Robert's interest in this line, so if he should some-day be a father he will, I hope, be some good to the mother. Elizabeth and Margaret fight over the one dirty baby left, so I am sure all [will] be happy when they get a new one.

The old Lap, his wife and daughter arrived today for Christmas. Robert, one of the native deer herders, has a young son. He has such a nice little wife, and he is very nice, so their baby must also be nice. Robert is asleep now so I must go to his baby.

December 24, 1902

MY DEAREST FATHER:

The Christmas exercises are at last over, the last little package to our different friends is ready to give, the tree trimmed with the children's gifts around it, and now for the first time in many days I breathe freely. Tomorrow we will have three white men to dine with us; Mr. Brown, Mr.

Dicky and Mr. Apple, and will furnish dinner for all of the native strangers, but this will be an easy task now that everything is ready, or nearly everything. I am almost worn out from working from early morn till late at night, and Herman has scolded until he is tired of doing so and I of hearing him, but I *am* glad that I have a Happy Xmas for my babies, and enough good things baked up to treat all of our friends. Tonight after chapel we had George, David, Christian and Jesse and wives come in to see our tree when we gave them each a bag of goodies and some little remembrance, Kawagleg also was here and we gave him a bag but no gift as we will send for him and his wife when he returns. How little it takes to make these people happy, and it makes us happy to see them so. Mary, George's wife, brought a pretty pair of boots for her little daughter (Elizabeth) whom she dearly loves. We miss Fannie so much; she always made presents for us all and was so happy over this time. Last year she gave her baby, Joe, and David's brother, Eddie (Elizabeth) such a pretty pair of boots. The exercises went off very nicely. Bro. Stecker held them, but the children were sleepy and grew very troublesome toward the last.

Mr. Brown has made a pair of wooden legs for Herman's patient of last Summer, and gave them to her for an Xmas gift. I hope they will prove satisfactory, for it is very hard for her to crawl around on her knees. I am too tired and sleepy to write more.

Hoping and praying with all my heart that a blessed happy Christmas may be yours.

Your loving daughter,

Ella

December 29, 1902

Yesterday was my thirty-first birthday, and for the greater part of the day it was not especially a happy one as Herman had left the day after Xmas for Ougavig for a ten day's trip, however I had planned to have the missionaries all over in the afternoon for cake and cocoa, and Mrs. Weinlick had promised to add ice-cream and cake as it was Anna Weinlick's fourth birthday. We were just talking it over, when Nellie ran in to say Herman was coming which proved to be true. The Ougavig and Tuluksak people are having a play so Herman said they could have their Christmas without him.[108] So David went on up while Herman returned, and afterall, my

---

108. Herman's refusal to visit the villagers during their winter festival period demonstrates the missionary's reluctance to participate in or encourage what they believed to be a heathen custom.

birthday turned out to be a pleasant one. I am glad Herman does not have to travel during this weather for it is frightfully cold. Mr. Stecker is at the coast, and I am sure he must be having a cold trip. Christmas was a very pleasant day. We had three white men for dinner, and the missionaries and two different men for supper. We furnished the dinner for the native strangers but George and David entertained them at their places so that all, natives and whites, might enjoy a happy Christmas. All of Elizabeth's relatives gave her presents. Bessie gave her a very pretty dress; David a dress; Mary a pair of boots; Christian a bag of fruit and cakes and Mrs. Weinlick, her God-mother, gave her a pretty red cashmere dress and a Turkish knit cap. The children were all very happy over their babies, especially Robert. He calls her Martha, and hugs her up-tight every night in bed. Herman gave me a beautiful pair of white deer boots, while I gave him eight new books which Miss MacManus had sent for me to give him. I sent to her for some toys and a Christmas gift for Herman last Winter, and all came in conveniently. This is a hard place to get Christmas presents. Elizabeth is having a hard time to go to sleep tonight, and I am getting tried sitting here beside her when there is so much to be done yet; school bread to be mixed and clothes to fold. Nellie is not with me now, only on Saturdays and wash days, and as Martha is a cripple, I have a great deal to do myself. My Birthday gift from Herman was a ten dollar gold piece with which I am to buy a new hat next year, but no I tell him. I will get something that will always last; something in silver for the table. Elizabeth has closed her little peepers so I will go.

Ella

Tuesday, January 6, 1903

You will think that I neglect you I write so seldom, but really Bethel is the worst place to get anything done. Someone is ever sitting around in the evenings, and during the daytime I am kept busy with my work. This is the longest cold spell we have ever known. For fifteen days it has been from thirty-four to forty-five below zero, and today a high wind makes it almost impossible to be out-of-doors. Mr. Stecker returned from the coast last Saturday having had a very hard trip, and not a satisfactory one. The natives had a great many complaints to make in all the villages over a story they seemed to have gotten from some source that the missionaries have put poison in all of the tea and tobacco. From where they get this report we know not, but it seems they are all always glad for all of the tea and tobacco they can get. Mr. Stecker talked Dutch to them anyway for believing such a story. Then at Quinhagak the night they were to have had communion, a native heathen dealt out ice-cream in the *Kashima*, which disgusted Mr. Stecker so he did not give communion. The native villages are all having their plays now and at such times it seems even our Christians put their God second. Our folks left here on one of the coldest days for Paimiut for the play, and I am sure had one of them been asked to make a trip on such a day for some other reason it would have been, "It is too bad! But the weather is too cold!" I wish the natives could be induced to give up some of their plays, for they give nearly everything away they have. But of course they are not like white people to look out for the future, they simply live for today and let tomorrow take care of itself, and are always the worse for it![109]

The mail carrier has not yet been heard from. Of course we all have our own ideas just why he does not come but I dare say the reason for not coming will be different than we have planned. If only he has not come to harm on the new ice on the Yukon. We had such a late Fall, and the first mail is billed to leave St. Michael on the first of December. We are all anxious about the present cold spell, and fear someone or ones are suffering from the cold. This is not like other years for no one saw the traders and missionaries go or come. We will soon begin to look for the second mail.

Wednesday, January 7, 1903

The wind is still blowing a perfect gale. We have had hard work to keep warm today. [We] have closed the sitting room, and are sitting and eating in our bedroom to save wood. But when this wind has spent its fury we hope to have it pleasant. The thermometer has gone up twenty-two degrees since yesterday morning, but with such a gale it seems far colder. I am very glad Herman is at home now for during such weather I am worried if he is from home.

---

109. Although many Yup'ik Eskimo outwardly embraced Christianity, some contemporary native clergy believe that in so doing the Yup'ik people never actually gave up their traditional beliefs. Instead of an all or nothing philosophy, "Christianity simply gave new form to old beliefs, [and] that in effect there has been no change" (Fienup-Riordan 1990, 69). To the early Moravian missionaries the Eskimos' desire to maintain traditional customs meant they were not fully committed to Christianity.

January 18, 1903

How shamefully I am neglecting your journal since we returned to busy Bethel. I have my work to do now, and since last Sunday have been trying to write some letters, so my time has been more than full. A week ago today, January 11, the mail arrived from St. Michael having been on the way since December 8. A Mr. Campbell, who claims to be one of the contractors, brought it. He had only six dogs and they not the best, and was one of the worst looking specimens we ever saw on such an expedition. Most of us doubt the truth of the statement that he is a contractor. He is probably only a carrier and a poor one at that. He had frozen one foot, though not badly enough to make traveling disagreeable. Though the mail was nearly a month late, he took his time while here and added only one more dog to his outfit. Mr. Koltchoff, our old friend, is to bring the second mail due now, but the past few days have been very stormy which may delay him. Mr. Koltchoff is an old-timer and will make all the time there is to be made. Mr. K. sent with the mail carrier each of the little girls and Anna Weinlick, a pretty handkerchief and Robert a pretty knife, and chewing gum for them all. It is needless to say, they all consider Mr. Koltchoff a very nice man. Robert very often asks me if I do not think him very nice. The children all, even to Elizabeth, are talking very much about the states now. Robert says he will not go to school for he does not like the boys and the boss down there. I am anxious that Robert gets in school next year for he is trying to write and draw all of his time of late. Margaret thinks there are plenty of children and papas and mamas down there, and nice dolls and dishes. Elizabeth said this morning, "Me too states, mama?" The little midget talks like a magpie from morning till night. She tells everybody that she is very bad in chapel which I am sorry to say is sometimes true. I made the dress David gave her for Xmas, and she wears the boots Mary gave her, and she tells everyone who asks her who gave them [to] her, that her brother gave the dress and her Anna the boots. Nellie often calls her "mother," and baby always answers her. She truly is rich in relatives. Of late baby is "I'm mama's darling," only when she wants to tease me she says, "I'm papa's boy." She is very polite just at present, saying please for everything she asks for, and thank you for all she gets. I hope she will ever be so.

The natives have been over the tundra to attend another play [and] returned today. George got in just in time to interpret for Herman in evening chapel. Mr. Stecker preached an English sermon this A.M. as he had no interpreter, and I for one was glad to hear something altogether English again. We are very fond of Bro. and Sr. Stecker, and find it a true pleasure to work with and for our superintendent. And then we are very glad to be relieved of this work too, for when Herman was superintendent it was much more work for him, and a little more for me as well. Of course we all always have plenty to do, but the hum drum work of managing everything is more than all the rest.

Monday, January 19, 1903

Another little native has entered into rest. Andrew's fourth baby, after suffering many months, passed away last night about eleven o'clock. After he had gone they sent for Herman to come over. He had done all he could for the poor little fellow, and I guess the parents wanted to see some sympathetic face in their house of trouble even though medicine could do no more. How my heart aches for the poor mother. She has had such nice children, and has had to part with them all, and all have died from the same trouble, consumption. But this is the way all of the poor native babies go, the old folks are going one by one and scarcely a baby lives to fill their places.

Herman is holding council with the Mountain Boy, David's father-in-law, in regard to his daughter becoming a Moravian. Before David married her the father gave his full consent to the marriage as well as the girl belonging to our church, but last Fall he sent word that she was never to take communion with us. This does not look well for a helper's wife to belong to one church and he to another.

I wish you were here to hear Robert talk to a deaf and dumb boy from the Mountain Village. He is asking him where he will sleep tonight and all sorts of questions, and is altogether out of patience that he does not answer. This mute is a very nice boy, poor fellow, he tries so hard to talk. I pity him so much. Another of our friends, one of the first we knew, Friday as Herman calls him, is visiting here also. He always seems to feel that he belongs to Herman, and always comes to us when here. We are always glad when our native friends come, so many have died during the past two years, and of those who are left few come as they have many other places to go now, and I cannot but feel that many of our people are drifting away from us, and growing indifferent.

Tuesday, January 20, 1903

The men were all out hunting today, all but Mr. Weinlick, but when it comes to hunting we never count him a man for he seldom goes. When he does, the other men have to jolly him up to it. But the hunt today was not much of a success. Herman got one rabbit, Mr. Stecker none, and Mr. Hinz got cold feet and had to come home. Jim, our adopted boy, shot two and one grouse. We really get hungry for fresh meat here. Ougavig is much the better place to live. There we had an abundance of fresh meat and fish. Nellie and Bessie were in to see their relatives tonight, and how glad the little chic was to see them, she fairly flew into Nellie's arms. Then she got down, went over to Bessie and said, "Hurry up and sing, I want to dance," so Bessie sung and Elizabeth danced. How I wish you had our darling baby with you. If you had, you would never get lonely; she is the liveliest little midget I ever knew. Just now she is singing as loud as she can possibly sing.

Herman's talk with the Mountain Boy resulted in nothing special. He however, said that when he gave his daughter to David he gave her to us, and he knew we would love her and teach her. He claims to be willing that she shall be a Moravian. But he also said that all of the villagers wish her to stay in the church in which she was brought up, the Greek church. They claim that they heard a voice in the mountains crying unto them to remain faithful to their own church. The trick is I think, they are afraid to belong to us. This is a very superstitious people, the heathen at least, and here the Greeks are no better for all they are taught is to cross themselves before eating, and bow and cross before the pictures of the Savior or the Virgin Mary, and are told that if they are Greeks they will go to Heaven. This is all they are taught, [and] that all other churches are wrong. Some years ago our helper there was sick and delirious or crazy for sometime. The people there claimed that the medicine or the instruction from here put the devil into him. It was at that time that they tried to kill John [Kilbuck] and afterward took the sick man out and let the dogs kill him. The Mountain Boy is the one who tried to kill John, and afterward led his brother out to his death. He is very sorry for all that happened, and for many years has been friendly toward all of the missionaries, but we believe they are just superstitious enough to be afraid to belong to another church lest their old trouble occur again. I am very sorry too that they are not Christians, for they are a very nice thrifty village, and such fine looking Eskimo.

Monday, January 26, 1903

This is Robert's sixth birthday. I wanted to have a dinner for him, but this morning we had such a storm no one could or would go out who could help it. Everyone was much concerned about stove pipes burning out, (such days are always the worst for that,) since last Saturday when Weinlick's house caught fire back of the sitting room stove, and everybody had to work long and hard before it was gotten under headway, so we are all on the look-out. Really we have only Providence to thank that two families, if not all of us, have homes and provisions now. Mr. Weinlick and Hinz who live in the house, yes, and the school boys, had given up the fight and were throwing their things out right and left. Were it not for Bro. Stecker and Herman the house would have surely gone. Bro. Stecker went upstairs and threw out some burning things and tried in a dense smoke to find just where the fire was while Herman tore the partition and ceiling out and threw water on the fire. Finally they did succeed in getting it out. When Mr. Weinlick was told it would be soon out he ran for a pail of water and threw it on, well, this exact pail did the work. It was "Betty and I killed the Bar." Mr. Stecker had inhaled so much smoke he had to go to bed for the greater part of the day, and is still feeling the effects of it. It is a blessing that it did not catch in the night for all then would have gone if some lives had not been lost. When we were told that Weinlick's house was on fire we thought little about it, for it is such an old story. We rather look for the alarm every so often.

The mail came in from St. Michael just after the fire excitement on Saturday, and leaves here tomorrow morning by Mr. Koltchoff.

But back to Robert's birthday. He had a very good time We gave him a jumping rope, a box of puzzle blocks and a pair of deer skin boots, and I made him a very nice cake with six lighted candles on. Then tonight, he had all of the school boys to eat supper with him, so he was very happy. Tomorrow I will try to have something for the missionaries; we have promised Robert to serve at least ice-cream.

I am very miserable just now from an abscess forming at the root of a broken tooth. My face is very swollen and painful. Herman wants to lance it or pull the offender, but I am resisting for my jaw is sore enough without that. I want to have a little ether, and Herman I think will give it although he seriously objects.

Tuesday, January 27, 1903

The mail left this A.M. and after the excitement was over Herman gave me ether and extracted my tooth, or rather the root, and then lanced the abscess inside (it was trying to break on the outside) and since, I have experienced a great deal of relief. This morning when I awoke I could scarcely bear to have my jaw touched while tonight, while still swollen, it feels almost well again. I took the ether very nicely, and although I knew everything that was going on, I felt no pain whatever. When Herman called for the knife I at first thought I would yell for fear it *would* hurt. Then I thought, well maybe it will not hurt much, and the next thing I knew Herman told his assistants to turn me on my side to let the discharge run out, and all was over. Oh, how good I felt too. I felt just like sleeping, it was such a pleasant dreamy feeling that ether gave to me.

Herman has not been feeling very well all day. He has evidently taken cold in some way, [and] he has some fever tonight and pain through the head and eyes, and is lying down with a pillow over his eyes as the light hurts them.

A native came in from the tundra today, and reports that a woman returning home by night from a play, was frozen from her feet to waist and died four days later. We fully expected to have some such reports for it was so very cold for awhile, and especially during the time of the plays between the different villages.

Poor Robert has not had his birthday celebration yet, but tomorrow is Mrs. Joaquin's birthday, and we expect to have a great time together in the evening in honor of both.

February 18, 1903

Nearly a month since I wrote in your poor old journal, but really there has been little to write about, save the very cold weather that lasted from before Christmas until a week ago, when in one night the mercury went up eighty degrees. For three days before it moderated we had from forty-eight to fifty-five below zero. As yet we have heard of no freezing, thank God for this. So many suffered from cold last Winter.

Herman left today for the up-river communion trip and will be gone probably ten days. He has waited so long for the outside mail to come in, but it does look as though it will never come, so Herman started without it. He may yet return before it gets here. The third and last mail from St. Michael is overdue too. Everybody would like the states mail to get in so letters might be answered by the last out-going, but it seems we are to be disappointed in this. I have not written one letter for the last mail, but Herman has written a great many.

My face is perfectly well again In fact it never troubled me after the abscess was lanced and the offender extracted.

We had a very pleasant evening on Mrs. Joaquin's birthday at our house in honor [of] Mrs. J.'s and Robert's birthdays. Robert was allowed to stay up of course, and was very happy especially over the ice-cream, but finally grew tired [and] wanted to go to bed.

I miss Herman so much tonight. I always do the first few days, but finally grow somewhat accustomed to being a grass-widow. Herman even took Laddie. He has always been our protector, and I feel lost without him. Foxie is here and a good watch dog. He always makes a great noise if anyone comes around. Of course I am not afraid, but I never like to be alone with the children, lest some of us get sick, but then we have always been alright and I trust will be in the future.

Friday, February 20, 1903

This is baby Hinz's first birthday, and such a large child. I never saw one so large for his age. I tell Mr. Hinz that is because he is an American.

Elizabeth is in bed, but not asleep, and telling me to hurry and come. She is looking at a magazine and talking partly in native and partly in English. She says, "Look at it! I guess machine! My picture!" Just now she is having prayer meeting. She sings, then raises her little hands and pronounces the benediction, says Amen, and begins all over again. Of late all I say to her she answers "All right mama," or "Jes (yes) mama." Nellie has a particular song she sings to her when she rocks her to sleep, and the little midget sings a part of it to her baby. She also tries to sing "Silent Night," and "Morning Star," but does not get very far with them. We think her the sweetest babe of all, but then Herman says the last is always the sweetest, and I guess its so.

Robert goes to school everyday, but of course Mr. Weinlick has enough to do without bothering with him, so he gives him all the paper and pencils he can use, so Robert spends most of his time drawing pictures. Mr. Weinlick says he uses a tablet about every three days. Last night he drew a picture of his papa he thought a master-piece, but then said papa looked much like a monkey with a pipe in his mouth.

Margaret, though much of the time happy, is not strong. I thought tonight when I put her to bed, how delicate she looks. We are very anxious to get her in a different climate, and hope it may prove a benefit to her. She was always so strong and well until she had first grippe, followed by measles and later in the year, whooping cough. Just two years ago we were all having our own trials with this terrible cough. It will be two years tomorrow night that Mrs. Weinlick's baby boy died of it. I hope we may be spared another trial of whooping-cough in our family. I often look at baby and think of the time when I was sure she was dead. When she breathed again it was as though she had been given back from the dead. Truly it is wonderful how so tiny a babe could go through so much and live. All I could do for her was to give her the best of care I knew how to give, and stuff her on milk and brandy. But the dear little chic is a picture of health and happiness now.

Saturday, February 21, 1903

Neck arrived today from Akiagamuit (now called by our properly speaking Germans, Akiagak) and brought a note from Herman whom he met between Akiachak and Akiak. The trail is very heavy, and Herman may return from Akiak. (It does me good to write, and especially so, to speak the name of the village the old way, much to the disgust, no doubt, of our two bright lights on the water.) It is sometimes amusing, and many times disgusting, to note how hard these two Labrador and Greenland men are trying to make all over the natives, and how utterly they fail for the natives when by themselves still speak their old way and probably will with only two to change it.[110] They have David and George and some of the other boys to help them when they can get them, and then they will ask how to say this or that. The boys will tell them, but no, that cannot be right, is it not so and so? No, they will say it is as I said. No, no, it must be, so and so, then the boys simply say nothing. Then, it must be so and so, it cannot be otherwise, now is it not? And then, either because the boys don't care, or are afraid, they will say, well perhaps it is. And then the great student has learned a wonderful thing. No one ever found it out before, and the one will run over to the other and tell the other one the wonderful

---

110. The "Labrador man" was Reverend G. Adolph Stecker who prior to his arrival in Alaska had spent sixteen years as a missionary in Labrador. The "Greenland man" was Reverend Ernst Paul Zucher who prior to his arrival in Alaska had spent twelve years working with the Natives in Greenland (Schwalbe 1985, 86 and 124).

discovery. But of course they do not know what the natives say of them. David says they are learning another language, and he guesses it is all right, but the natives will not understand them. I wish for their own sakes they would try to speak this language as this people speak it, and for the work's sake too, for they make themselves very conspicuous, and then without the slightest doubt the people are drifting away from us. It makes my heart ache to note the change in our people. They are nothing like they once were. They scarcely ever come from the villages unless it is for medicine or else in traveling they have to pass this way. I hope Herman will not turn back on this trip even if the roads are heavy, for I think the people need more work done among them, and then this will be the last time Herman will see many of them before we go out. Andrew at Ougavig is very anxious to see the doctor as his wife is very ill. She was very miserable when we left last Fall.

The children talk of nothing but the states. This morning Margaret wanted to know if the picture I have on my desk of Katie Kilbuck was Margaret. When I told her who it was, she said then she is a states girl? Robert wanted to know if the states people would be afraid of us, and I told him they probably would be. Margaret wanted to know if they are bashful. Baby simply looks on and listens, now and then putting in an exclamation point.

Sunday, February 22, 1903

Another windy day. The wind blows incessantly, but it is not cold, so for this we are thankful. Our eyes are ever looking down the river toward the gap where all teams come through bound for Bethel. Just as soon as one is sighted out go the field-glasses, and everyone starts to talk mail. But no, we look in vain. Mrs. Stecker, I am sure, every few minutes during the day goes to her south window and looks down the river. I tell her it is becoming second nature with her.

Elizabeth is in the kitchen entertaining callers. She is telling them all sorts of things. I was amused at her this morning. Martha was just about to drink tea, and Elizabeth asked her if she had prayed yet. Now she said, go ahead and pray, and she folded her hands, but Martha I guess was bashful, but Beth kept at her. She said my mama says, "Come Lord Jesus" and you must too, now hurry up about it.

Evening: Mrs. Weinlick came to the door this evening and said a light seemed to be coming from down river. We *all* ran out to see of course. All was excitement, [and] we could scarcely wait for the team to arrive, but finally it did get here, and it *was* the mail. But all are disappointed and angry, for Mr. Rock, who is Post Master, refused to open the mail bags, only the one addressed to Nushagak, so only a very few stray letters came for all; two for Herman and a German paper, and nothing for me. I have not been out but Mrs. Weinlick says the men, white missionaries included, are furious at Mr. Rock. I am disappointed, not a word from home even, but I know Mr. Rock too well to get angry or be surprised at all, it does not pay for one could be so many times. He is so unobliging in every respect.

Emmet came from Ohogamiut with a note from Herman to send to his father and brother who have been sick all Winter, some flour, mush stuff and rice. There is no one to support the family but Emmet, and he only a boy. His father is a staunch friend of ours, and is welcome to something to help him to gain strength. Herman has gone to Ougavig, for which I am very happy, for the natives are being neglected this year and we have so many missionaries too. But now that the mail is in, more plans can be made as Mr. Stecker thought something might have to be answered by the last out-going mail.

Tuesday, February 24, 1903

The mail left for St. Michael this A.M. and about two hours later the mail from there arrived at Bethel by a special carrier sent out by the mail clerk, a Mr. Brunell. He will leave tomorrow morning for Katmai. Mrs. Stecker and I made baking powder biscuits and crullers for him this afternoon for the trail.

Thursday, February 26, 1903

Herman came home about noon today after a very hard trip. He or David had to go ahead of the dogs on snow shoes much of the way up and back, but the trip was as far as the work goes, a very pleasant one. These communion trips are always blessed ones both to the people as well as the missionary, and require much thought and prayer on the part of the latter, in whom the natives have such confidence and come to him with all of their troubles to be guided by him in many ways, and many times he must decide for them whether or not they are fit to partake of the Lord's

Supper. This will be the last trip of the kind among our up-river natives until next Fall as they are soon all going to the mountains. Herman baptized both Lomuck's and Souil's babies. At the parent's request they were both named Mary.

March 4, 1903

Mr. Koltchoff arrived about noon today with the second mail. This time we fared better. I had four letters; two from Sadie, one from you, and one from Miss Whitaker. Herman also received several but none from home.

March 5, 1903

Mr. Koltchoff left this A.M. for St. Michael. Mr. Homemeiter, who has been living here since last October, went with him where he expects to get work for next Summer. Mr. Brown, who has been living here for two years, will leave soon for either St. Michael or Nushagak. Mr. Watson, a nice old man who has been here since Fall, will go with him thus we are losing many of our neighbors.

Thursday, March 12, 1903

Mr. Lind and Mr. Kemp, Mr. L's prospective son-in-law, arrived from up-river today for a visit. Mr. Lind at one time was a (good pretending) member of our church, but since he lives up river his life from all reports will not bear close inspection. It is said that he, his wife and oldest son and daughter and his relatives get thoroughly drunk whenever liquor can be gotten, then follows a general fuss with fists or knives. Mr. Kemp tells all this and yet he seeks to win the hand of the disreputable girl. The Catholic fathers will not allow the marriage as Mr. Kemp is a divorced man. I am more than glad that Mr. Lind is no longer a near neighbor of ours. When here in Summer he has offered some of our best boys whiskey to drink. We have a commissioner on the river now who, though not an especially good man himself, dislikes Mr. Lind, and I trust he will enforce the law on him in regard to giving or selling intoxicating drinks to the natives. I for one would be glad to see such a man landed in jail.

The Bethel Moravian congregation. Ella, wearing a white blouse and dark
skirt, can be seen in front at left looking at Robert and Margaret.
(Courtesy, Alaska and Polar Regions Department, University of Alaska Fairbanks,
Joseph Romig Collection, acc. #90-043-200N)

Sunday, March 15, 1903

We had a very pretty service in Church this morning when sixteen
boys and girls were confirmed, and six baptized. Mr. Hinz conducted the
entire service in native. Tonight Mr. Stecker administered the Holy communion. Mr. Hinz is making rapid progress in the language. In many
ways he is narrow minded on the language in as much as he thinks it has
never been properly spoken before, by whites or natives, but in time he
will see that the only thing to do is to adopt as it is spoken by everyone
else in Alaska. It will be with him like many others in this world, who
when they know the least consider themselves wonderfully clever. Mr.
Hinz truly deserves much praise for he studies from morning till night
and almost from night till morning, and of course he will in time master
the Eskimo [language]. But thus far, there has been no one who has won
his way so truly into the hearts of these people as did John [Kilbuck].
How dearly these people loved and still love their first leader, but it is

because he first loved them. I sometimes think where many of the missionaries fail today is in a lack of love as spoken of in the 13th Chapter of 1st Corinthians.[111] Truly a missionary does give all that he has, or better perhaps, all that he might have, and in fact may do all that is spoken of in this chapter, but do we all love, truly love, our people as we should? I am sure that in this, neither John nor Edith fell short. And it is my daily prayer that I too may love them enough.

Wedneday, March 18, 1903

The third mail arrived here this morning. I received no letters, Herman four: one from Bishop Oerter in which we are granted a furlough, and arrangements are made for it; and one letter from Herman's father; another from Edith to both of us; and the other, I have forgotten from whom.[112] Helmich's are coming back according to Bro. Oerter's letter.

Saturday, March 21, 1903

Herman and George left for Quinhagak this morning on a missionary trip. They intended leaving yesterday but the day was very stormy. The trail is very heavy after much snow falling, and Herman expects a hard trip.

Sunday, March 22, 1903

Mr. Brunell, the special mail carrier for the last mail out, and Christian arrived today from Nushagak. They camped with Herman last night at a little village a short day's run from here. Today has been an ugly one, the wind has blown a perfect gale all day. I am afraid Herman could not travel, and if he did, he has had a very hard day.

Nellie seems very happy that Christian is home again. He brought her some candy and a very pretty blue silk handkerchief, and himself a pair of shoes. I made a pair of wool pants last week that I had given him at Christmas, and as soon as he had eaten he dressed up in the new shoes

---

111. In this Chapter, Paul extols the importance of charity—Charity, a pure love, excels and exceeds almost all else.

112. A furlough was generally granted by the church as a rest for a year after which continued service was expected. Since Herman's seven year commitment was fulfilled in the summer of 1903, it is unclear why he was advised a "furlough" had been approved. It is possible that Herman had already presented his idea to operate a church-sponsored hospital at Nushagak after a year in the States.

and pants. Nellie and Christian are a very happy pair, and I too am very glad to see them thus. Jessie and Bessie are not so, but Bessie is the more to be pitied for while she can scold very well, she is not lazy, while Jessie is very good natured and equally lazy, in fact very provokingly so, and sometimes one can hardly blame Bessie for scolding. Bessie with her sewing and basket making, I am sure, buys most of the tea and sugar for the family.

Carmel Mission, Nushagak River, Alaska, December 30, 1904[113]

MY DARLING CHILDREN:

I have just run across this journal begun to grandpa over two years ago, and never finished it as you see. I thought sometime it would be interesting to you to read over some of our doing while yet together on the dear old Kuskokwim River, so am beginning your new journal here, having just closed a poor little excuse of one and sent it off for the states this morning.[114]

The past two weeks have been such busy ones for me, scarcely one night in that time have we gone to bed until after midnight preparing for a happy Christmas for those around us. The mail came in from the states a day before Christmas, the mail from the North three days later, and while we were *very very* happy to get good news from our two little folks, yet it gave me no time at this busy season to write one letter to the states not even to dear grandma, Mrs. Prizer, and Aunt Eva who are doing so much for you. There was simply no time. I have all of my housework to do, and so many callers to entertain that no time for writing has been allowed. The mail will leave for the Kuskokwim tomorrow then we trust there will be a lull, and I hope time for me to write for the next mail a month hence. We had long letters from Bethel. All there, natives and missionaries seem to miss us very much, or rather their doctor, and would like us to come back. Mr. and Mrs. Weinlick have another little girl. Annie is a big girl they say and often speaks of you. Mr. Weinlick asks about his boy Robert, and says he misses you very much. They have a very large

---

113. The Romigs left Alaska in the summer of 1903. In June 1904, they returned to the Nushagak River region where Herman operated a church sponsored hospital for the Natives and cannery workers in the area.

114. Robert and Margaret remained in the States with friends and relatives when Herman, Ella, and Elizabeth returned to Alaska to live at Carmel. Apparently the recently completed journal of which Ella spoke has not survived, thus the gap of over a year and a half in the material presented here.

school at Bethel now. Over fifty boarding scholars. Mr. and Mrs. Helmich live in our old house and have the girls, while Mr. [and Mrs.] Weinlick have the boys in their home and the large school building. I am sure they must be very busy with so many children to care for.

David's boy Johnnie, with whom Robert used to play, they say is a big boy now going to school every day.

Mr. and Mrs. Schoechert who live at Quinhagak, have a very dear little girl baby. I am sure Marie and Emily will be very happy to hear of a little new sister.

Papa is in the hospital dressing a native who was accidentally shot through the foot some weeks ago, and when he is through we are going out for a walk and to make some calls. So will not write more this time. I only wanted to make a beginning in your journal.

Affectionately,

Mother

January 1, 1905

MY DEAR ROBERT AND MARGARET:

May you both have a blessed happy New Year. We have thought of you and talked much of you today, and wonder what kind of a time you have had. Doubtless a very happy time. We have had a very pleasant time here at home. Mr. Kahlen, papa, Mrs. McClain, one of our white neighbors, myself and our two boys, George, and Moses, stayed up to watch the new year in. Bro. Zucher [was] too tired, and we too were very tired, but January first comes only once a year, so we stayed up to wish one another a Happy New Year as soon as the clock struck twelve. The boys and Mr. Kahlen went out and fired a few shots, and someone from the village answered. All said these few shots [were] as quiet as though no new year had come.

Last year, Papa, Aunt Sadie, Mrs. Fischer, a friend from Philadelphia, and I were at an annual show in Philadelphia on New Year's Eve after which we walked around looking at the beautifully illuminated buildings throughout the day, many of which were fine indeed especially the Public building that was almost [aglow] with electric lights from one end to the other. And when the many clocks struck the hour of twelve, bells rung, cannons were fired wherever permissible and all kinds of hideous noises were afloat. Quite a different celebration from that of last night here. A year ago today we stood on Broad Street about two hours waiting for and watching a large parade, had dinner at the "Young Friend Association," and in the afternoon we went to the Zoological Garden, Mr. Kahlen accompanying us. In the evening we had to return to Bethlehem in a heavy snow storm, as papa had to speak in the Nazareth church the following day. Aunt Sadie was to return to Wilkes-Barre on the eight P.M. train and missed it, so had to wait until the eleven getting in about three A.M., and had to be driven to Forty Fort in a cab at that hour for her school had to open on the second. This ended her first visit to the dear old city of "Brotherly Love."

Tomorrow will be our dear baby Elizabeth's fourth birthday, and once more I am going to make an effort to celebrate. The mail came on my birthday spoiling all of my plans for the day. Elizabeth told Mr. Tonie that she would have a large cake with four pretty candles on it, and he was to come over to dinner and she would give him two of her candles. Mr. Tonie was over to supper last night and we had, and enjoyed so very much, corn meal [indecipherable], papa and Mr. Tonie said the best they had ever eaten. How good it is to have milk and eggs. So many good things can be made with this addition. Tonight we had eggs for supper, the first in three months. Bossie gives very little milk now and will soon give none at all. How we will miss it, especially papa and Snooks.[115]

Papa had the service this morning, and Peter, one of our small school boys interpreted. Chris always did the interpreting, and we miss him very much since he is gone, but Peter did very well for the first time. Peter is George's younger brother. Papa asked George to interpret for him some time ago, but he was too timid to even try. But I think papa just struck the key note today toward George's interpreting, for he said tonight that he could interpret if the doctor would tell him the lesson before hand. He was just a little bit jealous, don't you think so? I was real glad to see Peter try. We can all do a great deal by just trying, and doing our best. No one ever expects more of us than our best.

Elizabeth just put her baby's arms around my neck and said she wanted to kiss me. When I had kissed her she said, "Now, that is because baby wants some clothes." Dear baby, I *must* dress her.

Papa, Mr. Kahlen and Mr. Guinther are all talking, and Snooks jarring my table, so I must stop for tonight.

Wishing you both a blessed Happy New Year.

Affectionately,

Mother

---

115. Nickname for Elizabeth.

Monday, January 2, 1905

Elizabeth has had such a happy birthday, and is now fast asleep with her Buster Brown, one of her birthday gifts. She had quite a number of presents. Mr. Guinther gave her a silk handkerchief and two cans of fruit; a white man from the other side of the river, Mr. Johnson (or as he is called "Klondike Johnson") gave her two dollars and a half in money; another white man, Mr. Fluer, gave her fifty cents; and Tall Olga, one of her very dear friends, gave her a bead cushion and a breast pin. Mrs. Zucher gave her a new red hood and a box of candy. I made a large cake with four candles on [it] and at dinner she lit them, and when Mr. and Mrs. Zucher and Mr. Guinther came to dinner Elizabeth took them to the dining room to see her "pretty birthday," as she called her cake. You both always called your cakes your "birthdays," do you remember? I wish you could have seen Elizabeth all day. She is always very happy, but today she sang and danced all day, and I am sure she and Buster were very tired when they went to bed. As soon as she opened her eyes this morning she said, "Mama is I four years old now?" I said, "Yes darling, you are four years old now." Then she said, "I am not three then, is I?" She is very proud of the fact that she is four years old. Margaret has just passed her sixth birthday and Robert's will soon be here too, and just think my boy will be eight years old. It makes mama feel older to think of having such a big boy and girl. And I guess you both grow so much that by the time we see you again we will hardly know you. Won't you laugh at papa and mama though, if they see you and [do] not know you? That *will* be a joke, won't it?

Papa is writing an article for a paper, and when I asked him, "How long will you be writing?" he said, "Well not until I am through will I stop if it takes all night, for I am in a writing mood." It *would* be real funny if papa were to stay up all night to write, for he never did such a thing. I am sure he likes sleep too well, and then it would not be wise either, for we need sleep as well as food. But it does make me laugh to hear papa talk of staying up all night. Mr. Zucher stayed up several nights last week to write, and poor man, he looks tired yet.

Moses and George took Nellie (the horse) for the first time for water today, and handled her very well too. Nearly everyone is afraid of Nellie, for she is pretty frisky, but now since Chris left, someone must get water and I am glad Moses and George did so well. Moses used to be one of our school boys on the Kuskokwim, and is a very nice boy. Maybe you remember him yet? He and George live with us and sleep upstairs. Moses says he is afraid to sleep upstairs alone. Papa is going to fix a bell up in their room with a string to pull it in our room so that we can awaken them in the morning to start fires. Moses and George think it a joke now, but maybe they will not see the joke when they have to get up every morning to start the fires.

I taught the children to play Muggino with the "Flinch" cards to-night (Robert and Mrs. Luring used to call it "Bamboozle") and they are having a fine time over in the girl's room. But papa is all through with his article (10:30 P.M.) and is hungry, so I must away to the pantry.

Good night

Mama

Tuesday, January 3, 1905

While the boys are washing for me, I will write a little in your journal for I am going to try real hard to write often from now on. We have not washed for over three weeks, and are washing now because our clothes are all soiled not because we want to. But now that Christmas and New Year and our birthdays are past we must get down to work again.

Papa and Mr. Kahlen are over in the new school-house painting and making ready to begin school over there in a few days. I guess Elizabeth will miss running over to school. She could always run through the halls to the old school-room, but now that she must go out of doors it will not be so easy. The new school-room is the old log house next to Mr. Guinther, and is a very cozy room.

Elizabeth is out with the boys dressing up in the soiled clothes from the basket. She has church, goes to Lancaster and "Millinois" to visit Robert, Margaret and Rachel, and part of the time plays school. George asked her how old she was this A.M. and she said twelve hundred, and George told her she was quite a young lady. Papa always bites her ear until she says she loves him twelve hundred so she thinks that *the* number for everything.

Monday, January 9, 1905

Well, the great washing and ironing days are past, and a goodly number of clothes [are] together for another day's washing. I washed for two days, and on the evening of the second day George very kindly offered to iron everything for me if I would trust him. Of course I let him help me for as he said I was very tired, so I played Crokinole with papa, Mr. Lori and Mr. Kahlen until ten o'clock and missed nearly every shot, then I left them in disgust and went to the ironing and we ironed until nearly two o'clock. George wanted to stay up all night and finish, he thought it great sport, and he did *very* well too. But I insisted upon his going to bed for he is not very strong and needs rest. As for Crokinole, a few nights after we all played again and papa and I won four out of five games, then we changed partners, and Mr. K. and I won two games. Of course I felt better over my success.

Mr. Lori has a very severe cold and feels miserable so we had him visit with us yesterday, and he spent this evening with us. We are always glad to see him, he is very jolly company, and then he is very lonely over home. His talk now is all about visiting Olga next year, and is making all his plans to go out. I am sure Olga will be very glad to see him too.

Papa, Elizabeth and I are going down to Clarks Cannery to visit Mr. and Mrs. Nicolson tomorrow if it is a nice day. We are having very fine mild weather for about a week, and if it continues we will enjoy this little three hours run, and a little change for two days. We expect to come back the following day.

Papa has had a very large sled made for the deer, and we had a great time testing it last Friday. There were fifteen people in the sled and nineteen dogs to pull us (We have no deer yet), and we all enjoyed the sport. Of course when we turned around the dogs were in a mess, and [they] had a good all-around fight, but that was part of the sport. Papa has made a new tent to go over the sled, and has a peep hole all ready to put up a stove, and says we will camp in the sled when on trips. Won't that be fun though?

Thursday, January 26, 1905.

MY DEAR ROBERT AND MARGARET:

This is my precious boy's eighth birthday, and all day I have been thinking of him, in fact both of you, and wish you were here that we might celebrate it together, and I am sure we would have a fine day together. One thing I am sure we would do, that is, we would take a ride in our fine reindeer sled for it is a most perfect day, and then of course, we would have a party too, but sometime we will all be together again I hope, and can have many happy birthdays. Papa, Elizabeth, George, Moses and I were all down at Clarks and had a fine time, and lovely weather. Returned the following day. When we were ready to start for home we found that four of our dogs had run away, so we made slower time for awhile, but when we were a few miles on our way Billie Powers came along with the run away dogs (they had come all the way home) so we made good time. We stopped at Mittendorff's and had coffee. A few yards farther on a white man called papa in to see his sick wife, and finally just about sundown, we arrived at home where Mrs. Zucher had a fine supper for us. The two following days I was busy with my work and making storm parkas for papa and Mr. Kahlen and a pair of trousers for Elizabeth to wear with her coat and vest, and on Saturday we went to the other side of the river where we had a very pleasant time until Tuesday when we returned, as it was Mr. Zucher's birth-day. We were all very sorry that we had not gotten off sooner or that Mr. Zucher had not been born a few days later, for everybody wanted us to stay longer, and we wanted very much to stay longer. But I must tell you about the trip some other time for I must go to my supper now. We have two patients in our hospital now, and it takes me just about all of my time to cook and wash dishes for four big men eat a little. Our patients' appetites are not sick, and I am very glad too for I would rather cook for hearty eaters than people with delicate or fussy appetites. George and Moses are down to the water hole filling cans for ice for which they get ten cents per can from papa, but in the meantime I must do all the work alone for nothing. But I must go, for we have chapel after supper.

So goodnight. May my darling boy have many very happy birthdays.

Mama

Sunday, February 5, 1905

MY DEAR CHILDREN:

Both patients are gone, one much better, the other, poor man, he has a trouble that will improve. After the last one had gone we had the mail carrier from the Kuskokwim for two days waiting for a storm to clear up then he started toward Katmai to meet the carrier from the South as he is very late, and as he started out without a guide, some fear he is lost or that something has gone wrong. However he has been this late before, and I dare say he will turn up safe and sound. I hope he will come soon and bring us letters from our precious little folks. The bell is ringing for chapel, so I must run over, but papa will stay with Snooks who is asleep, and says he will write in your journal for me.

February 5, 1905[116]

DEAR CHILDREN:

Mamma has gone to Chapel and I am watching with Elizabeth who is asleep, and have promised to write a little while mamma is gone.

Elizabeth is asleep in the bedroom with her little doll hugged tight in her arms as Pappa & Mamma are wont to hold her. And I am in the sitting room but I made a mistake on getting up from the sofa where I was reading and coming to write for I stepped on the head of a little doll and will likely be consulted in the office tomorrow by a mamma with a poor sick baby as Elizabeth sometimes calls herself.

My office is the scene of many domestic scenes between Elizabeth and dolls, and our fisherman gave Elizabeth a small tea set for Xmas and so that is brought in to use. I made her a small table and two foot stools serve for chairs and so at times when I am most busy I find myself the guest of the little family and must sit on a stool and eat crusts of bread and bits of sugar and pretend to drink tea, not forgetting when done to brag on the dinner and thank the hostess for the excellent meal I have enjoyed. Some of the dolls that have not eaten as they should are then given a special course of training and feeding and then the meal is over except the re-mains that the cook is often very tardy in cleaning away and over which we are apt to stumble.

Not long ago I was making a whip to use in driving dogs and as Little Joe or Elizabeth in boys' clothes, has to have the same things as her father we made her also a whip proportionately smaller. When the whip was done her mother said when she is tired of it I will send it to Robert, but she said, "Oh no, we must have it to drive dogs." But she told a stranger when she laid the whip down and was tired of it, her mamma was going to send it to Robert. Some days she brings in a whole armful of things to be sent to Robert or to Margaret and Rachel, but we do not send them, however we are glad she is not selfish and is willing to divide. The other day I was going to the P.O. at Nushagak and wanted Mamma and Elizabeth to go along. Mamma had bread to bake and could not go but Elizabeth went and the trader's wife gave her candy which she divided to

116. This entry made by Herman.

all when she came home giving to a native she liked two sticks and sending her last stick with a white man to his little girl. We went out riding in my big sleigh and at the same time hunting and as we came down the bluff to come home we let the dogs loose lest the sled might run on them and hurt some but the dogs are not so good to us as they howled and ran and drug pappa and eight boys in the snow and getting away ran home, but we got them back and made them go up the river a ways, for they were too lively, then we came home and the dogs always ran fast when we turned them for home because it was almost feeding time.

We are now going on a trip up the river to get some game, and Mamma and Elizabeth are going along, and also Olga's Papa and we expect to have a good time and get plenty of grouse and rabbits and other birds, little spruce grouse. We often speak of you both and are so homesick for you to be with us and help to make the trips and camp lively but we must not think about that too much or we are sad and do not enjoy ourselves. We hope soon to be all together and then there will be happy days.

We are expecting to be in the States next winter and then we hope to be all together in our happy home.

The chapel is now almost out and I will close for this time.

May God bless and keep you both pure and healthy and make you to grow up a useful Christian Boy and Girl.

Your loving

Pappa

Wednesday, February 8, 1905

Elizabeth has just gone to bed after a busy day, and papa and Mr. Kahlen are reading, so I will write to you. We have been out camping since I wrote you and such a time we had too. Papa wanted to take us on Friday last on a hunting trip, but I just could not go, for my work had to be done for over Sunday, and so he made me promise to go out for a little ride and to go on the hunting trip on Monday. Well, we went on the sleigh ride and had a hard time ploughing through the snow, for we started out over the tundra to look for grouse and found only deep snow. In going down hill one time we were afraid the sled would run over the dogs so papa unhitched them, and to show their appreciation they ran away from us and the miserable things they ran all the way home, so we had to sit in the sled until Moses and Nellie went down for them. When the boys were nearly home they met Mr. Kahlen coming with our run-a-way team. While the boys were gone for the team George went hunting and shot six grouse.

All day Sunday the wind blew and it snowed very hard all day, but not-with-standing, papa insisted upon our going on a camping trip, and I think he had enough of it too, for the snow was very deep, the boys had to run ahead on snow shoes nearly all the way. Elizabeth and I had to stay in the sled all the time for we would go in snow almost to our waists were we to step out without snow shoes. Papa made a tent and stove for the large sled, and we all slept in it. We were warm, but crowded, my back was nearly broken when I awoke the following morning. The wind had come up during the night and snow was blowing and drifting but still the men started farther from home in search of game. But after dinner they decided to start toward home as they had gotten game and the weather growing worse they decided to stay all night at the salting station about four miles above here and hunt today, but when once on the homeward stretch I insisted upon coming home for I had had enough for once so home we came, and very glad are we all for today has been a very disagreeable stormy day. I told Elizabeth to tell the folks that our trip was a "complete failure" so when they asked her if she had had a pleasant time she said, "No, the trip was a comflete pailure." The afternoon we started out we met a native with a sled who looked so badly and I said surely he cannot be well. No, said one of the boys, he is casumpted. I was so amused, but did not dare to laugh just then until Elizabeth asked if he was "cathumpted." Well, as George said, even if it was a hard trip we had fun. Poor George, he got wet through from running in the snow and tore one boot nearly off and broke a snow shoe, so if he thought it fun, I am glad he looked at it in that way. The hardest part for him was coming home with no game. The only thing killed was a black crow and he was forgotten.

But now I must go to set bread so will say goodnight. Papa is already asleep.

Mama

Thursday, February 9, 1905

This is papa's chapel night and after service we are all going over to the new school house for a little entertainment. Two men are going to debate as to which does the worse harm fire or water. Mr. Guinther takes the Water side, and someone we hope will take the Fire, but no one is willing, the poor men they are so bashful, but they really want to help. Papa has written a paper, everyone had the privilege of writing some little joke, or article, and Mr. Kahlen is going to read it. Papa wants me to sing but I don't believe I will this time, for when papa has evening chapel I have to sing so much and always feel tired afterward.

This has been a very stormy day. Yesterday everything out of doors was white, but today the little that is left is all covered with mud and water. Everyone is wearing either leather or rubber boots, and it is still thawing. I am afraid we are going to lose all of our pretty pure snow. Papa thinks the roads will be good now for another hunting trip, but I am not thinking about hunting trips.

Fannie has ten very cunning black and white puppies. Such fat little dumplings! I wish you could see them. Mr. Zucher had them brought in the little bathroom in the wood-shed this morning for they were nearly drowned out under the chapel steps. Well, I do hope they won't get itch. The others from last summer all have it, and even dear old Bossie has it too, but we are working very hard to cure it.

But now I must go to chapel, so good night.

Mama

Sunday afternoon, February 12, 1905

Papa and Mr. Kahlen have gone over to drink coffee with Olga's papa, so I will write in your journal. Elizabeth and I were going over too, but the weather is too bad. It has been raining and blowing all day so we decided to stay at home. Elizabeth says, "Why mama, it is bad but we can take you over in my little sled," but dear child it is for her sake I stay at home. The children around here, and grown people too, are nearly all down with Grippe, and we want to do our best to guard against it. Peter Krause, George's brother is the only one sick enough to go to bed in the house, and he is not very *sick*. Elizabeth has just brought an empty bottle out and tells me to "take it every time a day, and shake it well before taking." She is a great chic. Mr. Kahlen was trying to teach her chess last night, and after he had gone to evening chapel she stood beside me saying, "Now for instance, you move the King here or the Bishop or the Knight there," and so on. As soon as she awoke this morning she told us how an ugly black King took a pretty white Knight. Poor child, if she can not understand chess better than I can she will have a hard time. The little midget! She bothers me so I can scarcely write. She is spelling all the words on an Ainslie's Magazine, and when she has spelled one she will torment me until I tell her what it is. We have a great joke on Snooks now. She will run over to Mrs. Zucher's everytime I am out of sight, and yesterday I took a wooden soldier of hers, just the right size for a paddle, and spanked her a little. Well, she came home in a hurry, and now we tell her if she does not stay at home we will get a soldier after her.[117]

Elizabeth has been having phonograph music this afternoon; "just play" phonograph. She has the dinner bell for the horn propped up on a cup, and round pieces of paper for platters which I had to cut and mark for her. Two are "The Holy City" and "The Good Old Summer Time" her favorites. She sings "The Holy City" from morning till night some days. At first she sang instead of "Jerusalem," "Chris-a-lum-bus, hark, how the Angles sing." But now she knows how to sing it right. But now I must stop for Elizabeth won't give me a bit of rest, so Good night.

Lovingly,

Mama

Wednesday, February 15, 1905

I am almost too tired and sleepy to write tonight, but will write just a little. The folks around here are all sick, but I guess I told you before. Most of them are slowly improving; one little baby, papa thinks, will not recover. George too is *very* sick since Sunday night but he has not Grippe. Papa was afraid he might be getting appendicitis, but it seems to be some other very painful trouble. I miss him very much for Moses has a great deal of outside work, so I have just about all of the house work to do, and it takes just about all of my time.

The second mail came on Monday afternoon bringing letters from both of you. Margaret wrote a dear little letter on her birthday and sent a little sickle she had made at Kindergarten; and Robert too wrote us some sweet little letters. Mama treasures all of these dear little things from her precious far away darlings. And we are so happy to hear that they are both doing well at school and that you like to go. Some day you will both write long letters to us, and the writing and composition will be better, and

---

117. Scribbles appear on the bottom half of this journal page with Ella's note that "Elizabeth has written here to dear sisters, Margaret and [cousin] Rachel, and dear Robert, so I must write on the other side."

truly they will be sweet letters, but these first ones from your little hands will always be the most precious. From both Grandma's and Mrs. Prizer's letters we know you are, or were, both well. We always feel happier after the mail is in and we know you are all right. But we never worry about you for you both have such lovely friends and good homes.

I had only four letters this time: one from Mrs. Prier; two from Grandmas; and one from Mrs. Clegg at Valdez, and then of course your dear letters too, but they were in with the other letters. Of course papa had many letters, but then he writes more than I can possibly find time to write.

A gentleman from Juneau sent us some of the latest magazines for which we are very thankful. He sent me a January *Delineator*, and I must say that I don't like the new styles of [fashions]. The big sleeves are horrible! I am very sorry they are in style again. But of course *I* cannot regulate the styles, so why worry.

Elizabeth is coughing tonight. I do hope she will not get sick. We are hoping for cold weather, this cough is always worse in such warm rainy weather. It is just as it used to be on the Kuskokwim, the natives just cough, cough, cough. At evening chapel and Sunday services they keep up a perfect chorus throughout the whole meeting. When they come for medicine and sit around and cough, (and they make it as bad as possible that papa may fully realize how very serious it is with them) I just feel like sending them out, for it is very disagreeable to have them so near one at such times. It is very difficult to make them understand that they must go to the office for their medicine; they *will* persist in coming to my part of the house.

But now good night, I am very very sleepy,

Mama

Thursday, February 16, 1905

George grows worse, but papa is undecided as to just what is the trouble with him. The tenderness seems to seat itself first in one place then it goes to another. He eats very little and has a hard time to retain that, poor boy. I am afraid he will not recover. Thus far we are all well, that is, quite well though none of us feel perfectly well. Mr. Johnson's little baby, of whom I spoke yesterday, died last night at ten o'clock. His other little girl seems a little better.

Friday, February 17, 1905

George still seems the same. His pain seems less if anything but he is weak, very weak. Poor boy, he has no constitution to go on. His mother a native woman, was like all these natives, consumptive, and his father, a white man, was very weakly, was never known to be well here. So no wonder Peter and George are not strong. We who have strong healthy bodies can never thank God enough for such wealth or blessing than a strong healthy body, and let us never forget to thank Him for keeping us so well all these years, and first of all giving us such strong well bodies to begin life with.

Saturday, February 18, 1905

George seems really better today, [and] is more hungry and has taken and retained [a] good nourishing diet, but still has intense tenderness of the abdomen. Papa thinks he has an abscess of the liver and thinks seriously of operating unless a marked change for the better comes soon. I hope and pray George may get well, but of course God knows best and in all things will do for the best. George has been a very kind thoughtful boy toward mama, and I miss him very much now. When I have felt tired, or papa would ask me to go somewhere with him when I felt really too busy to please him by going, George would always say, and so heartily, "I will do all the work if you will only let me, and you go and lie down, or play some game with papa to rest you or go out for fresh air," just as the case may have been. Twice he has insisted upon staying up until twelve o'clock to help me with my ironing. All these little things have been [a] real help to me, and I appreciated them then and miss them now. I wonder if Robert remembers George. He loves you so much, and often speaks of you and the good times you all had when we were here a year ago last summer.

Sunday, February 19, 1905

George is still no better and papa told him that tomorrow he thinks best to operate, that no other help can be given, and George is willing for, as he says, he cannot stand the suffering much longer.

Monday, February 20, 1905

George has stood his operation very well. He was so brave about it all, and is doing very nicely tonight. We are all very tired, and I am especially tired for I have to help at all such times but have no one to help me with my work. People *will* get hungry, the house gets up-side down, and fires go out unless fed, and thus my time goes.

Thursday, February 23, 1905

Joshua, who went with Chris for the deer, returned this morning. The deer are on the way and by the last of this month we can look for them here. Papa will then go to the other side of the river to locate them and would like Elizabeth and I to go along. Joshua brought Laddie our old hunting dog over to us but he does not look as he did when we left him, but he is only very thin and we can soon fat[ten] him up, then he will be the same old Laddie again. Laddie used to run around with you so much I wonder if you remember him?

George's wound is doing very well but he has no appetite, and as he is very thin. He needs all the nourishment he can stand, but he is always so peculiar about eating. He eats so little of anything and so many good things he will not eat at all.

Sunday, February 26, 1905

Third and last mail came today but no letters came, only some old papers from Unalaska. How disappointed we all were. We will not hear from you for a long time now, not for three months and how long that seems now. Olga's papa is very happy over a very good picture of Olga he received today. How I wish we could get a good picture of you both especially of Robert for we have no good picture of him. Of Margaret we have a pretty good one. Papa and I were down to Nushagak today to see Mrs. Mittendorf and her baby boy born yesterday. We left Elizabeth at home as it had been very stormy all day, but soon after we left it got so clear and balmy we were sorry we left her at home for we all need fresh air. We are having our house painted throughout, and it is very unpleasant to live in such a smell all the time. We sleep over at Mrs. Zucher's in Aunt Mary's old room and will until the house is dry again and free from smell. I guess I will be pleased with the rooms in their fine new dress but just now I am not so well pleased. It would be better in Spring but then the men are all busy at the canneries, so I am afraid there is nothing to do but to make the best of it.

George improves but the little monkey, he will not eat to suit us, and he looks so thin and poor, but I guess he cannot eat.

Monday, February 27, 1905

We were down to Nushagak again today, this time we took Elizabeth along and how she enjoyed [it], but she was almost too tired and sleepy to eat her supper, and now she is fast asleep, and I am so very tired and sleepy I must say good night. I think the paint makes one feel so very good-for-nothing.

Tuesday, February 28, 1905

This has been such a beautiful day The sun has shone so brightly all day. It seems as though we are to have no more severe weather, this has been such a delightful Winter. The days that such a short time ago were so short, are already noticeably longer and the sun has much power. It snows nearly every night and the sun during the day melts the snow on the roof, and gradually our cistern is filling but I never use the water. I am saving it for the time when Moses will be gone to work at the cannery. Now he takes Nellie to the spring for water. The painting still goes on, and I am tired of it, *very* tired. Just now I am a little provoked with papa for he has asked the painter to play Crokinole, and I think he ought to be painting, our house is in such a mess, and I want the work done with, and get straight once again. I just feel like throwing the board out.

Mr. Campbell is spending the day with us. Mr. C. is the mail contractor, or one of them, and one of Robert's old friends Do you remember him? I had five men for dinner besides George, Elizabeth and myself to feed, and Moses had to get water for both houses and the barn so I had the dishes to wash. I wish I could learn to love cooking, for it seems I can do nothing else, but I don't like it.

Mr. Schniall started to the Kuskokwim with the last mail. Elizabeth and I sent Nellie and Christian a pound of tobacco. It is too bad, but these poor natives are not happy unless they have a chew, and Nellie is especially fond of it, and on the Kuskokwim they have only very poor tobacco this year, so I am sure they will be very happy to get some good. We had letters from Jim, Jesse and Christian and they all send love to you both.

Laddie looks like a new dog already, and he eats so much. One of our chickens died the other day, and I made soup for Laddie from it, and he was *very very* glad for it. Today he went out of doors, and when he saw Nellie he barked at her. I guess he has forgotten how a horse looks. Elizabeth was afraid of Laddie at first, but now she likes him very much.

March 21, 1905

Two natives from the other side of the river arrived while we were out for a sleigh ride with a message that the deer are here. Of course we are all, especially papa, very glad. Papa will leave tomorrow for the herd, but we (Elizabeth and I) must stay at home this time. Robert, one of our good Kuskokwim boys and Chris are with the deer. We had such a splendid ride this afternoon. Papa and Mr. Nelson hitched our and his dogs to our large sled and both families went for a trip to "Louie's Point," about fifteen miles above here. The roads were fine as well as the weather, and we made the run up and back in six hours and visited awhile with the natives at the Point. On our way home we met Mr. Kahlen who told us of the deer, and of course all talk is about the reindeer. Papa and Moses shot five grouse. Mr. Nelson bought a whole bag of smelts, and gave us a large panful and as soon as we got home I cleaned and fried them for we were *very* hungry.

Saturday, March 25, 1905

Papa came home today bringing Robert with him, and oh, how good it is to see one of our Kuskokwim boys again, and Robert seems equally glad to see us. He spoke in chapel tonight and Mr. Zucher was more than pleased with his address, and wishes we could have a good native helper here. We have no one to speak the native language here, that is, no interpreter. George and Peter both try, but as they were never allowed to speak Eskimo in the house, (that they might learn English the easier) it is not to be wondered that they cannot think in native.

Sunday, March 26, 1905

Robert left today for the other side of the river to join Chris and the deer, and tomorrow they will start for Wood River where the herd will be kept. Moses took him over and will help them up a little way with their provisions. Robert asked papa to give him communion before he left, and this morning before breakfast we took communion together. I wish we had more people here like those on the Kuskokwim for many there are really good Christians, but maybe if they were here with these white men and natives they would soon grow bad too. I always feel good to know that the best natives here are those who have come over from the Kuskokwim, and they are nearly all from heathen villages.

George is now getting well but had to have a second operation about two weeks ago, poor boy. He has had a *very* hard time, and we hope he may get really well now.

And Laddie, you will want to hear about him of course, well, he is a new dog already. Poor fellow, he had itch too but that too is better, and he is quite fat already. He wags his tail when anything makes him happy just as he used to do. Elizabeth is very fond of him and wants to call him Rosie, but we tell her that is a girl's name, "Well," she says, "even so I am going to call him Rosie for that is a *very* pretty name." Since I wrote in your journal papa and Mr. Kahlen made a trip to the other side, and I taught school for Mr. Kahlen, and liked it very much for the time, but I think that even though I don't like house work very well, I had rather do it than teach school. When papa and Mr. K. came home they brought one of the white men's children, Johnny Anderson, along whose mama had run away from his papa. He was a very cunning little fellow, always said his name was Charley Ansiton, he could not say Anderson, his papa's name is Charley. But he was here only a week when his papa sent for him, his mama had come home again. We were very glad when the little fellow went home for he was too little to be away from his mama.

Friday, April 14, 1905

We are all very happy today over the birth of Bossie's baby, a girl, and Elizabeth has named her Rosie and says she is her own little pet. Rosie is nearly all white and is very lively this evening. Laddie came in the barn to see her too but Bossie was cross. I guess she was afraid he would harm her baby. Laddie goes hunting nearly every day with George and Mr. Kahlen, and such a happy fellow you never saw when they pick up their guns and call him. But they get very few grouse now as they are getting scarce around here. We counted twenty-eight pound cans of deer meat and grouse last week.

Palm Sunday, April 16, 1905

A year ago today, that is, on Palm Sunday of last year, we were at uncle Will Romig's. Robert, papa, Elizabeth, and I, and if you remember we had such a splendid time there, there were so many little folks there, little cousins of ours. Elizabeth often speaks of them even yet. They were all such nice children, and dear Aunt Cecelia is so kind and patient. I wonder if Robert remembers that after church a year ago how he followed papa and mama who were out calling, crying with tooth ache, and how we took him to Dr. Reginis to have the tooth out. Well it was not much fun to have the pain of pulling, but it felt much better when the tooth was out. Poor papa had had an aching tooth for a long time, and he has been trying to kill the nerve and save the tooth, or rather I have been begging him to do so, but he often asks me to try to pull it. Poor papa, he says when other people have tooth ache they have a doctor to go to, but he has none.

We sang "Hosanna! Blessed is He that comes in the name of the Lord!" this morning! Papa, Mr. Zucher, Mr. Guinther, and George and Peter were the boys, while Mr. Kahlen, Mrs. Zucher, Ollie, Eliza, Elena and I sang the girls' part. And I think we got along very nicely considering the fact that we practiced it only twice. It was papa's service, and [the] address in native he had written and read it to the people, and they say they understood it very well. Our interpreters are so very poor, and they make miserable failures everytime they try to interpret, so papa has them to help him, and writes his little talks out, and it is a much better plan. Little Susie Zucher, (a little native girl) her own father's name is Big Trap, so Elizabeth calls her Susie Trap, but I was going to tell you about her. She is always so very naughty in church but somehow she has more respect for me than for anyone else. Just one look from me generally settles her for awhile. This morning she was cutting-up some, so I just took her in the seat beside me, and she was so frightened she never said boo all through service, and every now and then she would look out of the corners of her funny little black eyes at me then she would settle down even more quiet if possible. Tonight I did the same thing and she was as quiet as a mouse and finally went to sleep.

Monday, April, 17, 1905

Papa has just started for the other side of the river. A man over there has had a third stroke of paralysis and is *very* low. Two men came for papa and Mr. Kahlen. But it is so windy I am worried lest something happen to them, but God will care for them. I am very lonesome always when papa is away, but Laddie will watch, and Moses sleeps upstairs.

Little Rosie is doing splendid. She is so frisky and happy. She runs around her stall and kicks with all four feet, and makes fun for all of the children.

Tuesday, April 18, 1905

Papa and Mr. Kahlen did have a rough trip last night and a worse one back today as it was not only rough but they had much running ice to pick their way through but they managed to get through all right. Mr. Anderson (whom they brought over to the hospital) was very sea sick on the way over. Poor man! I guess he was glad to get here. Mrs. Anderson came along to take care of her husband, as Mr. Kahlen is teaching school. They have a little boy also, Freddie by name, so this means three more for me to cook for.

I was so glad when papa came home today, for I thought of him all last night and worried too, and prayed too. Why should we worry? God is everywhere to care for his children. And how good God is to us all. How kindly he cares for all of us though separated. I so often think of and pray for my two far away darlings, but I never worry for I *know* God does and will care for you both.

Elizabeth is sleepy, and I too am tired and not yet done with my work, so Good night.

Mama

Easter Sunday, April 23, 1905

A pleasant but very busy Easter. We were all up at 4:30 A.M. and all save me, up to the Sun Rise service at the cemetery at 4:45. Elizabeth was asleep, and we never like to leave her alone in the house.

Mr. Tonie and Mr. Kahlen took breakfast with us as Mrs. Zucher had all of the natives to drink tea over there. Our chickens just will not lay eggs for us, so no one save Elizabeth and our patient could have an egg, and we gave George, Moses, Elizabeth and little Freddie Anderson a large candy egg each.

Last Easter was the last Sunday we had with our precious boy. The following Tuesday we left for the West. Those were sad days leaving our two dear little ones, but God has been good to us all and kept us all so well and some day soon we hope to be together again. It will not be long until we can look for [a] steamer [and] there will come our letters. How anxious we are to hear from you both again.

Mama

Saturday, May 6, 1905

The first steamer came in sometime during the night, one for the Astoria Cannery at Nushagak. But we do not look for mail until the Alaska Packers steamer *President* comes. Papa and Mr. Kahlen were down for news. The cannery here at this place will not run this year, so it will be very quiet here all Summer. Of course we will not have so many bad Chinamen and Japs around, nor will we have steamers to take a ride on now and then, and we will miss them too. Mr. Anderson, papa's patient, is getting better it seems. Some time ago he did not know what he was talking about, and said so many very funny things, but now his mind is very clear, and [he] has more sensation in his poor sick side. He speaks very often of Mr. Johnson, the Alaska Packers Superintendent. "Big Johnson," he is called, for he is a very large man. Mr. A. and Mr. J. came from Norway on the same ship many years ago and are good old friends, and of course Mr. A. wants to see him very much.

Our little Rosie grows so fast, she is very large and frisky. She and George have great fun. When he tries to put her out-of-doors or in her pen she runs away from him or she kicks at him, and that of course George thinks very funny. George is well and strong again, fatter than we ever knew him to be, and he feels better too than ever before. He and Laddie are great friends. When George goes upstairs or out of doors Laddie will stand at the door and cry until we open it and tell him to go, then he just bounds after him. Laddie looks fine now.

Sunday, May 7, 1905

MY DEAR CHILDREN:

Papa was called to Nushagak to care for a man's toe that he had torn off on the way up from Astoria on the steamer, but the man had been drinking too much liquor and papa just left him until tomorrow. Mrs. Mittendorf sent Elizabeth six fine large oranges but we put them away till tomorrow. Oh, how good the oranges smell, they scent the whole house and make us *so* hungry.

Kyuksak and family came from the Kuskokwim bringing letters to us from the missionaries and many of the natives. Kyuksak's wife, Helen, was Robert's first nurse, and she was a very sweet pretty girl then, now she looks like an old woman. These native women all look old and worn so soon. Helen has had five dear little children, but all are dead, poor girl, she has not one left, only a step-daughter who is really a very ugly disagreeable child and always has been. Helen has joined her husband's church, the Russian Greek, and has even changed her name. The Priest called her Elena but she was baptized Helen, and we still call her Helen.

Monday, May 8, 1905

Just as soon as Elizabeth opened her eyes this morning she sat up and after rubbing the sleep from her eyes she said, "Mama what smells like oranges? I smell oranges, did papa buy some?" And papa said, go over and look in mama's drawer and sure enough she found some, and she fairly danced for joy, and of course she had to have one right away. Then I told her that Mrs. Mittendorf had sent them, and she said, "Well she is very nice, I love her very much." Mr. and Mrs. Bruntnook were to bring us oranges and apples this Spring but now they are not coming up, so we can hardly look for our treat.

Friday, May 12, 1905

Papa has gone to Nushagak and so I am going to give you his time. Papa and I always have a little after dinner chat. Between times are busy moments for us both now, as we have three patients in the hospital and papa does nearly everything for them, and I have extra cooking of course for we are eleven now instead of five. Ollie is with us again and she and Mrs. Anderson help me a great deal. Today they got dinner for me as papa forbid me in the kitchen. I am either too tired or too lazy to work. I guess I have Spring Fever.

George and Moses are working in the garden today. Moses and papa ploughed yesterday, and they and Nellie were a show for Nellie would go too fast and so papa had to half run while Moses rode the horse, but they ploughed the garden very nicely anyway, and Nellie was fine, only a little too fast. Our chickens I guess are sorry for their past laziness, for yesterday they gave us six eggs, and today three. We have only nine hens, and of course we can not expect too much of them.

I have just finished a new operating gown for papa from the white material I got from cousin Mabel last year and it is *fine*. The dogs tore two new gowns to threads last Winter, but I can make only one for papa as I have no more stuff. I am going to write and ask cousin Mabel to try to get some more for me. I wonder if she can? But now I must to work. Good bye.

Mama

Sunday, May 14, 1905

MY DEAR LITTLE ONES:

It is time to get supper for our patients, but I am going to steal time to write a few words to you.

We are getting another patient tonight. We have only three beds in the hospital and four patients. What shall we do with the fourth? Put him under the bed I guess. It looks as though [we] will have more work this year, and I am very glad, but I wish I could find some real good woman to help me. I am already tired and the season [has] only just begun.

The *President* has not yet arrived. We are all anxiously awaiting our letters, and maybe Mr. Hamilton will be on her too.[118]

Today is Mrs. Zucher's birthday and we have all spent most of the day together, that is between cooking periods. Papa and I, yes, and Snooks too took dinner with Mrs. Z. but just as dinner was ready four men came to the office and we had to begin without papa, but he finally did get in in time for a good dinner. But now good night, I *must* go.

Mama

Monday, May 15, 1905

Mr. Barnum, one of our neighbors from across the river, and Chris came yesterday, and today they with Moses and George planted our potatoes for which we are so glad for both papa and I are too busy to work much at gardening. Papa takes care of the sick, and I, well I am not a nurse, even if I am a nurse, but just an old cook, and when I have finished with this I am too tired to even think of going in the garden. We will have five cabbage, beets, and a few cauliflower plants to set out after awhile but it is too early yet for them, for the nights are still quite cold and it often

---

118. Bishop J. Taylor Hamilton, from church headquarters in Bethlehem, Pennsylvania, made a visit to Carmel to determine whether to continue the mission. His decision was to close the mission in June 1906 (Schwalbe 1985, 61–63).

freezes. I wonder if our little boy and girl will have a garden this Summer. I dare say Margaret and Rachel will plant flowers again. I wish you could bring us a handful of flowers now, as yet we have no wild flowers and the pansy plants we took up last Fall are all dead, so our prospects for flowers looks pretty slim. I sent George out today to pull grass for the chickens and oh, how *glad* they were for it. George scolded a little because the grass is not very high yet, but I told him that we all have work to do that is not altogether pleasant but still we must do it, and he should just skip along and think it fun. George is looking so well and he feels fine. He can yell just as loud now as Peter, which is saying much, for Peter *can* make a terrible noise.

Tuesday, May 16, 1905

While I am waiting for the kettle to boil…. Papa came in just then and I stopped to get the mail, for the steamer is in but we get no letters, not one, only some old papers. Well, the kettle has boiled and thirteen of us eaten once again, so I think I can write for a few minutes.

Dr. Robinson, the doctor for one of the canneries, came last night to see Mr. Anderson and Mr. Henry, two of papa's patients who are employees of the same company. He, Dr. Robinson, brought us some letters, but only one for me and that from Mrs. Wolf in California. So we have nothing from our dear little boy and girl. Mr. Johnson one of the superintendents, sent us a case of oranges, a case of apples and some lemons, and I need not say that we are more than glad for them. Elizabeth can have all she wants now, and she is very kind to remember us. His wife always sent very many things to the Mission, but God took her home last Summer just the day they were to leave for San Francisco. Mr. Johnson has always been General Manager of four canneries on the Nushagak, but this year two are closed. Some call him the King of Bristol Bay.

We are always planning to steal a few moments in which to get our garden seeds in, but find it difficult to do so, our hospital takes some time. Now that there are four in the hospital Mrs. Anderson is here most of the time and she is a *very* good help.

Wednesday, May 17, 1905

We got a few more letters today, and one of them from dear Robert and grandma, but none from our dear little curly head. But so *many* letters are missing that we hope soon for more. There are so many boats coming in the river always.

We were surprised and very much pleased to see how well Robert writes already. The dear little man. When we left him he could neither read nor write, now he can do both. When I think of it, I have to think how you both have changed in every way, and have grown too. Why, we will hardly know you, then how you will laugh at us. Robert's photo has never come to us, and now that I know about it I can hardly wait for it. Dear grandma and Aunt Eva, I am sorry they feel hurt lest the photo is not pleasing. Why of course it is if they think it good. I hope we will get pictures of both you and of dear Rachel, for we think of you almost as brother and sisters, and all our own children. I do hope we will soon get your photo. We want so much to see how you look.

Did I tell you that our things are all here, that is our provisions and clothing? Captain Bolton brought them on the *Indiana*, the ship we all went down on. They are not here yet, but the ship is in, and no doubt we will soon get them. We are so glad for we are nearly out of everything, and so many to feed everyday. And I am just about bare footed too; still have to wear fur boots for there are no shoes large enough on the river.

Ollie and I set out our little onions this afternoon, and tomorrow we will plant peas, radishes and carrots and lettuce.

One patient went home today and two more will soon go, then we will have only Mr. Anderson left unless some new ones come.

Captain Lutzens sent Elizabeth a very nice book. *Sara Crews* and *Little Saint Elizabeth* by Mrs. Burnett. I am just dressing Elizabeth's doll that sleeps. Poor little Margaret has been since Christmas without clothes. Isn't that a shame? Little Rosie is fine, so large and fat, and Bossie is still our good faithful old Bossie, giving so much fine milk to use. She gets much fresh grass now, and of course her milk increases.

But I must say good night now, it is very late,

Mama

Thursday, May 18, 1905

Just a few minutes until the folks are through with their dinners then we must all [get] to work again. This morning we washed and baked bread, and this afternoon we will iron.

While we were washing this morning we heard the first whistle and every chic and child ran to see from where it came. Mr. Kahlen rang the school bell three times, but no one came, everyone was curious. A steamer had come to this cannery for some things. There were always plenty of whistles here in previous summers, but this I guess will be a very quiet Summer. Robert used to be so very much afraid of whistles and said he would walk to Pennsylvania if the locomotives had whistles. But I guess he is not afraid now. Elizabeth came running in yesterday crying, and told us that two "Chinamans" were coming. Poor child she is so afraid of Chinamen, and declares she will not go to Nushagak nor across the river till they are gone, for she says "Chinamens are no good." Just now she is holding Margaret [her doll] up to the window for Bossie to see, and says that Bossie thinks her *very* nice. Elizabeth and Susie have great times at play. They very often play church just as you both used to do. One will ring the bell, then Elizabeth announces a hymn and after singing Elizabeth begins to preach and Susie is the interpreter. Robert used to always be the minister and said he would be a "really" one when he grew to be a man. I often wonder what my little man will choose for a profession. I often wish him to be a surgeon. Dr. Van Lennup, papa's old preceptor, sends us a little booklet of photos and a copy of a speech made by him at the opening of the new "William S. Elkins Memorial Clinic" presented to the Hahnemann Hospital by his daughter Mrs. George D. Widner of Philadelphia. And as I read it I wondered yes, and hope, that my boy will some day be a student in this magnificent clinic. But that is too far off, for he is only our own little boy yet.

We are having such a time with Rosie. She will not learn to eat. She just wants Bossie to feed her, but this morning George took some mush and milk out for the chickens and what do you think! Why Rosie just chased them away and ate it all up. But tonight she just will not have more, just a stubborn little monkey!

It was too cold and windy today to plant seeds, so we will try again tomorrow. I have made three attempts at writing this, and now I must go to bed.

Lovingly,

Mama

Friday, May 19, 1905

This is a real lovely Summer day, far too nice to stay indoors, but somehow people's stomachs *will* get empty. We are having two fine roast geese for dinner. Mrs. Nelson, one of our neighbors, gave them to us. Her father is a good hunter, and they give us much fresh game and fish. One goose had an egg in her, and Elizabeth ate it for breakfast. I have just made gelatin for the first time this year. We are *so* glad for the lemons for cooking. And as I sit and write I am breathing in the sweet fragrance of oranges that are just before me. Oranges have ever been my favorite fruit, and how I enjoy this splendid treat from Mr. Johnson.

Mr. Guinther left this A.M. for Clark's cannery where he will work this Summer, and we will miss him very much. Mr. Powers will soon go too, two of our very good neighbors. Mr. Guinther is counting so much on visiting with Olga next Fall. Mr. Kahlen has rented his little house, garden and dogs for the year.

Now to dinner, after dinner to garden.

Friday, June 30, 1905

It is over a month since I last wrote in this poor little journal, and much has happened since then. The afternoon after I had written here papa said I was to accompany him to Nushagak, so we hired a white man to set out cabbage plants with George, and I went along for a walk. The following day our goods all came; clothing and provisions. On the following Monday Mrs. Anderson declared herself ill and ran away home. Thus I was deprived of her help and she was a *very* good help. Mr. Anderson is still here and is improving now very nicely. We have had from two to five patients ever since I last wrote. George helps in the Hospital most of the time so the work manages to keep Ollie and I very busy.

Mr. Hamilton from the German Board arrived by the steamer *Nushagak* the day before yesterday, and today he and papa are around visiting the different canneries, and expect in a day or so to go up Wood River to see our deer herd.

We received a great deal of mail from outside by the *Nushagak*, and many letters from our two darlings and from the loving friends who care for them. We also received the long looked for photo of our precious boy, (and it is splendid of him) and one of Margaret and Rachel in some young man's lap, which is also very good. I was amused at Ollie when she saw it she asked why the girls had not pulled their stockings up before having a picture taken. (they have on short stockings). Will try to write more this evening. I must now make mosquitoe nets for papa and Mr. Hamilton.

Mama

Saturday, July 1, 1905

Papa and Bishop Hamilton started this morning for the Wood River, but they have a very stormy day, regular Alaska rainy day, and one for mosquitoes as well, but these are all good experiences for our visiting representative from Mission Board. It gives him a fair idea of some of the traveling experiences of the missionaries. But I am sorry for Bro. Hamilton for he is such a fine man, and a broad-minded far-seeing man on missionary work. He says that he called to see Margaret but she had already gone to bed and came to him very reluctantly. Poor child, I guess you were too sleepy. It was too bad that he called so late, for he was on his way to see your very own papa and mama and wanted to bring messages from you to us. But I am very tired from Saturday's work and have Elizabeth to bathe [and] to tuck into bed so will say good night.

Lovingly,

Mama

Sunday, July 2, 1905

Papa and the Bishop returned while we were at service this morning after an interesting though stormy trip. I had to come from service and prepare lunch for they were all *very* hungry. Of course, this is the normal condition of all Alaska travelers. There were two men from the launch to whom we gave lunch also. Mr. Johnson our very kind neighbor, had furnished a gasoline launch for the trip.

We are counting on a Fourth of July picnic, but as Bro. Hamilton has many little items concerning the work to attend to we may have to give up our picnic, but I hope not for the children are all counting on it so much. Elizabeth is especially anxious for the Fourth to dawn. Every few minutes she will say "Mama what is today?" "Well today is Sunday." "Well what is tomorrow?" "Monday." Then she will jump and fairly shout, "and the next day is the Fourth!!"

Chris came down with papa and the Bishop, and tonight the latter spoke to us all in chapel and Chris interpreted. He told us all about the long trip he had made, the many people he had seen and visited with, many of whom we know, among them Mr. and Mrs. Rock and Aunt Mary. And all had sent loving messages to all missionaries and natives.

But now the Bishop and Mr. and Mrs. Zucher have come in to spend the evening with us, so good night my precious darlings.

Mama

Friday, July 7, 1905

Today has been, I am sure, the very most trying one I have had since our return, and I am sure there have been many very trying ones. To begin with I have been almost too sick to be on my feet, but still I have had to spend the day serving meals for visitors and for about twenty working people. I have done my share. One of the cannery superintendents gave us seven thousand fish yesterday, and today papa has had four thousand cut and ready for drying for dog food, hence the twenty working people. Then this morning Mrs. Anderson with two friends, a baby, and her boy came over to visit her husband, and besides these were several other visitors and callers from morning till night. Then Bishop Hamilton and Mr. Zucher left this afternoon for the Kuskokwim sooner than they had expected, so their getting off of course made plenty of work for Mrs. Zucher, for Mr. Z. needs much preparing to get him off always. The Bishop was all ready in good time, and as calm and cool as though he were simply going out for a walk while poor Bro. Zucher was all excitement as well as very late in getting off. Papa feels good that so much has been accomplished in one day, while I feel only glad that night is here and I am able to go to bed.

Saturday, July 8, 1905

I am feeling better today but papa says I dare not work. He is always afraid these attacks might be appendicitis, so I can write some more to you.

We did not have our picnic on the Fourth, nor could we get one fire cracker. Such a quiet Fourth, why I scarcely believe there were five guns fired during the day. The children were *so* disappointed not to have some fire crackers. Other years Mr. Rock had gotten [some] from the Chinamen but this year there seemed not one bunch to be had. We gave them a nice dinner, a half pound of candy each and five cents, and what do you think they got for the money? Well, they each bought chewing-gum and such a chewing as we saw around here, and they are still chewing. Why I really believe that they chew all night too, it seems that their jaws are working incessantly. We had such a fine time last Fourth, Aunt Mary and the Rocks were still here and we had such a fine picnic. The men and boys had all sorts of fun and games but the games were cut short by someone coming for papa to see some Japs and Chinamen who had been fighting, several having been shot, one quite badly, who was papa's first patient in the hospital. But I am too tired to write more now.

Mama

July 25, 1905

MY DARLING LITTLE ONES:

What a time I do have trying to fill this poor little journal. I often think, "Well if Robert and Margaret were here I would have to do much for them, and I *will* take at least time to write to them, since they are absent from me," but somehow every minute of every day is taken and then many things are left undone. I can't explain it, but somehow there is no such thing as getting done here. I used to think that I would not work as hard as poor dear tired Aunt Mary did, for she always worked from early till late. But since I am in the harness I can see how it was with her; not choice but bare necessity if one would keep things moving at all.

We have two patients in the hospital now and a working man to [feed] three meals a day, and so many people who just happen in hungry at meal time, and as there are no hotels around here, it is "just walk out [to] my friends and have a bite," and sometimes when I am real tired I feel cross enough to bite myself.

I have been all alone since six o'clock this A.M.; not a chic nor a child about. Papa took Mrs. Zucher and the children out for their Fourth of July picnic, and I stayed at home to look out for the place and hospital. Mr. Johnson gave the *Swan* (gasoline boat) and two men for an indefinite time for our pleasure. Has he not a great big kind heart? I look for them soon now as the tide is coming in. Elizabeth was in her element at the thought of a picnic. Last Saturday, three days since, we were all around the river visiting all the canneries, and were so tired when we came home that we could scarcely walk. We climbed up and down the dirty wharves of six canneries, and finally arrived at Nushagak at low water and had to walk home. And it was *such* a close hot night with millions of hungry mosquitoes to fight. Papa carried Elizabeth who was *very* tired and finally went to sleep so you can imagine big fat papa puffing and blowing considerably before we reached home. And as it was dark and muddy, I got my feet *very* wet, and well, such a time you never saw. But Elizabeth and I both needed an outing, and I am sure it did us both good. Mrs. Davison, the superintendent's wife from the Whaler's cannery, was with us, and was almost worn out. It was good that the following day was Sunday and we could rest. But dear me, not much rest did we have for we had visitors the live long day. But there, it is eight o'clock, and I must run out to look for our picnickers, so good night.

Mama

Monday, July 31, 1905

MY DEAR ROBERT AND MARGARET:

We are all ready to start for the deer herd, so while we must wait for the launch I will write to you.

Elizabeth says, "Give me a ink pencil. I want to write to Robert and Margaret too." But I think from the way my pen works I will have to look for another. Well, here's the new pen, but Mr. Burgland is here with the launch so we must be off. We expect to call on Mr. Johnson first and are taking some fine head lettuce and cabbage over to him.

Good bye till tomorrow.

Mama

August 1, 1905

MY DEAR LITTLE ONES:

We returned this A.M. at 6 o'clock, after a very unsuccessful trip. First, we had a very rough trip across the river, [and] could not get in at Mr. Johnson's. When we arrived at the deer camp, [we] found boys and deer gone. After a little walk around the camp, we had lunch and then started toward home for the mosquitoes and sand flies nearly drove us wild. Part way down the river we ran aground and had to wait for the tide to take us off. Made Mr. J. a very early call this A.M., and got home for breakfast.

Pacific Ocean, Latitude 50° 7' North, Longitude 150° 29' West
September 3, 1905[119]

DEAR CHILDREN!

Mamma is telling me to write to you today as this is my birthday. Think, Pappa is 33 years old today and would like to have his little boy and girl with him.

Elizabeth said she would say good morning pappa a happy Christmas and so she did and before we were up she called out to Captain Bolton.

---

119. This entry made by Herman.

"You do not know whose Birthday this is?" and he said, "No," and she said, "It is Papa's" and she said, "Happy Christmas." Later in the day mamma gave Pappa a new purse with $10.00 in it for a present and Elizabeth went around with a new box of Cigars to all those men and said later, "A cigar, this is Papa's birthday."

Today we played Flinch and did all we could to be merry as it has been calm. The ocean has been as smooth as glass. Only the memories of an old swell rolls slowly inundating a smooth sea surface. The men have been feeding the gooneys today and some times they would tie two pieces of meat together and let two gooneys swallow it and fight over the string. The Captain says he is not satisfied with the day and says it is worse than two years ago when we all went out, as on that day we had high S.W. wind and today it has been calm.

Mamma is talking, and it is hard to write. Mamma will try [her] best to see you soon and so I will not write more tonight.

Much love from

Pappa[120]

Well, here we are on our homeward trip and [we] have been since the twenty-second of August. And ever since we came aboard I have intended to write to you, but the first few days we rested, for we were very tired from packing as we had to pack everything in less than a day the boat having to leave three days earlier than we expected. Then for two days after our rest we were all sea sick, and since then well, I have just put it off from day to day, for as you know Mama is a very poor letter writer.

We were over a week in [the] Bering Sea this time having head-winds. When we finally did get through the Pass we had fine wind for four days [and] were making from nine to eleven miles an hour, but for three days now or nearly three, we have had practically a calm. Captain Bolton has been very impatient all day; would not even play a game of Flinch of which he is very fond. Tonight when he went to bed he said, "There are better prospects for wind tomorrow," and seems to feel in a mood.

This is papa's thirty-third birthday, but it has not been a very joyous one for as Elizabeth said he had no cake with candles on it. I always like to make some kind of a party on our birthdays, but of course in the mid-ocean we must forget such pleasures. Elizabeth is already planning for her

---

120. This ends Herman's message. Ella continues this date's entry.

birthday. Dear child, she is going to give everybody cake and candy and a candle too, and she will have Robert, Margaret and Rachel to come to the party, and you will all have a very lovely time. Well, mama only hopes her wish may come true.

As it is late, already four bells (ten o'clock), I will say good night. Affectionately,

Mama

Pacific Ocean, September 4, 1905

We have a fine breeze, are spinning along at about seven miles an hour, and naturally Captain Bolton's spirit goes up with the breeze. I must write today for tomorrow it may be too rough, for as we say "after a calm, storm." We have had the bear skin up on deck, basking in the sun-shine. Papa read most of the time, while Bess at times played her accordion. Have I told you yet that she has an accordion? All of the girls at the mission have one so she thought she had to have one too, and we bought Elisa's old one for her. You would be surprised to hear her play. She plays nearly everything the other girls play, and other Aires besides. Her first piece was "America" her last "Blest Be The Tie That Binds."

Today the sailors are scraping the masts and all of the wood work that is not painted, getting ready to go into port. Before we were up this morning one mast was finished, scraped and oiled.

This is Labor Day in California, a holiday, and two years ago we arrived in San Francisco on this Holiday, but not this date. Labor Day is always the First Monday in September.

Elizabeth is making great plans for everybody when she arrives in Frisco. She says she is not going to the states first but to San Francisco. I think she has planned to buy everyone of her friends two or three mouth organs and some candy. She says when she sees you she will hug and kiss you and say "I am *very* glad to see you."

Mr. Guinther's ship *Star of Italy* left two days ahead of us, and Mr. Kahlen's *Star of France*, one day, so doubtless they will "beat us" out. Mr. Guinther is very anxious to see Olga.

Mr. Anderson, our old patient, is on the *Indiana* with us, and papa is caring for him. Mr. A.'s little boy, Freddie, is with him. Katherine Powers is also on board, Mr. Bruce the Second Mate is taking her out.

Do you remember Uncle Martin who was so kind to you all on our other trip out? He and Mr. Brown often took you all in the Forward Deck and Elizabeth used to show the Alaska pictures to all the men. Uncle Martin is on board again, just the same kind Uncle Martin.

Elizabeth, Katie, and Freddie have great fun on deck and playing in one of the fishing boats. We have a very cunning friendly kitten on board. The children dress her up and put her to sleep and cover her up, and she just lies there, such a patient little little puss. But the captain says she will never be any good to catch mice.

Supper is ready so I will say good night for this time.

Mama

P.S. Papa, and the Captain played Flinch against Mr. DeMent this afternoon, two games, and we beat them, and we are teasing them about it. Sometimes we play Bamboozle too and have lots of fun. I wonder if you ever play with the Flinch cards? I guess you have newer games now.

Pacific Ocean, Longitude 130° 28', Latitude 39° 19'
September 11, 1905

My dear little ones:

We have been counting on getting in Frisco by Wednesday, but our wind has left us so we are doomed, unless we get another breeze, for a few more days. Today we have almost a calm [and] are making about two miles an hour instead of ten. This trip has seemed *very* long to me, for while I have not been *real* sick for more than three days, I have not felt well one day. Somehow I cannot get used to the motion this time. Everyday I have had headache, and a very uncertain stomach. I counted very much on this ocean trip for a rest, but I guess I was too tired to begin with. Papa says I must stay a few days in Frisco with him to rest before starting on my long railroad trip. I will be very glad when this traveling is over and we are in a home of our own with *all* of our little folks with us again. For over two years we have been living practically in our trunks. It seems we were hardly settled at Nushagak until we had to tear up everything and get into our trunks again. Some people like to travel, and I *ought* to, but I don't. It is the hardest work for me.

The captain got down the last "Tell us where we are thing," (Elizabeth's name for chart) yesterday, for the coast, and we were measuring off the miles, and we who twisted in the wind planned to get in Wednesday noon, but captain said, "Now don't count your chickens till they're hatched." Good advice, was it not?

Elizabeth had to go to bed this afternoon first for being naughty at the table, but she did not sleep, and finally papa said, "Well if you will be good you may get up now, but you are not to go down on the main deck." But we soon found her down with her arms around Uncle Martin's neck. There she thought she was safe. But not so. She had to go to bed again while we played Flinch in the cabin. At first she did not mind, but after awhile she said, "Papa, don't you know you are cruel to your child?" We all had to laugh at this. The little midget does say some very old fashioned things sometimes. But we soon let her go, and she was real good till bedtime.

We have a beautiful moon tonight, so I think I will go on deck for a walk. Maybe we can kill some rats or a rat. Last night one of the men killed one that was running up and down one of the sails. Now good night darlings.

Mama

September 12, 1905

Still a calm and no promise of wind. We are only 260 miles from shore, but what of that in a sailing boat with no wind. Two schooners, one steamer and one ship were seen this morning before we got up. We were in time to see one schooner, but they were so far that only a sailor could tell what they were.

Papa got his typewriter out this A.M. and wrote eight letters, one to each of you too, so if I do not write you letters you will still get papa's, and I will send this poor little journal as soon as it is full, and I will try to fill it soon.

We played Flinch this afternoon and Papa won every time but one. Papa and Captain Bolton then played against Mr. DeMent and me, and they beat us again. Wasn't that *too* bad? I think so anyway. Now they tell us we don't know the first principles of the game.

Elizabeth must go to bed now so good night.

Lovingly,

Mama

Thursday evening, September 14, 1905

MY DARLINGS:

We dropped anchor in San Francisco Harbor about three hours ago, six o'clock, after a long tedious trip of twenty-three days. We were favored with a fine sailing breeze during Tuesday night which lasted till yesterday noon, then it went down long enough to discourage us but soon came back again. When we first got up this morning we saw many vessels of all kinds, and soon saw land, but all were dim as we had a dense fog. We worked hard all day to get in and for awhile were afraid we could not make it. Finally a tow boat came out to us at four P.M. and at six we were at anchor. The Alaska ships have been straying in for about a week, many came in today, some ahead some behind us. That was one reason we had to wait so long for a tow, so many were ahead of us.

Elizabeth has been very happy all day, singing and dancing and telling everybody that she would soon see her brother and sister. The other day she asked where we would go first, to San Francisco or the states. We were afraid that the health officer would not come to us until morning (until a physician comes aboard and examines everyone on board the yellow flag must remain, and until that goes down no one is supposed to go aboard or leave the ship), but the officer was very good this time. He simply came along side, asked if any one had died and whether all on board were well, and when the Captain said "All are, and have been well," he said take down the flag, and left us. Nearly everyone has gone ashore, but as it was late and cold we decided to wait until morning. We will *all* be *very* glad to get on solid ground again. Papa and Elizabeth are long asleep, so

Good night.

Lovingly,

Mother

The Grand Hotel, San Francisco, September 16, 1905

MY DEAREST MARGARET AND ROBERT:

Here we are in the heart of noise and commotion, so called civilization. We came ashore yesterday at noon, [and] found our good old friend Captain Lutzens waiting for us. He had been here at the hotel several times inquiring for us. After a nice little chat about Alaska and friends here we have in common, he took us out to the dearest little restaurant where we had a most delicious dinner, and needless to say, we *more* than enjoyed [ourselves]. Oh, *everything* tasted so good to me, for I had eaten so little on the *Indiana*. Elizabeth ordered and had "cold ice cream," and said "it is just fine." We are waiting now for Captain Lutzens who is to take us over to visit with his family at Alameda. This will be a treat to us all, especially Snooks, for the Captain has three little folks. Their baby girl's name is Alaska. But I will tell you all about them when we return.

Elizabeth, while I write, is holding prayer meeting. Yesterday she stood at the window here looking at the men on the street at work. After awhile she said, "Mama, is that out on deck?" But I guess she will soon forget all about ships and decks. All the way out my head ached, but since we came ashore I never think of my head, so I guess it does not ache, eh?

I don't like civilization anymore. If I could take all of my little folks to Alaska and have good schools and associates for them I would be willing to start today, but I guess I will learn to like all this noise soon again, I hope so any way.

Elizabeth is [so] interested and excited over everything that she has no appetite, so I told her last night if she would eat all of her supper and drink a glass of milk I would get some nice candy for her. Of course she ate the supper. This morning she ate her breakfast for some apples. Of course I won't always pay her for eating, that would be wrong, but just now all is strange and exciting for mama's little girl, so I do this to encourage her. The Captain will soon be here, so I will not write more now.

The Grand Hotel, San Francisco, September 19, 1905

MY DEAR ROBERT AND MARGARET:

I will just begin where I left off last Saturday. Captain Lutzens went over to his home for the day. Alameda is a beautiful place, like one large garden, the sea air so fresh and pure, and it is such a quiet place where as this place is so noisy. Why, one can scarcely hear one's self think between the heat and the noise. I am thoroughly tired of it all. Why, here in our room we can scarcely hear one another speak, and the noise begins early and lasts late. But back to Alameda. The Lutzens have a very lovely home and such fine grounds for the little ones to play on. Their boy Paul is about Robert's age only very light, while the girl has light hair and dark eyes and is nearly as old as Margaret. The baby is a very sweet blue-eyed flaxen-haired fair little lass, a perfect German type, and such a fat cunning little midget. I think I told you her name is Alaska. Isn't that funny? I am sure I wouldn't name a baby Alaska and I like Alaska *very much*.

We had such a fright over our little girl out at Alameda. She and Gretchen were playing together in the afternoon and I missed Elizabeth for a few minutes, and when I asked Gretchen where she was she said she had run down the street alone, and on the street the trains run on full length. Papa started out for her, and when he stayed so long I started too, and finally papa found her about eight blocks away and on the rail road street, and two trains had passed while she was away. Dear little girl, she was very warm and tired when papa found her, and while she was laughing it was a nervous little laugh. We were very glad when we found our precious little chic, she could so easily have strayed away from us. [She was] lost long enough to cause us all much trouble and worry. Papa has put a tag on her underwear now with our address on, but we take good care to keep her very near to us.

We stayed in Alameda until about nine o'clock when the Captain came over with us enroute for [the] Astoria. On Sunday afternoon we started for the Park but when we came to Divisadero Street we decided to get off and look for Mrs. Joaquin, whom you of course remember. We soon found them. They live about fifty steps from where we stepped from the car. We spent the afternoon and evening with them and had a very pleasant time talking over old Alaska times. Mrs. Joaquin has a little girl nearly two years old now who looks like her papa. Ule Ryfcogle and his wife came to see us too. They have a darling baby boy and [a] year old with blue eyes and curly hair just like his papa's. You remember Ule Ryfcogle, Mrs. Joaquin's brother? Mrs. Joaquin lives with her mother who is a very kind motherly woman. Elizabeth and I are going up to their place tomorrow to do some washing and ironing.

Yesterday we went shopping. First we bought Elizabeth a new coat and hat of which she was much in need, and over which she is the happiest creature around. Then papa had to have a new coat and vest and shoes. After dinner papa went around to see some physicians while Elizabeth and I took a rest. Toward evening Captain Bolton and Mr. DeMent came to call, but papa was out so Elizabeth and I entertained them. After they had gone papa came in with Mr. Kahlen and we all went out to a restaurant for dinner.

This morning we all went to "The City of Paris," a large store, and mama bought a new suit and hat, papa selected both, and I am very glad, for I like him to be pleased with my clothes. We have had to buy dresses for Elizabeth and shirt waists for me as our own clothes are too heavy for this intense heat. I am sorry we must buy so much for things here are very high, and I can make my own and little folk's things if I only have the chance. But then a doctor can't afford to look too poor, and under the circumstances the only thing to do is to buy. While everything costs very much here, I have never found a city in all my travels where I have been as well satisfied as here. On the whole I think this a good country in which to live. The climate [is] *fine*, and fruits and vegetables more than plentiful. With these to live on anyone can live surely, and I hope and pray that soon we may all live here together. Just now papa has Chris Peterson outfitting him in clothes. Chris is one of our Creole boys from Nushagak who was raised on the Mission. He had saved some money and wanted to come out with us. Papa did all he could to persuade him to remain on the Nushagak but he was too anxious to come so papa has arranged to send him to grandpa in Kansas. They have just come in and Chris looks splendid in a new blue serge suit and black hat.

Elizabeth was to rest while I write but she is and has been singing or dancing all afternoon. She has two of her dolls, Joshua and Katie, putting them to sleep and is telling them not to cry now but go to sleep. When she is in she wants to go out and when out she wants to come in again. Poor child, she is tired and restless and will be glad for more freedom, and she is growing very anxious to see you both. She asked today how we would get to you, if we would have to walk? She often says, "Come now Mama, let's go down on the street, I'm full of fun, I want to run and play with the children." She has caught a very disagreeable cold somehow. Two nights ago papa had to get up at twelve o'clock and go for medicine. He was afraid she would have croup, but she slept well after he had gone out, and now she is very nearly well again. Papa bought the Snooks a new pair of shoes on Friday, and today she said, "I think papa ought to get me some new shoes, don't you?" When I told her she already had a pair, she said "Oh no, they are old now." The shoe dealer gave here a purse, and then of course she had to have some money in it. When papa gave her ten cents she wanted "plenty," so he exchanged it for twelve pennies, then she was satisfied for awhile, then wanted to exchange some for "white" pennies.

Elizabeth and I are planning now to start for Chicago next Monday morning on the Santa Fe Limited. In that event we will soon see our boy. It will be very lovely to see our two darlings again, but it will be very hard to leave dear papa alone here. He will be very lonesome without Mama or babies, but we will all pray that soon we may be all together again.

Elizabeth is getting very restless now so I will say good-night.

Mama

September 20, 1905

I have been trying to fill your journal to send before I come so you may enjoy it more, for when you have mama you will not care so much to read her journal, but some how it won't get full. And so I guess I will just send it today anyway.

Papa has gone out to attend the Homoepathic Clinic this A.M. and to call on his old classmate Dr. Engle, or as they always called him at College, "Bismark." It is now two P.M. and he is not yet here, and Elizabeth and Mama are getting very hungry.

Elizabeth and I were around to "The City of Paris" this morning to try on my suit, but we came right back, as it was so warm and dusty. Just now she has gone with one of the maids to some other rooms. The dear little girl gets so lonely. She often goes out in the hall to visit with an elderly porter in uniform who sits near the Parlor all the time. Elizabeth likes him very much and calls him Foxy Grandpa.

Mr. Kahlen and Chris have been waiting a long time too for papa. Chris will start for Kansas tonight. Papa bought his ticket this morning, and also mine for next Monday. So Snooks and I will soon be with Robert, and after a little visit with him we will start for our little girl. If dear Grandma and Aunt Eva will keep Robert we will leave him there till we return.

Evening. Mr. Kahlen took Chris to his train, and by this time I guess he is on his way, this is his first trip by rail and I hope it will be an interesting one, but I guess he will often be lonely, traveling alone and everything new and strange is not very pleasant. Poor Chris, I cannot but pity him, for I am sure he will not be satisfied out here. He had saved some money but by the time he was fitted out and had his ticket, he had but little left, and making money here is not as easy as in Alaska.

After dinner this evening we took Elizabeth up to the "Emporium" to the toy department, and how she did enjoy looking at the many toys. Some customer fell in love with her seemingly, and took her all around to see the things. She gave her a real pretty book and asked her to go out to the St. Francis to dinner, but she was a stranger to us, and anyway Elizabeth would be troublesome at such a place. The lady kissed and hugged Elizabeth and told us she would like to steal her. But of course we could not spare one of our little folks.

We took breakfast yesterday and today in a vegetarian restaurant. They serve no meats or coffee only cereal coffee. Everything is very clean and the food nicely prepared, but somehow we crave heavier foods for our other meals. I guess we are poor vegetarians.

Tonight Elizabeth ate the best meal she has eaten since we came ashore so we let her have two small dishes of ice cream, "cold ice-cream."

Elizabeth and papa have gone to bed. I am very sleepy too so will say good night.

Mama

September 21, 1905

My dear little ones:

Mrs. Brownbrook and Leslie her son, spent the evening with us. Mrs. B. is not looking very well nor does she feel well. And she thinks if only she could get to Alaska again she would be much better, she seems to feel very keenly the disappointment over their not getting to Nushagak this past Summer. You of course remember Mr. Brownbrook the Superintendent of one of the Nushagak canneries?

Elizabeth and I spent the day with Mrs. Joaquin and her mother. I did some washing and ironing, and washed my head. While I was busy every minute, I still enjoyed every minute talking over old Alaska times, and chatting with mother Ryfcogle who reminds me very much of dear grandma Ervin who is now in Heaven. And then it *was* such a treat to get away from this noisy room 27.

Morning, September 23, 1905

Have just been out to breakfast and did some shopping too. Papa is out looking for rooms. We want to get in cheaper and more quiet quarters. I would like so much to see papa located before I go East. Our dear, dear, papa will miss us so much. But he is going to be very busy this year, if he can get but little pay practice he is going to study, and care for poor people who need a doctor as much, and more than the wealthy but have no money to pay one.

Now I am going to close this poor excuse of a journal and send [it] to Margaret first as I will see her last and, she can enjoy this till I come, then she can send it to Robert to keep this time.

It has been a great pleasure to write these few pages to my absent darlings. I am only sorry I had so little time for it. We will soon be together then we will not need journals.

With a great deal of love to you both.

Mother

Epilogue

By June of 1906 the Romigs were homesick for Alaska and again returned to Nushagak, where Herman planned to open a government hospital and to oversee a mail-route contract that he had secured between Bethel and Quinhagak and Koserefsky on the Yukon River, forty miles down river from Anvik. In addition, he served as the Alaska Indian Service Superintendent of Schools at Nushagak.

There is no clear record of Ella's life during the years following missionary service. Apparently, journal-keeping was something she did only while in the service of the Moravian Church. She and her family remained in southwestern Alaska until 1910 when they relocated to Seward where Herman opened a private practice. During their several years in this southcentral Alaska community a fourth child, Howard Glenmore, was born to Herman and Ella on January 28, 1911.[121] In 1914, Herman accepted a position as surgeon for the Alaska Railroad Hospital. Eventually, the family left Seward to live in Nenana, Fairbanks, and finally Anchorage as Herman's responsibilities with the railroad medical service shifted.

When the Romigs moved to Fairbanks in 1920, the family settled into a large two-story house near the corner of Eighth Avenue and Cushman Street. In 1922, Elizabeth was a student at the new Alaska Agricultural College and School of Mines (now the University of Alaska Fairbanks), and she became friends with fellow co-ed Margaret Thomas. Margaret, who did secretarial work for Herman during her student days, recalls that she was "always made welcome" in the Romig home.[122] In 1923, Elizabeth served as maid-of-honor to Margaret when she married biologist Olaus Murie.

In 1923, Ella was initiated into the Pioneer Women of Alaska, the elite organization that chose for its membership women who had arrived in Alaska prior to 1901. Elizabeth Romig filed an application for membership which caused some controversy and eventually resulted in an amendment to the group's constitution. Ella was elected into

---

121. Joseph Herman Romig Family Papers, Series 1, Box 1, Folder 1.
122. Margaret E. Murie, personal communication with editor, October 1993.

Left to right: Ella, Robert, Margaret and Elizabeth relax in
Golden Gate Park in San Francisco, 1906.
(Courtesy, Alaska and Polar Regions Department, University of Alaska Fairbanks,
Joseph Romig Collection, acc. #90-043-969N)

membership on September 1, 1923, and the minutes for that meeting
reveal that Elizabeth's application also came under consideration:

> Moved and carried that balloting on the application of Elizabeth
> Romig be postponed to another meeting. This was due to the fact
> that some of the members object to Native Daughters of the

Left to right: Margaret, Howard, and Elizabeth in Seward, 1912.
(*Courtesy, Alaska and Polar Regions Department, University of Alaska Fairbanks,*
Joseph Romig Collection, acc. #90-043-986N)

Golden North being called Pioneer Women, and it was deemed best to await a larger attendance of members, Miss Romig being a Native Daughter.[123]

The minutes of the December meeting advised that, "In view of the fact that Miss Romig is a Native Daughter and therefore according to our amended constitution not eligible to membership, it was moved the initiation fee be returned to Miss Romig with a letter of explanation."[124] Although the records show that Ella was a full dues-paying member until her death, the minutes for the organization do not reflect any activity with the group.

As the Romig children grew to adulthood, the family continued to enjoy outings together as they had in Bethel, and many photographs taken

123. Pioneer Women of Alaska, Minutes, September 1, 1923, Clara Rust Collection, Box 9, Folder 242, Archives, Alaska and Polar Regions Department, Elmer E. Rasmuson Library, University of Alaska Fairbanks.

124. Ibid., December 1, 1923.

The Romig family home in Fairbanks at the corner of Eighth Avenue and
Cushman Street, summer 1923. Left to right: Margaret Romig Hannon,
Elizabeth Romig, Margaret's daughter Pat, and Ella.
(Courtesy, Alaska and Polar Regions Department, University of Alaska Fairbanks,
Joseph Romig Collection, acc. #90-043-765N)

in the 1920s and the 1930s show them enjoying picnics at such places as Harding and Birch lakes south of Fairbanks. When Herman and Ella settled in Anchorage, they bought a cabin south of town where they spent the summers in the solitude that nature provided.

In 1936, Ella suffered a stroke which left her in failing health. That August all of her children and her six grandchildren gathered at the "Moosehorn Ranch" cabin for a reunion. This was the first time in sixteen years that the entire family had been together.

On January 1, 1937, Ella had wished to get out of doors, and in the afternoon she and Herman took a drive to their cabin. When they returned home around 4:00 P.M., Ella became ill, and early that evening she died peacefully. Her death was headline news the next day in the *Anchorage Daily Times*. A funeral followed a few days later at All Saints Episcopal Church, and she was buried in Anchorage.

Ella Romig did not see herself as an extraordinary woman, and would probably be surprised to think anyone else did. Her day-to-day life in southwestern Alaska was challenging, but she considered the hard work,

Ella and Herman in the early 1930s.
(Courtesy, The Anchorage Museum of History and Art, Anchorage, Alaska,
Romig Album #3, Image #BL85-63-326)

primitive living conditions, isolation and loneliness the composition of her chosen way of life, not hardships. Her ability to deal with whatever came her way was fueled first by her strong Christian faith, and second by her love and dedication to her family. She was in control of where she went, what she did, and how she accomplished her goals. Only God had a commanding power over her, recognition of which she regularly and humbly acknowledged. Margaret Murie described Ella as having "a very calm, dignified manner, but also a quick sense of humor."[125] Undoubtedly these traits provided the foundation that allowed Ella Romig to stand out as one of Alaska's dedicated pioneer women.

---

125. Murie, 1993.

Works Cited

Anderson, Eva Greenslit. *Dog-team Doctor, The Story of Dr. Romig.* Caldwell: The Caxton Printers, Ltd., 1940.

Baker, Judith M., Associate Director for Public Services, Hahnemann University Library, Philadelphia, PA. Correspondence with editor, July 23, 1993.

Coates, Kenneth. "The Discovery of the North: Towards a Conceptual Framework for the Study of Northern/Remote Regions," *The Northern Review* 12/13, Summer 1994/Winter 1994.

Encyclopedia Britannica, 1910 and 1994 eds. S. v. "George Dewey."

Fienup-Riordan, Ann. *The Real People and the Children of Thunder: The Yup'ik Eskimo Encounter with Moravian Missionaries John and Edith Kilbuck.* Norman: University of Oklahoma Press, 1991.

Fortuine, Robert. *Chills and Fever: Health and Disease in the Early History of Alaska.* Fairbanks: University of Alaska Press, 1989.

Gilfillan, Molly. Personal communication with editor, February 1993.

Grinnell, Elizabeth, Editor. *Gold Hunting In Alaska.* Elgin: David C. Cook Publishing Company, 1901.

Jackson, Sheldon, L. L. D. *Education in Alaska, 1894–95.* Washington, D.C.: Government Printing Office, 1896.

_____. *Education in Alaska, 1897–98.* Washington, D.C.: Government Printing Office, 1899.

_____. *Education in Alaska, 1898–99.* Washington, D.C.: Government Printing Office, 1900.

_____. *Education in Alaska, 1903.* Washington, D.C.: Government Printing Office, 1904.

Jeffrey, Julie Roy. *Converting The West: A Biography of Narcissa Whitman.* Norman: University of Oklahoma Press, 1991.

Lenz, Mary and James H. Barker. *Bethel The First 100 Years*. Bethel: A City of Bethel Centennial History Project, 1985.

Michel, Bernard E. *The Moravian Church, Its History, Faith and Ministry*. Bethlehem, PA: The Moravian Church in America, 1992.

Murie, Margaret E. Correspondence with editor, November 1993.

Orth, Donald J. *Dictionary of Alaska Place Names*. Washington, D.C.: Government Printing Office, 1967.

Oswalt, Wendell H. *Mission of Change In Alaska*. San Marino, CA: The Huntington Library, 1963.

Pennsylvania. Census Records, 1880 and 1900.

Pioneer Women of Alaska Papers. Clara Rust Collection. Archives, Alaska and Polar Regions Department, Elmer E. Rasmuson Library, University of Alaska Fairbanks.

Rennick, Penny. *Alaska Geographic, The Kuskokwim*. Volume 15, Number 4/1988. Anchorage: Alaska Northwest Publishing.

Romig, Ella Mae Ervin. Membership application. Daughters of the American Revolution. Washington, D.C.

Romig, Joseph Herman. Family papers. Archives Alaska and Polar Regions Department, Elmer E. Rasmuson Library, University of Alaska Fairbanks.

Schwalbe, Anna Buxbaum. *Dayspring on the Kuskokwim. The Story of Moravian Missions in Alaska*. Bethlehem, PA: The Moravian Church in America, 1951; updated edition by Gertrude and Harry Trodahl, Bethlehem, PA: Department of Publications, 1985.

Smelcer, Clarence. Personal communication with editor, February 1995.

Unity Synod of the Unitas Fratrum, or Moravian Church. *The Ground of the Unity*. Herrnhut, German Democratic Republic: Moravian Church, 1981.

Weisberger, Bernard A. *Reaching For Empire*. New York: Time Incorporated, 1964.

Index